Using

Access 97

Using

Access 97

F. Scott Barker

with
Diana Barker

Using Access 97

Library of Congress Catalog No.: 96-72197

ISBN: 0-7897-1050-1

100   99   98   97   6   5   4   3   2   1

Interpretation of the printing code: the rightmost double-digit number is the year of the book's printing; the rightmost single-digit number, the number of the book's printing. For example, a printing code of 97-1 shows that the first printing of the book occurred in 1997.

Screen reproductions in this book were created using Collage Plus from Inner Media, Inc., Hollis, NH.

Composed in *ITC Century*, *ITC Highlander*, and *MCPdigital* by Que Corporation.

Credits

Publisher
Roland Elgey

Publishing Manager
Lynn E. Zingraf

Editorial Services Director
Elizabeth Keaffaber

Managing Editor
Michael Cunningham

Director of Marketing
Lynn E. Zingraf

Acquisitions Editor
Martha O'Sullivan

Product Development Specialist
Melanie Palaisa

Production Editor
Tom Lamoureux

Editors
Kate Givens
San Dee Phillips
Nick Zafran

Assistant Product Marketing Manager
Christy M. Miller

Strategic Marketing Manager
Barry Pruett

Technical Editor
Jim O'Connor

Technical Support Specialist
Nadeem Muhammed

Software Relations Coordinator
Patty Brooks

Book Designer
Ruth Harvey

Cover Designer
Dan Armstrong

Production Team
Marcia Brizendine
Jenny Earhart
Maribeth Echard
Nicole Ruessler
Staci Somers

Indexer
Craig Small

To our children: Christopher, Kari Anne, Nichole, and David.

About the Author

F. Scott Barker holds a Bachelor of Science in Computer Science, and has worked as a developer in the database field for over 12 years, and with Microsoft Access for the last six.

Working at Microsoft for two years, Scott was a member of the Microsoft Access and Fox Pro teams. Since leaving, he has been contracting with Microsoft and the Access team developing in-house tools used throughout Microsoft. With his company, Applications Plus, Scott has also been doing contract development for other companies in industries including banking, medical, and insurance.

Scott has trained for Application Developers Training Company and others all around the U.S. and is a frequent speaker at Access Conferences throughout the world. Through his classes and conferences, Scott has trained thousands of developers and users. He was also rated one of the top Access speakers at TechEd95 U.S. and he spoke at European TechEd96.

Scott is also a partner of LBI, which specializes in sponsoring Office conferences with Microsoft around the world. To see information about conferences, go to **LBIInfo.com** on the Internet.

He has been a Contributing Editor and is currently writing for *Access/Visual Basic Advisor* magazine. Scott has also written for *Database Advisor* magazine and *Smart Access*.

Besides authoring *Using Access 97*, Scott has recently authored *Access 97 Power Programming*.

Scott lives in Woodinville, WA, with his wife Diana and four children: Christopher (9), Kari Anne (6), Nichole (4), and David (2).

Acknowledgments

I want to thank my wife, **Diana Barker**, for jumping in and helping me to make this book what it is today. I couldn't have done it without you!

Thanks to the crew at Que for giving me the opportunity to create another book, and in particular thanks to the New User group: to Acquisitions Editor **Martha O'Sullivan** and Product Development Specialist **Melanie Palaisa**, we stuck with it! To Production Editor **Tom Lamoureux,** Assistant Product Marketing Manager **Christy M. Miller**, and **Lorna Gentry**, Senior Product Development Specialist, thanks!

A special thanks to Technical Editor **Jim O'Connor** for being right on top of the text, and making sure this book was correct technically.

As usual, thanks to some of my clients for putting up with me in my book-writing frenzy: **Caster Technology** and **Microsoft**.

Thanks to the Microsoft Access team for coming up with such a powerful product!

We'd like to hear from you!

As part of our continuing effort to produce the highest possible quality, Que would like to hear your comments. To stay competitive, we *really* want you, as a computer book reader and user, to let us know what you like or dislike most about this book or other Que products.

You can mail comments, ideas, or suggestions for improving future editions to the address below, or send us a fax at (317) 581-4663. For the online-inclined, Macmillan Computer Publishing has a forum on CompuServe (type **GO QUEBOOKS** at any prompt) through which our staff and authors are available for questions and comments. The address of our Internet site is **http://www.quecorp.com** (World Wide Web).

In addition to exploring our forum, please feel free to contact me personally to discuss your opinions of this book: I'm **73353,2061** on CompuServe, and I'm **mpalaisa@que.mcp.com** on the Internet.

Although we cannot provide general technical support, we're happy to help you resolve problems you encounter related to our books, disks, or other products. If you need such assistance, please contact our Tech Support department at 800-545-5914 ext. 3833.

To order other Que or Macmillan Computer Publishing books or products, please call our Customer Service department at 800-835-3202 ext. 666.

Thanks in advance—your comments will help us to continue publishing the best books available on computer topics in today's market.

Melanie Palaisa
Product Development Specialist
Que Corporation
201 W. 103rd Street
Indianapolis, Indiana 46290
USA

Contents at a Glance

Table of Contents

Part II: Creating a Solid Foundation for Your Database

Part VII: Rounding Out Your Database

23 Fine-Tuning Your Database Application   331

24 Importing, Exporting, and Linking Information   341

Introduction

A letter from the author

Dear Reader,

I have trained literally thousands of people in databases over the last 10 years, the last five using Microsoft Access. The amazing thing is, regardless of whether I am at a conference in Nice, France, for Microsoft, or training for a company in Bismarck, North Dakota, I don't get tired of teaching people Access. I really enjoy it when people catch on to a concept or get excited about a tip I demonstrate for them.

Access 97 is a very powerful application that can help you handle your business or personal tasks. Take this book one chapter at a time, and by the end of it, you will be comfortable with using most of the features of Access 97.

Some may be wondering why my wife, Diana, is sharing cover credit with me. I have been training developers a good portion of my time, so I needed someone to bring me back to earth with users. This person had to be comfortable with computers, intelligent, but couldn't be familiar with Access 97. All this was in order to keep an eye on what I was putting down on these pages. Diana was perfect for the job. In the past, she has had a job supporting users on PCs, so she knows computers. She also has helped in software seminars as an assistant, so she knows what it takes for users to understand new software. Lastly, she has no problem pointing out my mistakes to me.

How the book is organized

This book was written to give you as much information about most parts of Access 97 so you can get started as quickly as possible. This book also aims to give you the best foundation for creating solutions to your database problems with Access 97.

Part I: Beginnings

In the Beginning…there was the database. So that's where I start, in Chapter 1, by explaining exactly what a database is compared to what you have been doing by hand for years. I then give you a taste of Access 97 in Chapter 2, where I show you how to get into Access 97 and I give you a quick tour of the Access 97 database screen, menus, and toolbars. Chapter 3 covers Help, including how to use a little guy called the Office Assistant. Chapter 4 explains the various ways to create a database and open existing databases.

Part II: Creating a solid foundation for your database

I live in the Pacific Northwest where there are a lot of evergreen trees—big ones. The only reason they become big and do not blow over is because they have a good solid base, with roots going deep into the ground. The same is true about working with databases in Access 97. Tables are the roots for storing and working with information in Access 97. Chapters 5 through 9 look at various ways tables are used, and how to use them together—by creating relationships—to come up with a good base for your system. You will also learn how to enter and change your information in the tables.

Part III: Finding information in your database

After you have the information in your database, you need to be able to work with it. Chapters 10 and 11 show you how to locate information in your tables, as well as how to filter out information that you don't want to see for a session. You will also learn how to sort your information with just one or two clicks of the mouse.

Part IV: Viewing your data with queries

Like tables, queries are a major part of working with your information in Access. Queries allow you to view your information in different ways, summarizing the information. Chapters 12 through 16 take you through the tasks of showing what a query is, to using them to update large sets of your data automatically.

Part V: Working with forms

Forms allow you to control how data is entered into your tables. There are a number of ways to use forms to help create a good-looking interface for the information you are storing in your database. Chapters 17 through 20 show you the basics of using forms and form controls when working with your information.

Part VI: Reporting information

Of course, having the information in the tables doesn't do much good if you can't report it in a convenient and attractive manner. Chapters 21 and 22 show you how to use Access 97 reports, first the quick and easy way, and then by taking those same reports and enhancing them.

Part VII: Rounding out your database

After you have learned how to use the various objects, tables, queries, forms, and reports individually, it's time to see how to put the pieces together for a cohesive database application. Chapter 23 discusses using the Switchboard Manager for tying your forms and reports together; it also gives performance tips to help complete your application. Chapter 24 shows you how to bring information in from other places such as spreadsheets and other databases. In Chapter 25, you will be working with Access 97 and other applications to share tasks such as mail merge with Word, and copying data straight from Access to Word and Excel. Chapter 26 discusses the Internet and what you can do with it and Access 97.

Examples in the book

You can create all the examples in the book as you work your way through the chapters. I happen to have an interest in videos, so I have you create a video library that you can use to check tapes in and out to loan to friends. You should be able to follow from page 1 through the end of the book and re-create everything discussed here.

Part I: Beginnings

1

Welcome to the World of Databases

● **In this chapter:**

- What is a database?

- What is a database application?

- Introducing Access 97 objects

- How do I use menus in Windows?

- All the things an Access 97 database can do for you!

Although more complex than word processing, databases aren't impossible to use. . . . .

J ust four years ago, it was not very likely that Microsoft would include a database application with its Microsoft Office suite. Databases were just too hard to use for the average person. Not so anymore. Now, anyone who can use a computer can use a database. A database is almost as easy to use as any other Office product.

What are databases?

Databases are electronic filing systems. For example, say you have a small business, and for this small business you keep specific facts and information, such as name, address, or orders, for each of your customers. These facts are kept on sheets of paper that will in turn be kept in a manila folder. You also keep another folder that is full of pages, with information on vendors for your business.

If you transfer this real world information to a database, you would say that:

- Each manila folder is a database *table*.
- Individual pages are *records* in a table.
- The information on the pages are *fields*.

Take a look at Figure 1.1 to see the analogy in action.

Two of the most important reasons for creating a database are:

- **Time savings**   It is much quicker to add, change, delete, and *find* information when it's in a database. You can create reports about your data quickly because it's all automatic.

- **Accuracy**   Your information will be more accurate because you only have to add, change, or delete it in one place. The reports you create will be accurate and contain only the information you want to see.

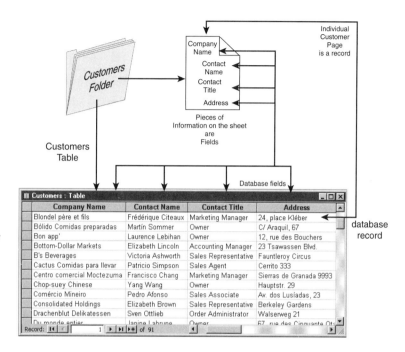

Fig. 1.1
Databases store on the computer what you've been doing for years by hand.

What is a database application?

As mentioned earlier, a database stores information. A *database application*, such as Access 97, goes a step further by allowing you to work with the information. This includes adding to it, updating it, and deleting it. A database application also allows you to create reports.

NOTE **I want to point out here that Access 97 is what is known as a** relational database. Rather than putting all your information into one table, you organize information by *subject* and create a database table for each subject. A relational database, then, has two or more tables of data that are connected by a common field called a key field.

For example, if you were creating a database for a small business, you may have a Customer table (containing the name, address, phone numbers, and so on of each customer) and an Orders table (containing the invoice numbers of each order placed by a customer, as well as the items ordered, cost, and so on). Your tables would also contain one field that is the same in both tables, such as a CustomerID field. This common field would "link" the two tables together and allow you to find information about any of your customers and the items they have ordered from you. Relationships are further discussed in Chapter 7, "Understanding Relationships Between Tables."

Some examples of database applications

A good place to look for examples of database applications is Access 97 itself. One of its great features is the Database Wizard. This actually creates a whole database application for you, using *templates* that already exist. I show you how to use the Database Wizard in Chapter 4, "Creating and Opening Databases," but for now take a look at Figure 1.2, and see some of the types of applications that you can create.

Fig. 1.2
The Database Wizard can give you a great jump-start if the type of application you need is included in its list.

Access 97 has a wide variety of databases.

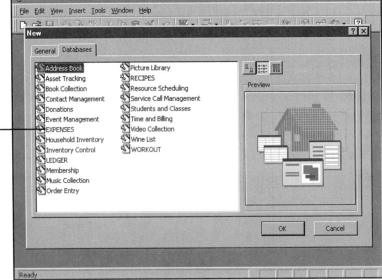

66 *Plain English, please!*

You may have heard of **templates** from working in Word for Windows or some other word processing package. In Word, you have templates for brochures, faxes, memos, and so on. These are document shells that exist to get you started in creating the type of document you need. Database templates do the same thing, only instead of documents, they create database applications. 99

You can see further descriptions for the list of database templates (shown in Figure 1.2) in Table 1.1. I have listed the templates beginning with the letters A through L. There are more templates available than those listed here.

Table 1.1   Available database templates in Access 97

Template name	Description of template
Address Book	Address information
Asset Tracking	Asset information including depreciation, maintenance history, employee information, and vendors
Book Collection	Books, authors, and quotations
Contact Management	Contacts (people) and phone calls
Donations	Contributors, pledges, and donation campaign information
Event Management	Event information including attendees, pricing, registration, event type information, and more
Expenses	Expense details, reports, and employee information
Household Inventory	Information about household inventory such as appliances, furniture, and so on
Inventory Control	Buying and selling inventory, purchasing, vendors, and supplier information
Ledger	Transaction information, accounts, and account categories

The templates create the various *objects* that make up the database application.

 Plain English, please!

When referring to **objects** in this book, I am discussing the main tools that make up Access 97, such as forms, reports, tables, and queries.

A database is for more than just storing information!

While storing information is definitely one of the main purposes of a database, you need to be able to use that information after it's in the database.

So, finding and creating reports about your information are examples of other tasks performed as well. These tasks are what this book is about, along with the objects that perform them for Access 97. Access 97 uses tables to store information, similar to the one shown in Figure 1.3.

Fig. 1.3
Tables are used to store information.

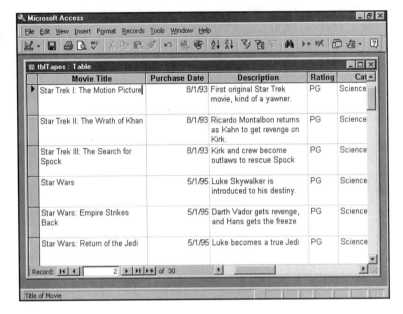

Maintaining and viewing your information

After you create your database and add data to it, you have to be able to view and maintain the information. There are various methods used for this in Access 97. You can:

- Import information from other sources. You will do this when you have other applications, and you need to work and maintain existing data in those applications. Importing is discussed in Chapter 24, "Importing, Exporting, and Linking Information."

- Use forms to enter and edit information. Forms enable you to maintain the information conveniently. Forms are discussed in Part IV, "Viewing Your Data with Queries." (See Figure 1.4 for an example of a form.)

- Use queries and filters to view your data in various ways. You will need to view your information in different ways so that you can make decisions based upon that information. Queries and filters are discussed in Part III, "Finding Information in Your Database."

- Queries can also be used to make changes to your information. This includes deleting, adding, and editing data.

Fig. 1.4
A form, such as this Tape Information form, allows you to update your stored information.

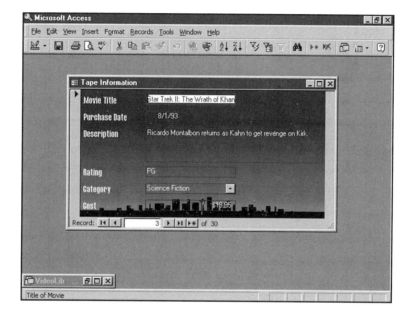

Forms allow you to create an attractive means of getting information into your database tables. For instance, let's say you are a banker taking a credit application from a customer. You could create a form that looks similar to the paper credit application. When you enter the information about the customer on the form, it is actually being put into your database table, which saves you and the customer time and reduces the possibility of making errors.

Creating reports from the information in your database

Storing your information in a database doesn't do much good if you don't have a means to report it. You can create reports in Access 97 like the one you see in Figure 1.5.

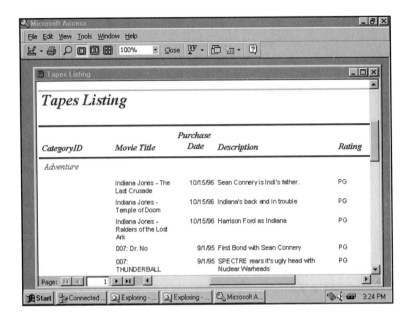

With Access 97 reports, you can view the data on-screen with Print Preview, or print it on paper.

Making the computer do the boring work for you

After working with Access 97 awhile, you will find there are jobs that are performed again and again the same way. When you find yourself doing a task that is repetitive and, well, boring, there are a couple of methods you can use to make Access perform the tasks automatically: Access 97 macros and Visual Basic for Applications (VBA).

Access 97 macros are different from other macros you may have used in Excel or Word. These products actually allow you to record keystrokes and associate them to a key combination. An example of this is formatting selected text as italic, by using the key combination of Ctrl+I.

For Access 97 macros, you have a set number of actions you can combine to perform the tasks you need automated. You can see a macro for opening a form in Figure 1.6.

Fig. 1.6

Macros can be used so that you don't have to open the database window to open a form.

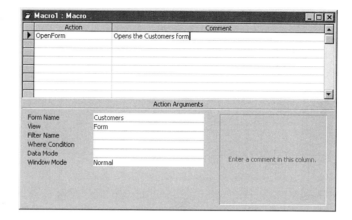

The other method for automating tasks is with Visual Basic for Applications. You would use the Module object type and write the VB code to automate your tasks. This method offers more control but requires more programming knowledge of VBA than macros. I would say that this method is for power users and beyond the scope of this book.

Access 97 will handle the automating tasks for you. You will see this when you use the Command Button Wizard, introduced in Chapter 20, "Controls that Especially Enhance Forms." The Command Button Wizard creates the necessary VBA code and places it in your form without you having to hassle with it. This is true of various commands that you create with the Command Button Wizard.

You can see some of the VBA code created by the Command Button Wizard in Figure 1.7. This code opens the same form that the macro did in Figure 1.6. One of the benefits of using VBA is that you can put error trapping into the code, where with a macro you can't. That means that if a problem occurs when you open the form with a macro, Access 97 will stop and give you a couple of error messages, whether you want them or not. With code, you can control what you see when an error occurs, or not even show a message.

Fig. 1.7
This VBA code, created
by the Command
Button Wizard,
performs the same task
as the macro displayed
in Figure 1.6.

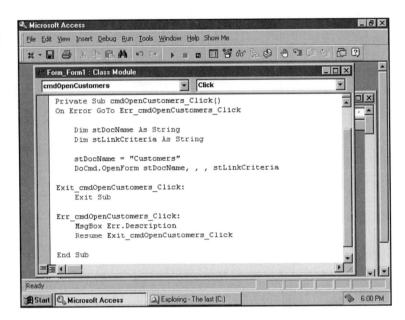

```
Private Sub cmdOpenCustomers_Click()
On Error GoTo Err_cmdOpenCustomers_Click

    Dim stDocName As String
    Dim stLinkCriteria As String

    stDocName = "Customers"
    DoCmd.OpenForm stDocName, , , stLinkCriteria

Exit_cmdOpenCustomers_Click:
    Exit Sub

Err_cmdOpenCustomers_Click:
    MsgBox Err.Description
    Resume Exit_cmdOpenCustomers_Click

End Sub
```

2

Introducing Access 97

● **In this chapter:**

- **Starting Access 97**

- **Taking a tour of the main Access 97 Database window**

- **What are menus and toolbars?**

- **Taking a close look at dialog boxes**

- **What's on the status bar?**

There's no time like the present to open Access 97 and learn what it's all about . . . . ➤

Access 97 is a very large application. You may be nervous about working with an application that does more than just help create documents or crunch some numbers. Well, don't be nervous. While Access 97 is a large application and does a lot, the Access team at Microsoft has put forth a great deal of effort to make it as user-friendly as possible.

Having said that, there are quite a few tools that you have to learn about. First, take a look at how to start Access 97.

Starting up Access 97

When you or someone else installed Microsoft Office 97 on your computer, Access 97 was also installed, and shortcuts to the Access 97 program were created.

❝ *Plain English, please!*

A **shortcut** is a command that is created to start a program, possibly located somewhere else in your computer. The nice thing about shortcuts is that you don't have to know or care where the actual application is located; the shortcut "finds" the program and opens it for you. ❞

There are many ways you can open Access 97. Two options are shown in Figure 2.1.

Fig. 2.1
Here are two ways to start Microsoft Access.

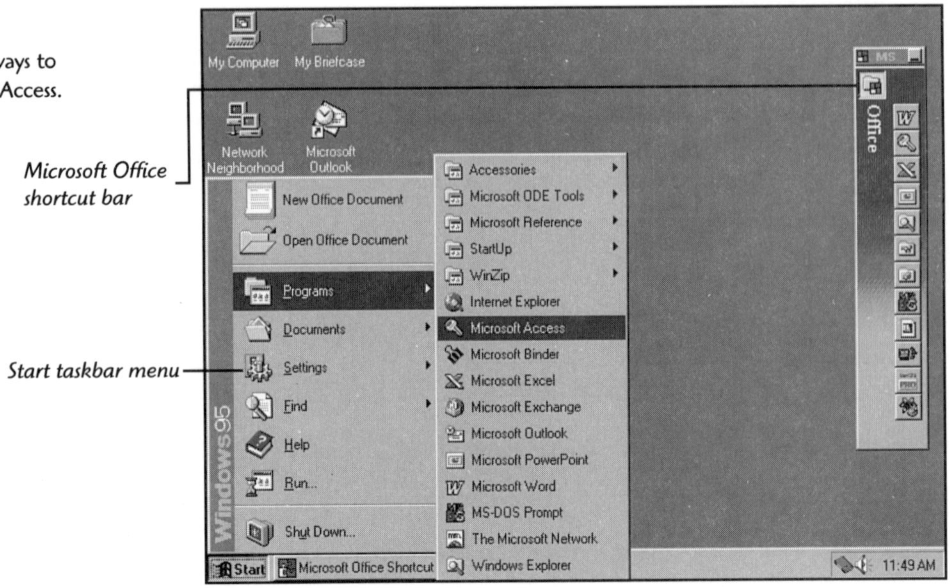

Microsoft Office shortcut bar

Start taskbar menu

Starting Access 97 from the Start taskbar menu

The first way to open Access 97 is via the Start menu. Here's what you do:

1 Click the Start menu button, located on the Windows 95 taskbar. In most cases, the taskbar is located at the bottom of the screen; although it can be moved to other locations.

2 Choose Programs. A submenu is displayed.

3 Locate Microsoft Access in the submenu and select it. Access 97 now starts.

The second way is even easier, provided the Microsoft Office shortcut bar is open and displays Microsoft Access as one of its shortcuts. This may be located on your Windows 95 desktop (on the computer screen, not your desk). The Microsoft Access button appears on the Office shortcut bar only if you, or your computer expert, have told the shortcut bar to display the button.

Q&A *Why don't I see a set of buttons like the Microsoft Office shortcut bar?*

If you don't see a Microsoft Office shortcut bar like the one displayed in Figure 2.1, it may be at the top of the screen, or you may not have your computer set up to open it on startup. Check with your Microsoft Office guru about how to get this program to run.

If the shortcut bar does not have the Microsoft Access icon displayed, you have to add it. Read the next section to learn how to add Access 97 to the shortcut bar; otherwise, skip to the section "Starting Access 97 from the Microsoft Office shortcut bar."

Adding Access 97 to the Microsoft Office shortcut bar

Adding Access 97 to the shortcut bar is not as painful as it sounds. Here are the steps:

1 Double-click any spot on the shortcut bar that does not display a shortcut button. The Customize dialog box is displayed.

2 Click the Buttons tab. In the Show these Files as Buttons list, you see a list of buttons you can include on the shortcut bar.

3 Click the Microsoft Access check box. A check mark indicates that the button will be displayed on the shortcut bar (see Figure 2.2).

4 Click OK. The Microsoft Access icon now appears as a button in the shortcut bar.

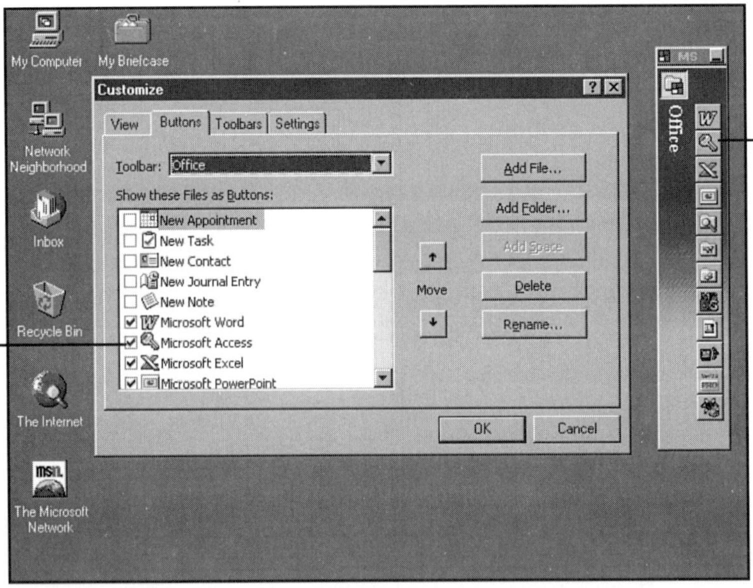

Fig. 2.2
Adding Microsoft Access to the Microsoft Office shortcut bar is easy with the Custom-ize dialog box.

Click here to put a check mark next to Microsoft Access.

The Microsoft Access icon appears here.

Q&A **What if I don't see Microsoft Access in the immediate choices?**

You then have to click the scroll bar on the right side of the Show these Files as Buttons list. If you can't find it by scrolling through all of the choices, then bug your favorite computer guru to show you how to use the Add File command.

❝ Plain English, please!

A **tab** is used to specify a page of information on a dialog box or form. These are the same as the tabbed dialog boxes used in Office products, such as the Options dialog box in Word and Access 97. You can also create your own tabbed forms. This is covered in Chapter 20. **❞**

TIP **Follow the steps just given to add shortcuts to some of your other** favorite Office applications, such as Word and Excel. That way, your applications are only a click away!

Starting Access 97 from the Microsoft Office shortcut bar

Starting Access 97 from the shortcut bar is even easier than working with the Start menu. All you have to do is click the Microsoft Access button, and that's it.

NOTE **The methods just described are successful as long as Office was** installed with the defaults. There are other ways that Access 97 can be opened. You can create a shortcut on the Windows 95 desktop or you can open Access 97 by double-clicking the .exe file through Windows Explorer.

Opening Access 97 for the first time

When you have started Access 97 by using your favorite method, the Access 97's opening screen is displayed. If this is the first time you have opened Access 97, you see the screen shown in Figure 2.3.

Fig. 2.3
Access 97 starts with a friendly face that belongs to the Office Assistant.

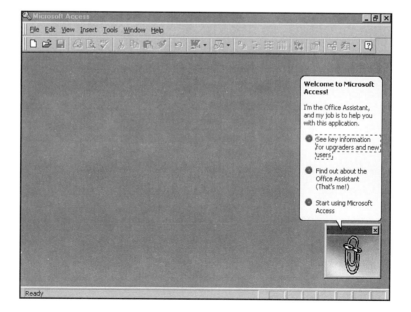

The little guy that appears in the bottom-right corner of the Access 97 window is what is known as the Office Assistant.

The Office Assistant helps you as you work with the various Office 97 applications and is covered in Chapter 3, "Getting Help When You Need It." The choices the Assistant gives you in Figure 2.3 are:

- **See key information for upgraders and new users** This is where you can find out about some of the features that Access 97 includes. Differences between versions of Access also appear here.

- **Find out about the Office Assistant** Explains what the Office Assistant does for you when in Access.

- **Start using Microsoft Access** Lets you get going using Access 97.

Click the last choice: Start using Microsoft Access.

You are now given Access 97's opening dialog box. This dialog box, shown in Figure 2.4, lets you choose between creating a new database, using either a blank database or the Database Wizard, and opening a current database.

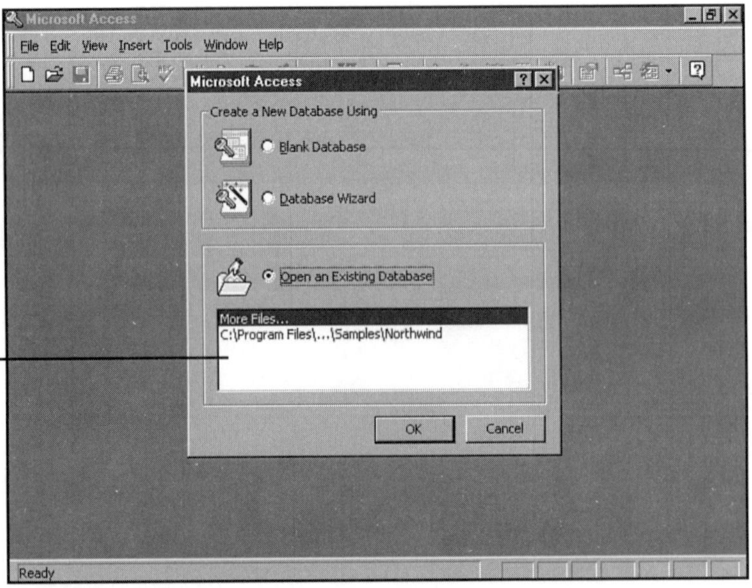

Fig. 2.4
The Access 97 opening dialog box appears whenever you go into Access 97.

Recent files list —

Notice that Access 97's sample application, Northwind, is displayed in the list of current files, even though you haven't opened Access 97 before. Northwind is a great demo database application provided by Microsoft that gives you examples of how to use some of Access 97's most common and powerful features.

 TIP **There are two other samples databases—Orders and Development Solutions**—that are also supplied by Microsoft. These are located in the same directory as Northwind. Later, when you get comfortable working with Access 97, you may want to take a look at them.

Because Microsoft was nice enough to give an example to start with, let's take advantage of it. Click the file Northwind.mdb that is listed at the bottom of the opening dialog box, in the recent file list, and then click the OK button.

 Plain English, please!

I mention Northwind.**mdb**, even though only Northwind is displayed. As with other files, databases have what is called a file extension. This consists of three characters that designate what kind of file it is. In this case, mdb stands for Microsoft Database. Whether this extension is displayed or not depends on your settings in Windows Explorer.

 TIP **You can also double-click the name of the database that has been opened** before in the recent file list, instead of highlighting it and clicking the OK button.

You then see the opening screen of the Northwind Traders sample database application, shown in Figure 2.5. Click OK. You are taken to the Database window, showing the Northwind database.

Fig. 2.5
Access 97 comes with some sample databases to show you how to use it.

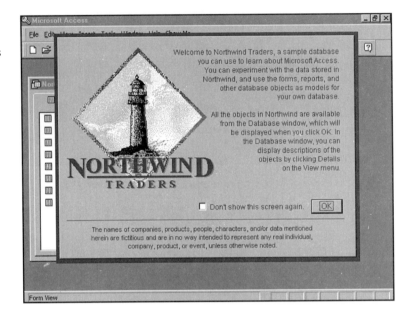

Taking a look at the Database window

The Database window is where you do most of your work. You can see the Database window in Figure 2.6, with the Tables tab displayed.

Fig. 2.6
You can think of the Database window as your command center for working with your database.

These tabs represent Object types that can be found in the database.

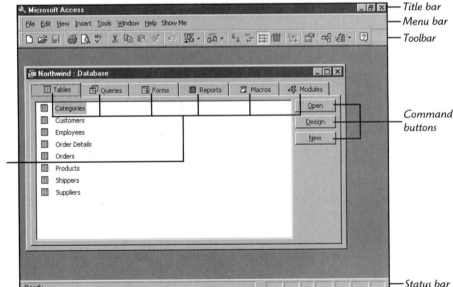

The tabs that are displayed along the top of the Database window allow you to switch to whichever object type you happen to be working on. The tab that is in front is the "active" or current object type. Simply click another tab to switch to another object type.

 Plain English, please!

As mentioned in Chapter 1, an **object** in Access refers to one of the major tools that you work with. These are tables, queries, forms, and reports. Macros and modules are also considered objects, and are used to automate some of the tasks that are extremely tedious. I cover the various objects in the rest of the book, starting with tables in Chapter 5, "Learning the Basics About Database Tables." 99

The nice thing about the way the Database window's tabs are organized is that they appear *left to right* in the order that you will use them when creating your own database. For example, you start creating your database by creating tables, moving on to queries, and so on.

The command buttons, which appear down the right side of the Database window, allow you to:

- **Open**   Open or Run the specific type of object whose tab you have chosen. For instance, you open a form, run a macro, and preview a report.

- **Design**   Open an existing object in the Design view, where you will modify the object.

- **New**   Create a new object of the current object type with the New button.

These commands are discussed throughout this book as you look at the various objects.

When you first create a database, there are no objects listed in the area below the tabs. But as you create your objects, they are added to this area. You can see from the Northwind database, shown in Figure 2.6, that it contains a variety of objects.

As with other Windows applications, you have menus and toolbars that provide commands and utilities for working in Access. Each Access 97 object type will display its own custom toolbar depending on the *view* you're using.

The menu bar remains the same for all object types, but the submenus change depending on which *view* you are in.

 Plain English, please!

> In Access 97, you can open objects, such as a table, in different **views**. For instance, a table can be open in Datasheet view, where you enter data, or Design view, where you modify the structure of the table itself. You are shown the different views as you work on each of the objects. 🙦

What is a menu and what does it do?

Just as restaurant menus present you with choices, menus in an application also give you choices in the commands that can be performed.

Sometimes when you choose a command from a menu, you may get what is called a *submenu*. You can see an example of a submenu in Figure 2.7, where the File menu has been selected and is displaying its submenu choices.

Fig. 2.7
You can choose commands from Access 97's various menus and submenus.

Command icon (same as toolbar)

Command executes

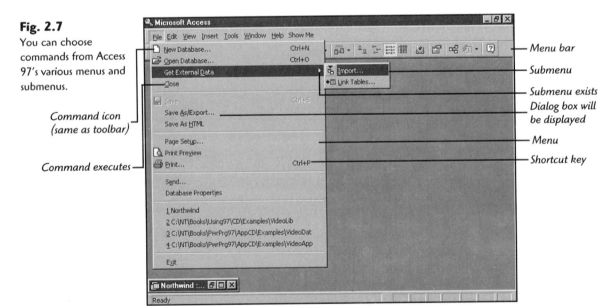

What do all the commands on the File menu do? Don't worry, as we work through creating a database, you'll be introduced to these commands and several others on the menu bar. And, after a while, you'll realize that many of these menu commands are the same no matter which object type you're working with.

When you select a command on the menu bar, a menu is displayed listing all the commands associated with that particular menu item. Menus and submenus are a bit more advanced in Office 97 than in previous versions. Here is a list of items to note about Office 97 menus and submenus:

- The icons to the left of the command are identical to the icons in the toolbar button of the same command.

- Some commands have shortcut keys that are displayed to the right of the command.

- If a submenu exists for a command, an arrow will be to the right of the command.

- An ellipsis (…) indicates that a dialog box will be displayed. Plain commands will execute when you click them.

 Plain English, please!

> A **dialog box** is a separate window that usually takes input for a particular task. You are then able to accept changes you have made or cancel them. For more information about what you will see in dialog boxes, as well as in other windows in Access 97, see the next section "Getting familiar with Access 97 dialog boxes."

Getting familiar with Access 97 dialog boxes

When you choose a command that has an ellipsis to the right of it, you'll find yourself facing a dialog box. A dialog box means that the computer needs additional information from you before it can execute the command you selected from the menu or submenu. As shown in Figure 2.8, there are several ways to enter information into a dialog box, depending on the kind of information that is needed. These various data-entry methods are also known as *controls*. A control can be anything from a command box to a text box or drop-down list.

The following list explains all the dialog box controls shown in Figure 2.8 and how to use them:

- **What's This? button**   This button provides help for other controls displayed in the dialog box. For example, if you have a question about what an option or command button does, click the What's This? button, and then click the command you want to learn about. Access 97 gives you an explanation of what the control does. More information on this control is in Chapter 3, "Getting Help When You Need It."

- **Close button**   Click this button to close the dialog box.

- **Tabs**   Click a tab to switch to another page of information.

- **Text box**   This is one of the more common controls. Click the text box and enter the required information. This can be anything from a number to a title of a file to a text description.

- **Drop-down list or combo box**   This supplies a list of values you can choose from. You can either click the text box and enter the value, or click the down arrow to the right of the list and choose a value from the list.

- **Check box**   Click this control to place a check mark in the box. A check mark indicates that the feature or control is "on," or activated. Click the box again to remove the check mark and turn off the control.

- **Option group**   You can only turn on or activate one of the controls in an option group at a time by clicking the radio button. A dot indicates the control is on. Click the radio button again to turn off the control.

- **Radio button**   Radio buttons are used in an Option group to make a selection.

- **OK button**   Click this button to accept the changes you've made in the dialog box and close it.

- **Cancel button**   Click this button if you want to reject the changes you've made in a dialog box. The dialog box closes.

You will also be using some of these controls in creating your own forms, discussed starting Chapter 17, "Creating Forms the Quick Way."

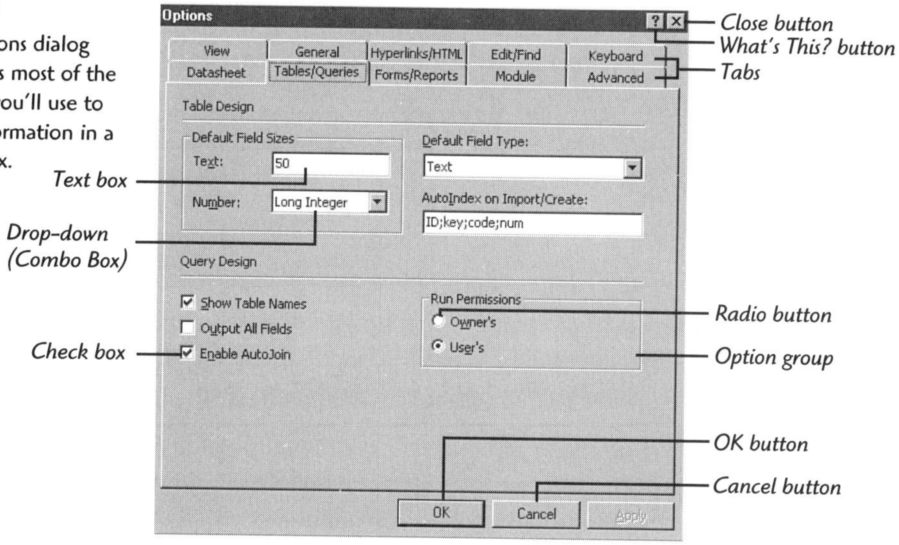

Fig. 2.8
The Options dialog box shows most of the controls you'll use to enter information in a dialog box.

Text box

Drop-down (Combo Box)

Check box

Close button
What's This? button
Tabs

Radio button

Option group

OK button

Cancel button

Using toolbars for quick action

Generally, toolbars contain the commands that the Microsoft Access team thought you would use most often in the particular area of the product you are in. Just as with menus, you see different toolbar commands for different areas in Access 97. If you have a question about what the button does, place the cursor over the button, and a ScreenTip appears, as seen in Figure 2.9.

Fig. 2.9
ScreenTips can help you figure out what the commands are on the current toolbar.

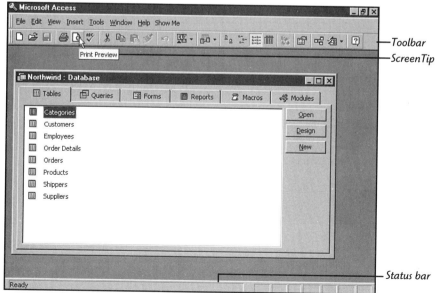

Toolbar
ScreenTip

Status bar

Q&A   ***Why is it that even though I move the cursor around on the button I am interested in, the ScreenTip doesn't show up?***

The reason the ScreenTip doesn't show up is because you *are* moving the cursor around. Just place the cursor over the button and take your hands off the mouse. The ScreenTip then appears.

The status bar

The status bar, located at the bottom of the Access 97 window, is used to display messages to you as Access 97 performs its tasks.

For example, any time you execute a command—such as printing a report or saving a file—or place the cursor over a menu item or button, the status bar displays some additional information about the task that is being performed, or will even tell you that a command can't be executed because certain conditions do not exist.

You have now seen some of the tools that are provided throughout Access 97. Now it's time to take a look at how you can get help when working in Access 97.

Getting Help When You Need It

● In this chapter:

● **What are the different ways to get Help in Access 97?**

● **Meeting the Assistant for your Help needs**

● **Taking advantage of context-sensitive Help**

● **Looking up topics with the index**

● **What's this "What's This?"**

One of the big secrets to learning Access 97 is knowing how to get Help when you need it. . . . . >

One of the things that users in Access use most is Help. Even when you have been using Access for years, it is such a big product that you can't remember everything. The folks at Microsoft know this, and they have been working hard with every release to come up with a better, more "user-friendly" method of giving you Help.

When you open the help menu on the standard toolbar, you find there are a number of ways to get Help in Access 97.

Table 3.1 provides a short description of each. I delve into them in greater detail throughout the chapter.

Table 3.1 Types of Help in Access 97

Help title	Description
Microsoft Access Help F1	This is where you get most of your Help while in Access. The Assistant is activated and answers questions you have.
Contents and Index	This is the traditional method of getting Help. You can find the topic you need Help on in a table of contents type listing, look it up in a index, or create a search for it.
What's This?	After choosing What's This?, you can point to an object on your Access 97 window and Help gives you a description of that object.
Microsoft on the Web	Everything you want to know about using Access 97 on the Internet and the World Wide Web, but were afraid to ask.
About Microsoft Access	Tons of system information about Access 97 and the computer that you are running it on.
Context Sensitive Help	Although not on the Help menu, Access allows you to press F1 wherever you are in Access 97, and Help attempts to bring up information directly relating to that topic.

Help from the Office Assistant!

The best way to describe the Office Assistant is to think of the movie *Star Wars*. In this movie, the hero, Luke Skywalker, meets one of his mentors named Obiwan Kanobi. Now, Obiwan, also known as Ben Kanobi, gets taken out by Darth Vader in the middle of the movie. Although Ben is now history,

Luke can hear him saying stuff like, "Use the Force, Luke," when Luke needs him the most. That's how I picture the Office Assistant.

When you choose Help, Microsoft Access Help, your Office Assistant window appears on the screen. You can see the Office Assistant in Figure 3.1.

Fig. 3.1
The Office Assistant waits to help you learn Access 97.

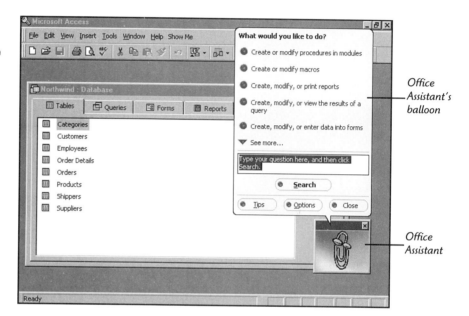

TIP

If you are in the Database window, instead of using the menu, just press F1. Obiwan, I mean the Office Assistant, appears.

The Office Assistant answers all

To get the fastest results from the Office Assistant, type in a question where it says Type your question here, and then click Search. For this example, type in the term Database window, and then click Search, or press the Enter key. You then get a list of possible subjects to narrow the topic (see Figure 3.2). Notice that even though it says to type a question, any term will work.

If you see the topic you're interested in, click the blue dot beside the Help topic, and the explanation is displayed; or, click the blue down arrow for more choices.

The Office Assistant takes the place of any messages you receive in Access 97, such as error or save messages, while it is displayed.

Fig. 3.2
Using specific phrases
helps the Office
Assistant quickly find
your answers.

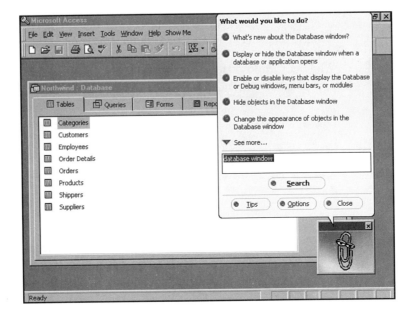

Changing the Office Assistant options and choosing a new Office Assistant

Because the Assistant is an intricate part of working with Access 97, it is worthwhile to show you how to change some of the options for the Office Assistant. To change options, click the Assistant to display his main question box (balloon). Click the button entitled Options (refer to Figure 3.1). Access 97 then opens the Office Assistant dialog box (see Figure 3.3) that allows you to change options and choose the various assistants located in the Assistant Gallery.

The options that are set as defaults for the Assistant work well for most people most of the time, but we all have our own way of working. Turn the default settings off by clicking the box next to the feature to remove the check mark; or turn options on by clicking the box so the check mark appears. If you want to reset the Office Assistant options back to the default settings without saving changes, click Cancel.

When you're satisfied with the options, click the Gallery tab. Page through the various Assistant "personalities" by clicking the Next and Back buttons located at the bottom of the Gallery page. You'll probably get attached to one assistant over the others. For example, click the Next button until the Genius is displayed, as shown in Figure 3.4. This guy is my favorite.

Fig. 3.3
By setting these options to reflect the way you work, you will get along better with the Office Assistant.

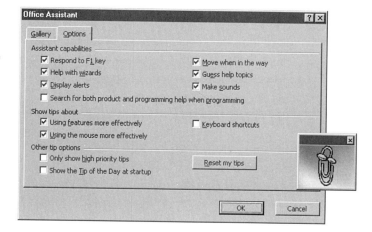

Fig. 3.4
The ClipIt assistant looks a little jealous of the Genius, because the Genius is about to replace him.

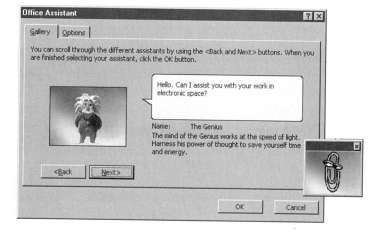

Click the OK button, located at the bottom of the Office Assistant dialog. Your assistant now changes to the Genius.

Plain English, please!

When talking about personalities and the Office Assistant, there are a number of characters that are included that have different animated features. They all serve the same purpose. Each just has different "cute" movements they perform. 🙶🙶

TIP **The Office assistants have a number of features besides showing** Help. They have sound and are animated so they can break up the monotony of the workday. To see some of the animations the assistant can do, right-click the mouse on the assistant, then choose Animate! The assistant will then perform a movement. If you do this a few times, it will show various entertaining movements.

Your Genius assistant is now ready to help you throughout the rest of this book, but if you'd rather not take advantage of his help, you can dismiss him by clicking the Close button on the upper-right corner of his window.

Using Access 97's context-sensitive Help and the What's This? feature

Just like a good spouse who is sensitive to your needs, Access 97 takes care of your Help needs by being there with the topical information whenever you press F1.

Working directly with context-sensitive Help

To test this out, restart Access 97. When you get to the Microsoft Access opening dialog box with the choices of Create a New Database Using or Open an Existing database, press F1. Because the Open an Existing Database option is selected, a Help screen pops up to explain that option (see Figure 3.5).

Fig. 3.5
Use context-sensitive
Help to get informa-
tion about a particular
feature.

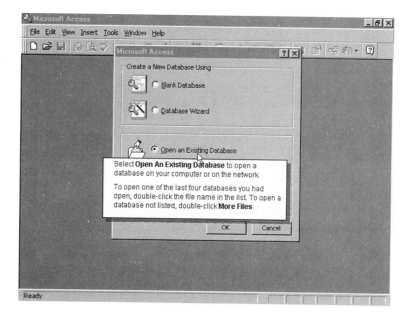

For another example, choose Blank Database in the group Create a New
Database Using. Now press F1. You get a description of all the choices within
the Create a New Database Using option group (see Figure 3.6).

Fig. 3.6
When you have a
number of choices for
a group of actions,
they are all described.

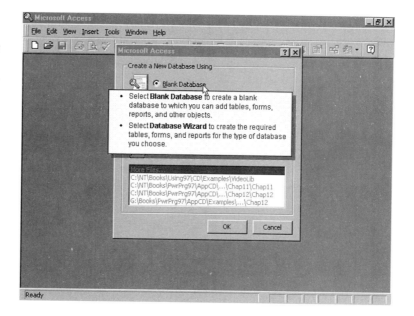

TIP **When you press F1 in some areas of Access 97, you see a full** screen of information. This is the full Access 97 Help system, rather than just the description boxes that usually appear.

Looking at the What's This? feature

There are times when one of the following occurs:

- You are at a place in Access 97 where there are so many possibilities that you need help.

- You are at a location in Access 97 where the place that has the focus is not what you need immediate help on.

When you are in one of these situations, you can use the What's This? Help feature to point to a specific item on the screen. Access 97 tries to help you with the topic you point to. If you are still at the Access 97 opening dialog box, click the Cancel button. The Access 97 screen opens with no Database window. Now, say you want to get more information about the Open Database toolbar button (the second icon from the left with the open file folder). Do this:

1 Choose What's This? from the Help menu. You see a pointer with a question mark attached to it.

2 Click the left mouse button on the Open Database toolbar button. You get a description similar to the one in Figure 3.7.

TIP **In some dialog boxes, when you can't get to the menu choices,** you can click the right mouse button, and <u>W</u>hat's This? is one of the choices on the menu!

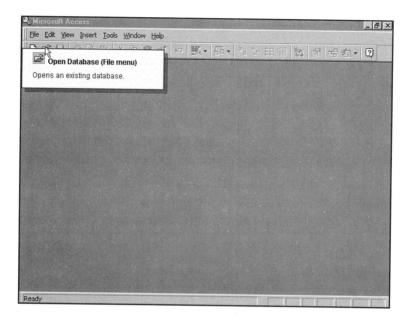

Working with the Contents and Index dialog box

One of the oldest forms of Access 97 Help, and still a very useful one, is the Contents and Index dialog box. This Help feature is great to use when you have:

- Questions about how an area of Access 97 works

- A specific item you want to look up

- A topic or phrase to search for

Finding Help with the Contents page

Using the Contents page is like looking at a book. You see the titles of the chapters in the Table of Contents. Then, based on the title, you read further into the chapter to see if the specific topic is there.

For example, if you want to find out how to get started working in the Database window, you would:

1 Choose Help, Contents, and Index. This opens the Help Topics dialog box. The first tab displayed is the Contents tab. The closed book icon indicates there are additional topics below the current topic.

2 Double-click the topic Creating a Database and Working in the Database Window. The closed book icon changes to an opened book. You then see more choices indented under this topic. The icon that looks like a page with a question mark on it denotes a page of information. Click the topic to read a description of the item. You'll also see more closed books, which means there is at least another level of topics to be displayed.

3 The topic you are interested in, Working in the Database Window, has a book by it. This means there is another level of information, so double-click it. You then see the topics listed in Figure 3.8.

Fig. 3.8
You can examine choices more closely to find the topic you are interested in.

Opened topic

Page of information

Additional level of information

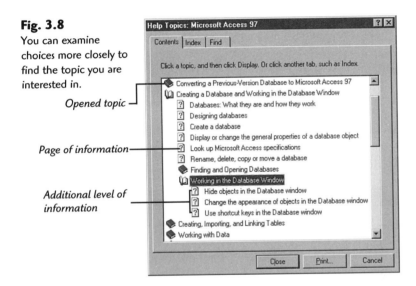

You can now double-click the topic that you are interested in.

Looking up a Help topic in the Index tab

If you have a specific item you are interested in, you can look it up in the Index tab. Just do this:

1 Click the Index tab in the Help Topics dialog box. Let's look up the same topic, Database window, using this method.

2 In the text box 1. Type in the first few letters of the word you're looking for; start typing the words database window. When you get as far as "database w," Access 97 displays all the items you need in list 2. Click the index entry you want, and then click Display (see Figure 3.9).

Fig. 3.9
One or two words can
bring forth a good
number of topics.

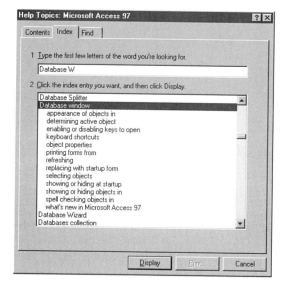

Using Find to find Help

The last tab on the Help Topics dialog box is the Find tab. This tab lets you locate information on any topic, provided it is included in the list of Help topics. Before locating information on topics using Find, you have to create the indexed file.

Creating the indexed Find file

To create the indexed Find file, while still in the Contents and Index Help dialog box, do this:

1 Click the Find tab. You then see the Find Setup Wizard (see Figure 3.10). This creates an indexed file to help you locate words and phrases.

2 For now, accept the default of Minimize database size (recommended) and click Next. You are brought to a new page that tells you to click Finish.

3 Click Finish. Access 97 now creates the file that will allow you to locate words and phrases. The amount of time this takes will depend on the speed of your computer.

Fig. 3.10
Here you get to decide
how big you want your
search file to be.

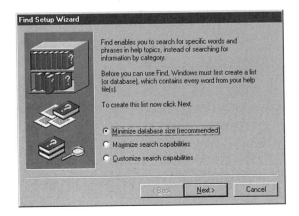

This completed indexed file will now be used whenever you click the Find
tab. Creating the indexed file only has to be done once, unless you want to
change the size of the file. You can now get help using the Find tab.

Finding Help for a word or phrase

To locate a word or phrase within the indexed Find file, type it into the first
field, 1. Type the word(s) you want to find (see Figure 3.11). For example,
type the word "database." As you do, Access 97 fills up the second list field
with words that match your search, and the third list field displays a number
of topics that relate to your word.

In the third list, highlight the topic that you want to see and click Display to
take a look at it.

Fig. 3.11
Another way to find
Help is using the Find
tab.

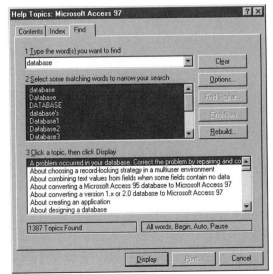

Getting Help for Access 97 on the Web

One of the coolest new features of Access 97 and Office 97 is the capability to use these products with the Internet and World Wide Web.

By choosing Help, Microsoft on the Web, you will see that Access 97 displays a submenu where all the commands have the Internet Explorer icon beside them (see Figure 3.12).

Fig. 3.12
These menu items all connect you to various Web sites.

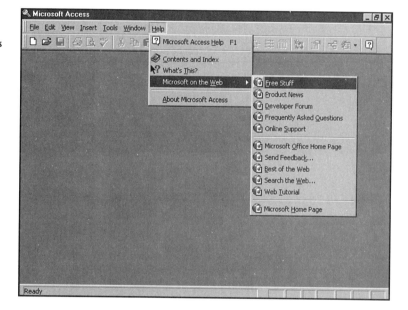

To access any of these commands, you must first have a Web browser—such as Internet Explorer or Netscape Navigator—installed, and you must have an account with an online service or Internet Service Provider that lets you access the Internet. Choose any command off the menu, and Access 97 automatically connects you to your online service or ISP, starts the browser, then goes to the Web site that the command indicates.

A good example is to choose the Web Tutorial command. To do this:

1 Choose Help, Microsoft on the Web, then Web Tutorial. At this time, the Internet Explorer, or whatever browser you are using, starts. Then, you are asked to sign on to your online service (in my case, Microsoft Network) or ISP (see Figure 3.13).

2 Log in by typing in your user ID and password or however your Web browser requires you to.

After you have logged in, the browser, having been told where to go, brings you to the Web site, which, in this case, is An Internet Tutorial.

Take a few minutes now to visit some of the other Web sites on the Microsoft on the Web submenu.

Finding information about Access 97 and your computer system

The final place you can look for Help actually gives you information about your system rather than specific help for Access.

To see some of the information, choose Help, About Microsoft Access. Access brings up an information window that displays the registered user and the Product ID. You can then click the System Info command button.

For the most part, you'll never have to go to this screen. But there are cases when you may run into problems and find the person who is helping you needs you to read some of the information to him or her over the phone. So, it is a good thing to at least know where it is located.

Creating and Opening Databases

● **In this chapter:**

● **How do I open a database that already exists?**

● **Creating a database**

● **Save time using the Database Wizard**

Opening an Access 97 database is a piece of cake. Creating an Access database isn't. But Microsoft has provided some useful tools to help you organize your information into database tables and prevent (or at least reduce) trouble. . . . . ⊜

Whenyou are working with Microsoft Word, creating a new document is pretty easy, as is opening a document. The same can be said of Access 97 databases. You need only learn the right commands to get into any database.

In Chapter 2, "Introducing Access 97," you learned how to open an existing database when you first start Access 97. Now it's time to learn more about opening an existing database with Access 97 already open.

Opening an existing database

To open a database, follow these steps:

1 If Access 97 is currently open, close it by double-clicking the X in the upper-right corner of the Access 97 window, or choose File, Exit.

2 Open Access 97. If you need a refresher on starting Access 97, refer back to Chapter 2 and the section "Starting Up Access 97."

3 At the Opening dialog box, click the Cancel button. You are now faced with an empty Access 97 window, as shown in Figure 4.1.

4 Choose File from the menu at the top of the screen. Located at the bottom of the File menu shown in Figure 4.2, you see what is called the Recent Files List. Make a note of the path displayed on your computer for the Northwind database. In this case, the default path is:

C:\Program Files\MicrosoftOffice\Office\Samples\Northwind

 TIP **A quick method of opening this file is to position the cursor over** the file in the Recent Files List, and double-click. As a default, the Recent Files List lists the last four files opened.

5 Choose Open Database from the already opened File menu. You now see the Open dialog box, shown in Figure 4.3.

Using the path noted in step 4, locate the Northwind database using steps 6 through 8. (Notice from Figure 4.3 that I start in the My Documents Folder. This is the default setting for opening and creating databases.)

Fig. 4.1
Here is the Access 97 window with no database currently open.

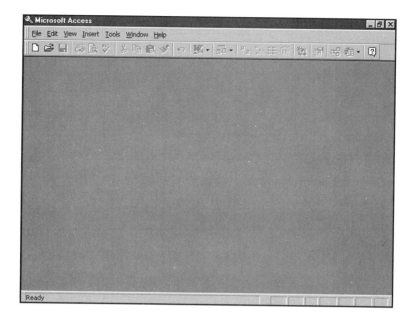

Fig. 4.2
The Recent Files List saves you from having to locate files every time you want to open them.

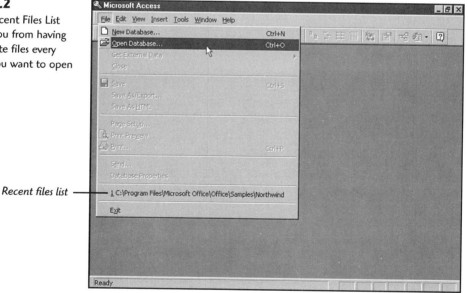

Recent files list ——

TIP **If you want to change the default setting for opening and creating** databases, choose Tools, Options. Click the General tab. You can then change the Default Database Folder property, and click OK. After this, when you go to open or create a database, you start out in the folder you just chose.

Fig. 4.3
This Open dialog box is
used to open existing
databases.

Start location ——

Up One Level button ——

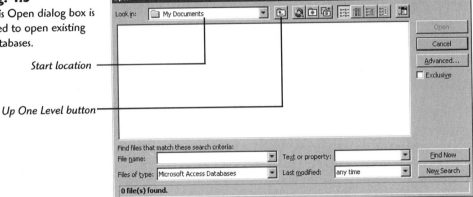

6 Click the Up One Level button once to bring you to the top directory on your machine. Listed in your folders is Program Files.

7 Double-click Program Files, then continue to choose the folders along the path for Northwind.mdb. In the case of Figure 4.3, it is C:\Program Files\Microsoft Office\Office\Samples. When you get to the Samples folder, you see Northwind displayed in the Files window, as shown in Figure 4.4.

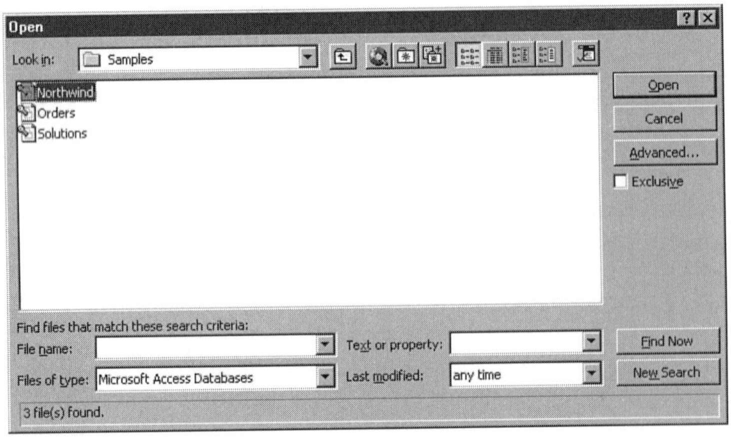

Fig. 4.4
Opening the
Northwind database.

8 Click the Northwind database, and then click Open. Click OK to display the Database window for the Northwind database.

Now choose File, Exit to exit Access again. This is so you and I can start from the same place for creating a new database.

Creating new databases

There are two ways to create a new database:

- Create a blank database. This creates a database with no tables, queries, forms, reports, and so on.

- Create a database using the Database Templates supplied by Microsoft Office. This creates a full-fledged database application with predefined forms, queries, and reports that are designed by answering questions asked by the Wizard.

I am going to discuss how to use both methods.

Creating a Blank Database

Creating a blank database is actually the simpler of the two methods. You are going to create a video library, called VideoLib, for your first database (because videos are one of my hobbies). You will then use the VideoLib and the Northwind databases as examples for learning all the features of Access 97 throughout the remainder of the book. To create a blank database, follow these steps:

1 Open Access, then click the New Database button. The New dialog box is displayed, as shown in Figure 4.5. You may notice that there are two tabbed pages on this dialog box: General and Databases.

Fig. 4.5
The New dialog box allows you to create a blank database, or choose from other database templates.

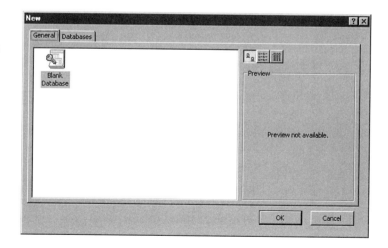

The General tab contains the template for a blank database, and the Databases tab contains the database templates that you were introduced to in Chapter 1. You learn a lot more about these in Chapter 5, "Learning the Basics About Database Tables."

2 Click the General tab.

3 Click the Blank Database icon, and then click OK. The File New Database dialog box is displayed, as shown in Figure 4.6.

 TIP **Notice that, as with opening a database, the default folder this** database will be saved in is called My Documents (unless you changed your default save directory). You may have to locate this at a later time, so be sure to keep a record of your folder name somewhere.

4 Type VideoLib in the File Name text box, as seen in Figure 4.6, and then click Create.

Fig. 4.6
Creating the new database called VideoLib.

Type the database name here.

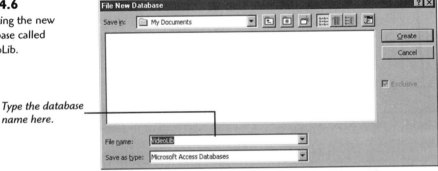

The VideoLib database is created, and the empty database is displayed on your screen, as shown in Figure 4.7.

You will come back to the VideoLib database in the next chapter, when you see you how to create tables, but now I want to show you how to use the Database Wizard to quickly create a database application. Close the VideoLib database by choosing File, Close. You should now be back at the blank Access 97 window.

 TIP **You can click the X in the upper-right corner of the database** window to close the database quickly!

Fig. 4.7
Your first database:
VideoLib.mdb.

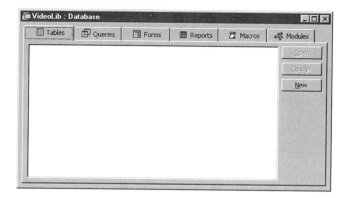

Creating a database using the Database Wizard

The database wizard gives you a method for creating small "standard" type database applications. The various database templates supplied organize information and create tables and fields that are "typical" for each particular database, but may not be exactly what you want. If needed, you can change these tables and fields, which is covered in Part II, "Creating a Solid Foundation for Your Database." Many of the other concepts discussed in this section appear in greater detail throughout the rest of the book.

Starting the Database Wizard

To create a database using the Database Wizard, follow these steps:

1 Click the New Database button. The New dialog box is displayed, shown back in Figure 4.5, which gives you the General and Databases tabs.

2 Choose the Databases tab. You now see a window full of database templates that you can use to create the database you desire (see Figure 4.8).

3 Click the Book Collection template. You see a picture displayed in the Preview area.

4 Click OK and the File New Database dialog box is displayed, which allows you to name your database (see Figure 4.9). Leave Book Collection1 in the File Name field. Click Create.

Fig. 4.8
Creating a new
database application is
easy using the database
templates.

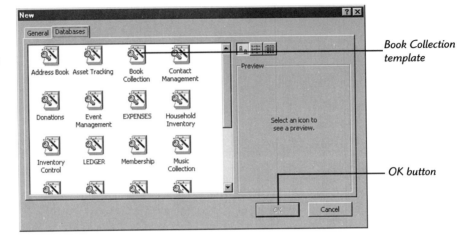

Book Collection
template

OK button

Fig. 4.9
We'll use the default
name assigned by the
Database Wizard.

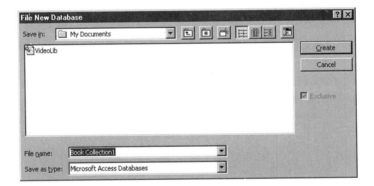

5 After the computer works for a bit, the first screen of the Database
Wizard appears, and a brief summary of the kinds of information in the
Book Collection1 database displays (see Figure 4.10). After reading
which tables will be created, click <u>N</u>ext.

TIP **If you are in a hurry and want Access 97 to pick the style (back-**
ground and fonts) for the forms and reports, click <u>F</u>inish. Access 97 does all
the work for you by creating the application immediately.

Fig. 4.10
This screen explains what information you will store (what tables you create) using the current Database template.

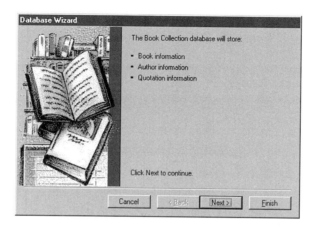

Choosing the information to include in your new database

The next screen identifies the tables that will be created, and what information to include in each table (see Figure 4.11). Tables are introduced in Chapter 5.

Fig. 4.11
Choose which fields you want in each table.

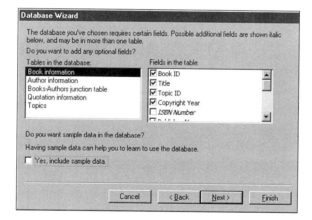

By clicking the different entries in the Tables in the database list box, the Fields in the table list on the right reflects the different fields that the Wizard will include (by default) in the selected table.

At this point, you can place or remove a check mark to decide whether you want to include various fields in your table. If a field is required, Access 97 does not let you un-check it, and displays an error message box to that effect.

Book ID is one of these fields. If you un-check Book ID, you will get the message "Sorry, this field is required and must be selected."

If you want to include sample data in your new database, click the check box for Yes, include sample data. This is a good idea if you've never created a database before because it gives you guidance as to the types of data that you can enter in each field. Click the Next button to move on to the next page.

 TIP If you decide to change one of your answers, simply click the **Back** button to return to this screen and make the change. Click Next until you locate the screen you left. To stop the Wizard at any time, click the Cancel button.

Choosing the style of your forms and reports

You see the page that allows you to specify how you want your forms to look (see Figure 4.12).

Fig. 4.12
Create a look for your forms that you will enjoy working with.

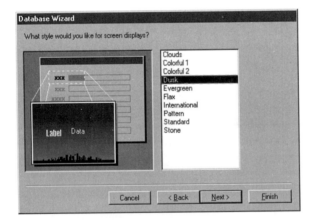

By choosing from the list of styles on the right, you change the graphic on the left to reflect your current choice. Choose Dusk, then click Next.

 Plain English, please!

Styles in Access 97 consist of bitmap graphics for the background of your form, as well as fonts and special effects for your controls. You see more about styles in Chapter 18, "Introducing Forms Design and Properties." **"**

In this screen, you choose a style for your reports. I use Corporate, which is the selection displayed in Figure 4.13.

Fig. 4.13
Reports created by the Database Wizard can have the style you choose.

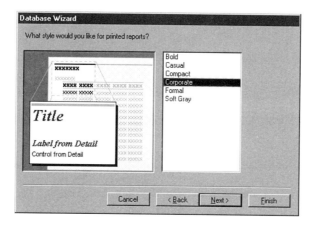

Click the Next button to move on to the next page.

Specifying a title for your Database

This next page, shown in Figure 4.14, asks what you would like the title to be, and supplies one for you called Book Collection. The Title name will be displayed on the application's main switchboard and is not used as the file name.

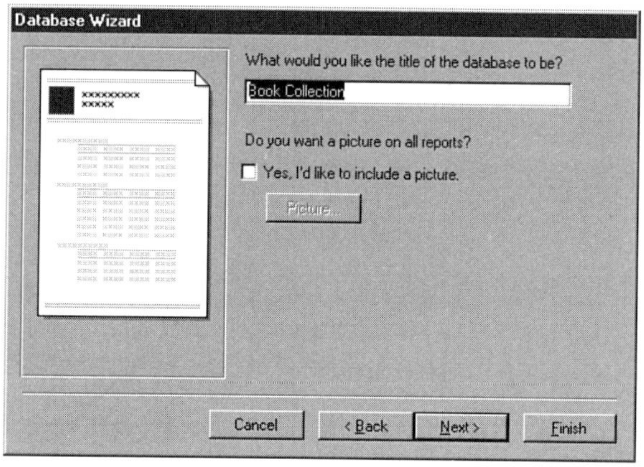

Fig. 4.14
Give your database application a title.

Plain English, please!

A **switchboard** is a form with command buttons that control what forms and reports you open in your application. Most applications created with Access 97 have a main switchboard. The Wizard creates the main switchboard for the current application. Chapter 23, "Fine-Tuning Your Database Application," discusses the creation of switchboards.

If you have a graphic image handy, perhaps a company logo, then you can include it by clicking the Yes, I'd Like to include a picture check box. This feature is beyond the scope of this book, so you can play with that on your own.

Click the Next button to move to the last page.

Finishing up and viewing the new database

This page asks if you want to start the database when Access 97 is finished creating it (see Figure 4.15). The default is Yes.

Fig. 4.15
Make sure you have answered the questions correctly before you click Finish.

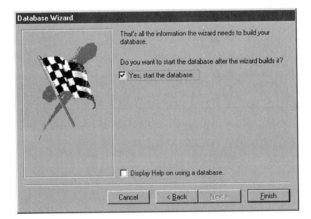

 CAUTION Up to this point, you could click the **B**ack button if you forgot any information or made a mistake. After you click the **F**inish button, however, you have to either start over from scratch with the Database Wizard, or modify the database yourself.

Click Finish. Access 97 then cranks out your new database application. This can take a few minutes, depending on the speed of your machine.

When it is done, you have just created—well, Access 97 just created—a full-fledged database application (see Figure 4.16).

Fig. 4.16
The Database wizard created this database application.

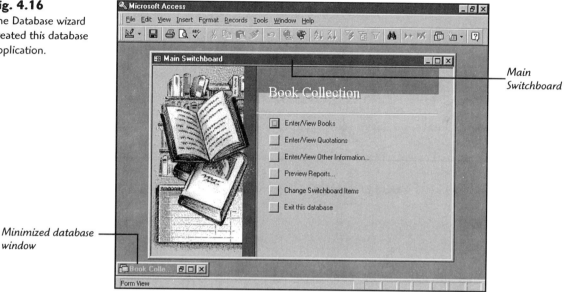

Minimized database window

Main Switchboard

Notice in Figure 4.16 that when you create the application, the main switchboard displays. You can also see the database window minimized to an icon. When you create your own databases, as we did when we created a blank database, you have to create your own main switchboard.

I will leave it up to you to click the switchboard choices and look at the various forms and reports created for this database.

Part II: Creating a Solid Foundation for Your Database

Learning the Basics About Database Tables

● **In this chapter:**

- **How tables play a part in the database**

- **Looking at two methods for creating a table**

- **Working with fields**

- **Entering information into your new table**

In Access 97, all your information is stored in tables. Tables are used by other Access 97 objects to display and change your information . . . . ▶

Tables are the foundation of an Access 97 database. You maintain your information within Access 97 tables, and tables are the source from which other objects such as queries, forms, and reports display and edit your information. You will learn more about using tables as sources for other Access 97 objects starting in Chapter 12, "Query Basics 101."

In this chapter, you learn to create database tables in the Datasheet view and the Design view. You create three tables in the VideoLib database. (We created this database in the last chapter.)

 TIP   **There is a third way of creating tables, using Table Wizards.**
This method is discussed in Chapter 8, "Saving Time with Table Wizards."

You will quickly create the first table, called tblRatings, using the Datasheet view. You will then use the Table Design view to create the other tables, called tblTapes and tblCategories. Creating tables in Design view is the more complete and recommended way.

 Plain English, please!

What are the features of Datasheet view and Design view? You can view Access 97 tables in two ways: Datasheet view and Design view. Datasheet view allows you to see the actual information stored in the table. It displays the information in a spreadsheet-type format that allows you to scroll around and browse through your information, with columns (fields) going across and rows (records) going down.

In Design view, you are actually modifying the design, or structure of the table (telling Access 97 how and what kind of information you want stored). You will learn more about Design view in the "Creating a new table with Table Design view" section, found later in this chapter. **99**

Open the VideoLib database by choosing File and then double-clicking the VideoLib entry in the Recent Files list, located at the bottom of the File menu.

TIP **If you don't see the VideoLib database at the bottom of the**
File menu, choose File, Open Database. Then locate the VideoLib database
using the Open dialog box, as described in Chapter 4, "Creating and
Opening Databases." In this case, because VideoLib.mdb is in the My
Documents folder, simply highlight it, and click Open.

The main database window appears, as shown in Figure 5.1.

Fig. 5.1
When you open the
database, the main
database window
appears. Notice the
Tables tab is the first
tab on the left.

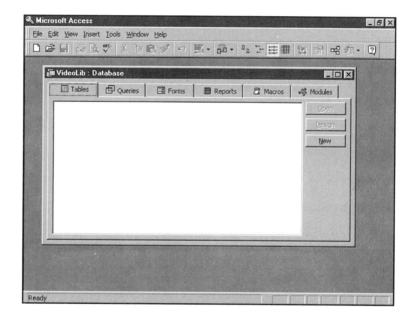

Creating a table with Datasheet view

When using Datasheet view to create tables, you specify field names for each
field. Access 97 then takes a best guess at what type of data is going to be put
into the fields, based on the information you typed into the fields in the first
record. For example, if you type "1" in a field, then Access 97 will set the data
type of the field to be Number. Type an "A" and Access 97 specifies a Text
data type. You will learn more about data types in the section, "Taking a
quick look at data types."

To create a table in Datasheet view, select the Tables tab (see Figure 5.1).
Notice the three buttons down the right side of the database window: Open,
Design, and New. You can click only the New button at this time; however,
here are the features of each button:

- **Open**   Opens an existing table in Datasheet view, allowing you to view, add, or edit information.

- **Design**   Opens an existing table in Design view, allowing you to view and change the table setup.

- **New**   Creates a new table using various methods.

Click the <u>N</u>ew button to display the New Table dialog box in Figure 5.2.

Fig. 5.2
The New Table dialog box gives you a number of ways to create new tables.

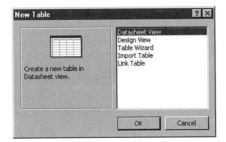

In the New Table dialog box, select Datasheet View and click OK. You are then given a Datasheet view with column headings Field1, Field2, Field3, and so on, all across the top of the datasheet, as shown in Figure 5.3.

Fig. 5.3
This datasheet is waiting for you to add your own fields.

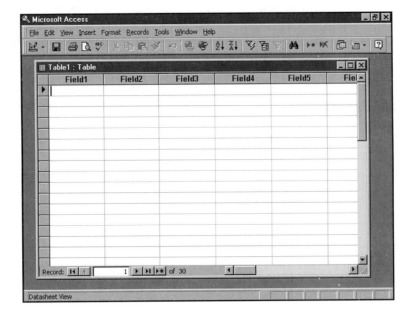

You may notice that the column headings are not descriptive. You can create your own column headings to name the fields that make up the table.

Naming fields in the table

When creating field names for your table, be sure to give them descriptive names. For example, if you create a table to store movie ratings, such as the table we'll create in this chapter, you may want to provide field names such as those in Figure 5.4.

Fig. 5.4
Naming your fields so they make sense can save a lot of hassle in the future.

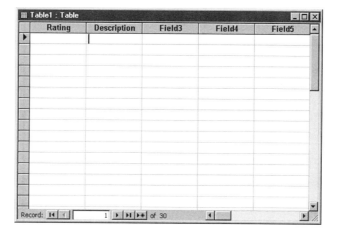

I will show you how to add these field names in a moment. First, here are some Access 97 guidelines, along with my tips, to keep in mind when naming fields.

> You can use up to 64 characters for your names. Don't be too wordy when creating your field names because you will be referring to the field names throughout your application, and it can be a pain to keep typing them out. For instance, for a field for the year-to-date sales, don't use: "YearToDateSales," use "YTDSales." And you also don't want to make the name so short that the meaning is totally obscure when you look at it. For example, the more obscure way to say the YTDSales would be YTDS. Most people recognize that YTD is year-to-date, but the S is not descriptive enough for Sales.

> You can use all letters, numbers, spaces, and special characters except the exclamation point, a period, an accent grave (`` ` ``), and brackets ([]). I don't recommend using spaces and special characters when specifying

your field names, or naming other Access 97 objects. Although Access 97 allows you to use spaces and special characters, you save many steps (and problems) later if you do not use them when naming your fields. To make the field name easier to read, you can capitalize the first letter of each word, for instance, "last name" becomes "LastName." You may be thinking, "But it really looks stupid not to have a space between the words last and name." Just hang on; you will see in Chapter 9, "A Closer Look at Field Properties," how to display spaces nicely for column headings and labels for your fields.

Do not use leading spaces. Access 97 will give you an error if you move out of the field name if you try to use a leading space.

❝ *Plain English, please!*

I mention using up to 64 **characters**. What is a character? When you type on the keyboard, you are using characters. Letters, digits 0 through 9, and other symbols are all characters. This means that you can use up to 64 combined letters, digits, or symbols for a field name. ❞

To create fields, follow these steps:

1 Place the cursor over the column heading you want to rename and double-click. The column heading will appear highlighted; you are in edit mode.

2 Type Rating and then press the Enter key.

3 Repeat the first two steps for the second column, using Description for the second field name (see Figure 5.4).

Now let's put data into the table.

Adding your information right away!

The great thing about using the Datasheet view method is that you can enter your information immediately, without switching to another view. To add data:

1 Click the first space in the Rating column and type G for the first rating.

2 Press Tab or Enter. This moves the cursor to the first space in the Description column.

3 Type the description for the Description column.

4 Press Tab or Enter again. This moves the cursor to the next row.

5 Repeat the first four steps for each rating, until you've added all the information, as shown in Figure 5.5.

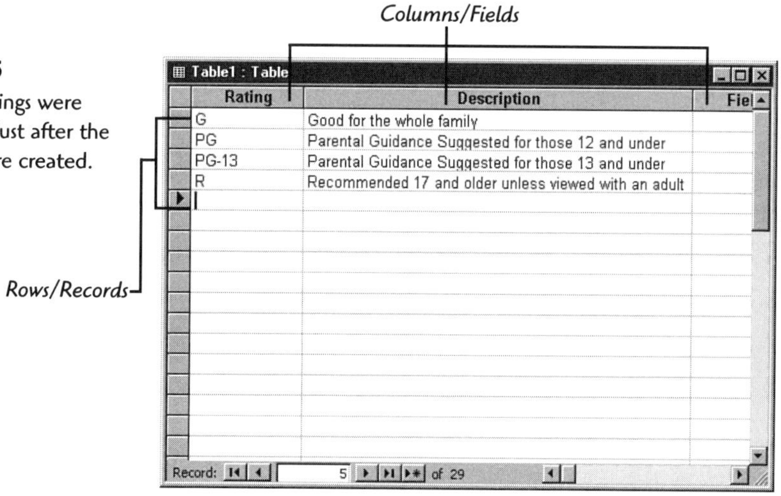

Fig. 5.5
These ratings were entered just after the fields were created.

Columns/Fields

Rows/Records

66 *Plain English, please!*

Fields and **records**, **columns** and **rows**. If you have used spreadsheets before, then you are probably familiar with these four terms.

- Fields hold specific pieces of information that define an item, usually displayed in a vertical column. In our example, Rating and Description are fields.

- Records are a set of related data fields that define an item, usually displayed in a row. In our example, a record, or row, is all the individual pieces of information stored together for a particular videotape.

In Figure 5.5, each row is an individual record of data that we entered. This row contains the fields Rating, "G" and the Description, "Good for the whole family." 99

Now that you've added some data to your table, it's a good time to save it.

Saving the table

After you have placed data in the table you created, you should save it. To save the table:

1 Choose File, Close. You are then asked: Do you want to save the changes to Table1?

2 Click Yes. You will then be shown the Save As dialog box.

3 Type tblRatings in the Table Name field, as seen in Figure 5.6.

 TIP When you want to save the table and continue working, you can choose File, Save or click the Save button on the toolbar. I recommend saving often; unlike other Office products, Access 97 doesn't have an automatic save feature. So whenever you make a significant change to your database, save the object you happen to be in.

Fig. 5.6
The name of the new table is tblRatings.

4 Click OK to save the table. A message box appears indicating there has not been a primary key specified for this table. Primary keys are discussed later in this chapter in the "Setting the Primary Key" section.

 Q&A **Why is there a tbl at the beginning of this table's name?**

Although not required, you may want to put the prefix tbl on tables and qry on queries to clearly distinguish between the two objects. Tables and queries can appear in the same list and can have the same or similar names. Using these abbreviations at the beginning helps you quickly find the file you want to open.

5 Click the No button. You then see the new table in the Database window, as seen in Figure 5.7.

Fig. 5.7
You have now created your first table, tblRatings.

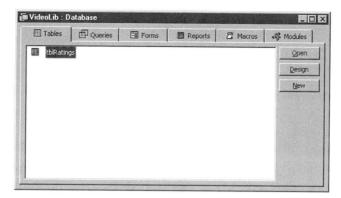

Creating a new table with Table Design view

When you create a table using the Table Design view, you specify more of the properties for each field. This includes the length and type of information used in the field. After creating a table with Design View, you know what you have told Access 97 to do. With Datasheet view, you can't set all the properties the way you want. You must open the table in Design View and change them.

 Plain English, please!

You can use **Properties** to describe a characteristic of an object, such as a field, form, or report. For example, Field Name describes the name of a field. Data Type describes the format of the data used in the field, such as numbers, text, or date.

In the main database window:

1 Click the Table tab; then choose New. The New Table dialog box appears.

2 Choose Design View and click OK. You are now in the Table Design view and are working with the Table Design window as seen in Figure 5.8.

Fig. 5.8
Welcome to the Table
Design view.

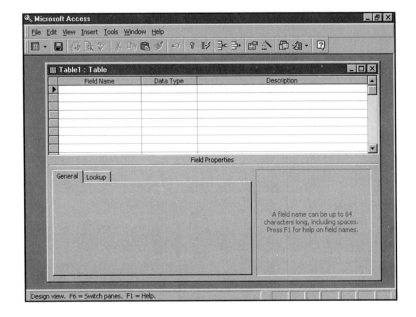

Working with the Table Design window

The Table Design window consists of four main parts: Field Name, Data Type, Description, and Field Properties. Remember, the purpose of the Table Design view is to help you specify the structure of the table for storing information.

Place the cursor in the first space in the Field Name column and type MovieTitle. Next, press Tab or Enter to go to the next column: Data Type. Notice there is a default given for the Data Type column of type Text.

 Plain English, please!

A **default** choice is the choice that the computer fills in if you don't select another choice. Although you can save time using default values, take a close look and make sure it is the correct choice. Defaults exist strictly for your convenience. To keep a default value, you press Tab or Enter to move on to the next choice.

Taking a quick look at data types

Of the various properties you will specify for a field, the data type is one of the most important. By picking a particular data type, you tell Access 97 what kind of values you want to store in the field.

TIP **If you want to know more about the various data types, I cover** them in more detail in Chapter 9, "A Closer Look at Field Properties."

The MovieTitle field is a Text data type. Click the drop-down list in the Data Type column and choose Text (see Figure 5.9).

Fig. 5.9
Access 97 Data Types cover just about every type of situation for different types of information.

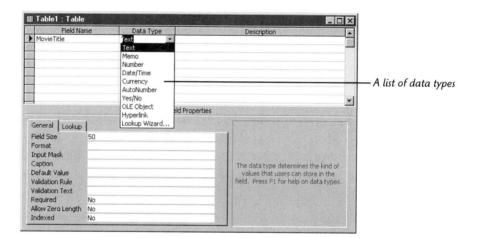

A list of data types

TIP **There are some cases where you create fields that are of type** Text, even though the field contains numbers. For example, fields like ZipCode and Phone are considered text fields when used in tables because you do no calculations with a ZIP Code or phone number. The rule of thumb is, unless you are going to perform arithmetic operations with the numbers in a field, use the Text data type.

There are many additional items to watch for when choosing data types. Take a look at Chapter 9 to learn more about them.

You may have also noticed that when you choose the value for the Data Type property, the values in the Field Properties area below changed based on your new values. This is because the field properties depend on the type of data you enter in the field. We will look again at those properties in Chapter 9, so don't worry about them now.

Enter the description

You can use the field description property for three different purposes:

- To describe the field in Design view.

- When entering your data in Datasheet view. The field description appears in the status bar as you move from field to field.

- As the status bar Text property for controls on forms. Chapter 20, "Controls that Especially Enhance Forms," discusses forms and controls.

In the MovieTitle field's Description property, type "Title of Movie" and press the Tab or Enter key. You then move to the next field in the table.

Adding more fields and saving the table

Now that you have created a field, specified its Data Type, and filled in its Description, you should add a few more fields. Go ahead and enter the information for the rest of the fields so your table looks like the one shown in Figure 5.10.

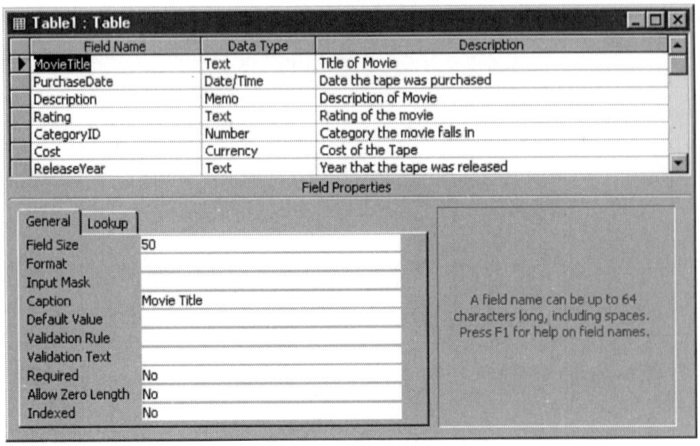

Fig. 5.10
Here are most of the fields used in the new table.

TIP   **In the PurchaseDate field, fill in the name of the field and then** press Tab or Enter. Now you should be on the Data Type field. At this point, press the D for Date/Time and Access 97 automatically fills the field in for you, using AutoExpand. You will see this in other areas of Access 97 as well.

After you fill in the rest of the fields, save the table by choosing File, Close. In the Save As dialog box, type tblTapes for the Table Name; then click OK. You see the message shown in Figure 5.11.

Click Yes in the dialog box. Access 97 creates a new field called ID set as the primary key, and saves the table.

Fig. 5.11
Use primary keys to uniquely identify each record.

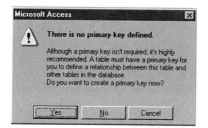

What is a primary key?

When working with tables, you want to make sure each record is different in some way. Handle this by creating a primary key field. Relationships, discussed in Chapter 7, require you to use primary keys. You may also need to find a record based on a unique value.

An example from the real world would be to use a Social Security number for the primary key field. Even if you have 100 "John Smiths" in your table, each one should have a unique Social Security number.

At first glance, you may think to use the MovieTitle field as a primary key. Think again. The reason the MovieTitle does not make a good primary key field, is that you may have two movies with the same title—for instance, the original *Kiss of Death* was made in the 1950s and was made again in 1995. Both films have the same title, so the MovieTitle field does not contain unique information for each record.

This is a common dilemma when thinking of a field to use for a primary key. Sometimes it's easier to let Access 97 do it.

Letting Access 97 create the primary key

When Access 97 created the primary key field, it created a field called ID, which is of the data type AutoNumber (see Figure 5.12).

 **Plain English, please!**

> When Access 97 creates an **AutoNumber** type field, each record will automatically have a unique value for that field. This value can either be incremented by Access 97 for each new record (the default), or generated randomly. When an existing table adds a AutoNumber type field, Access 97 will assign the existing records values as well. **"**

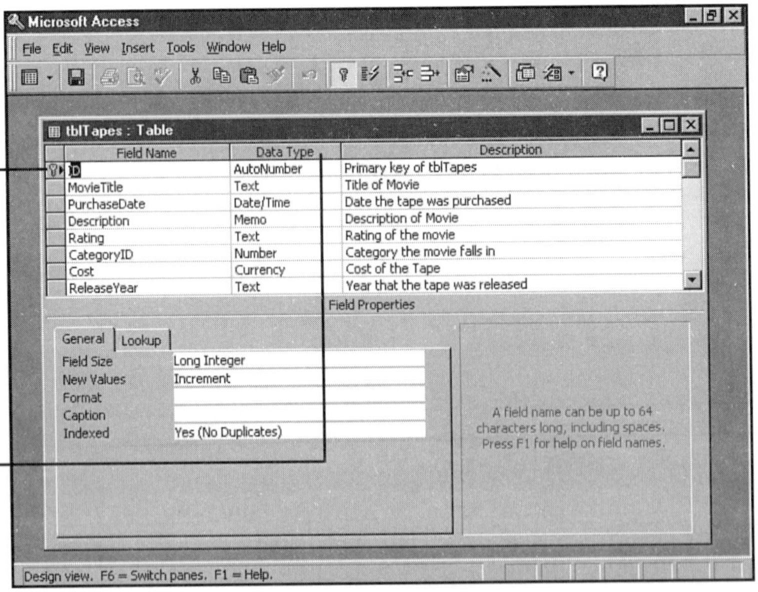

Fig. 5.12
The field called ID created by Access 97 and set to data type AutoNumber.

Primary Key symbol—

AutoNumber data type—

Creating the primary key

If you prefer to create your own primary key, here are the steps:

1 On the Tables tab in the main database screen, highlight the tblRatings table.

2 Click Design and tblRatings appears in the Table Design view.

3 Click the Field Selector for the Rating field. This is the gray bar on the left side of the Table Design grid by each of the fields. When you click here, the whole row appears highlighted.

4 Choose Edit, Primary Key or click the Primary Key button on the toolbar. The Primary Key symbol appears in the Field Selector next to the Field Name Rating, as seen in Figure 5.13. Choose File, Close and save the table.

Primary Key symbol

Fig. 5.13
The Rating field set as the primary key.

Field Selector

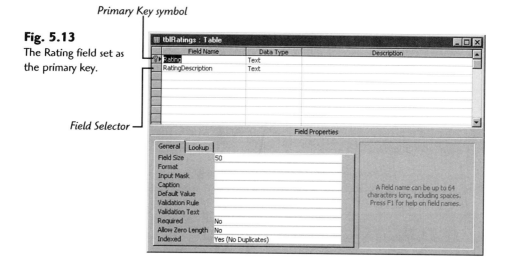

Here are some last notes about primary keys:

- Primary keys can consist of data types other than AutoNumber, as seen by the Rating field, which is Text.

- Creating a primary key also creates an index. Indexes make for quicker searches and sorts, discussed in detail in Chapter 9, "A Closer Look at Field Properties."

- If the field you are making a primary key has data already in it and the data is not unique, Access 97 displays an error and does not create the primary key.

Using what you learned

Taking what you have learned in this chapter, create one more table:

1 Using the Design View method, create a table called tblCategories. Table 5.1 shows the fields that need to be set.

Table 5.1   A table called tblCategories

Field name	Data type	Description
CategoryID	AutoNumber	Primary key for Categories
Category	Text	Category Description

2 Then set CategoryID as the primary key.

3 In Datasheet view, fill the table with the data you see in Figure 5.14. Notice you only have to fill in the Category field, since the CategoryID is an AutoNumber.

Fig. 5.14
Entering data into the tblCategories table.

6

Maintaining Your Information with Datasheets

● In this chapter:

- What are datasheets again?

- How do I enter information into a datasheet?

- Changing the look of datasheets

- Saving data and eliminating mistakes

Once you create an Access 97 table, you can immediately start entering information using datasheets. . . . . ⊙

Datasheets are the quickest way to enter your information into your Access tables. They allow you to enter information in a row/column setup very similar to spreadsheets.

To get a quick glimpse of a datasheet again:

1 Start Access and open the VideoLib database as described in Chapter 4, "Creating and Opening Databases."

2 Click the Tables tab.

3 Double-click the tblTapes table. The tblTapes datasheet appears. In Figure 6.1, you see the tblTapes with information already entered. The records that you see in Figure 6.1 have been entered in order to show you how to use datasheet features.

You will be adding your own records in the "Adding records" section found later in the chapter. For now, sit back and relax while I explain the parts of the datasheet displayed in the figure.

Fig. 6.1
The different parts of a datasheet serve various purposes.

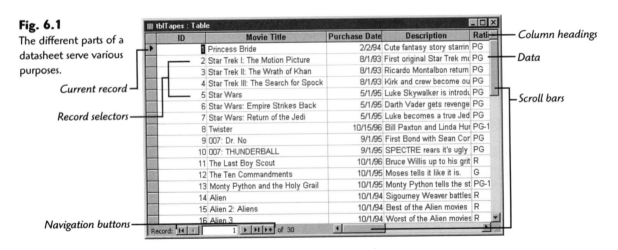

Current record

Record selectors

Navigation buttons

Column headings

Data

Scroll bars

Q&A *Instead of seeing the tblTapes table in Datasheet view, why do I just see the name of the table highlighted, with the cursor blinking at a letter in the name?*

If this is the case, then you double-clicked too slowly and instead did two single clicks. When told to double-click, you need to do so rapidly. Otherwise, instead of showing the table in Datasheet view, you told Access that you want to modify the name of the table.

Looking at column headings and data

Although column headings and data were discussed in Chapter 5, I want to mention them again briefly as a refresher. Column headings are either the name of the field, or Caption property, if it is filled in. (The Caption property will be examined more in Chapter 9, "A Closer Look at Field Properties.")

Data is the information that you type into the table for storage. The remaining items require a bit more examination.

Keeping track of individual records with the record selector

Use record selectors when you want to select the whole record versus individual fields of a record. You can also use the record selector to keep track of what is happening with a record. Some of the statuses that you can see are:

- **Current Record**—This arrow appears when you click the mouse in any field of a record. This arrow indicates this is the active record.

- **New Record**—The asterisk, which is always seen in the last record, is where you add a new record to the table through the datasheet.

- **Editing Record**—This pencil appears when you begin to edit any of the fields in the current record.

- **Locked Record**—This is one you will not see very often unless you are working on a networked system and somebody else is editing the current record(s). This prevents the simultaneous update of the same record.

Remember that you will use the record selector to affect the whole record. By clicking the gray square, the whole record appears highlighted. You can then perform tasks such as deleting the record or copying it to duplicate the information. We will discuss how to delete records later in this chapter, in the "Deleting records in a datasheet" section.

Moving around the datasheet using navigation buttons

Use the navigation buttons, located at the bottom of the datasheet, to move from one record to another in the datasheet, as shown in Figure 6.2.

Fig. 6.2
Use the navigation buttons to move forward and backward through the datasheet.

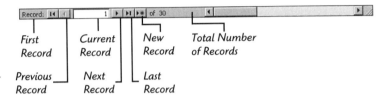

The other navigation buttons are very convenient to use to jump to the first and last records, and a new record. Play around with the various navigation buttons to acquaint you with their functions.

Q&A *Why is the Previous button dimmed in Figure 6.2?*

The reason the Previous button appears dimmed is that the current record is the first record in the table. Access 97 knows it can't move back another record so it dims the button. The same occurs with the Next button when you are on the last record, which would be the new record.

Scrolling through the datasheet with scroll bars

Whenever you have more then one page of information, either vertically or horizontally, Access 97 displays a scroll bar for one or the other, or both. You can see this in Figure 6.3.

When you click the mouse on either of the scroll bars, the datasheet scrolls in that direction. You can also drag the gray bar to move through the recordset. When you do this on the vertical scroll bar, you will see a ScreenTip that displays the record you are scrolling to, as in Figure 6.4.

Fig. 6.3
Use these scroll bars to see different parts of the datasheet.

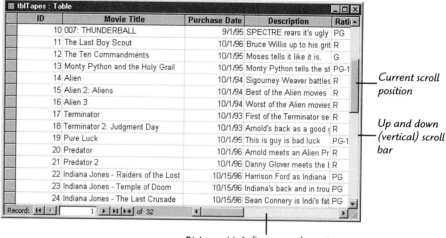

Current scroll position

Up and down (vertical) scroll bar

Right and left (horizontal) scroll bar

Fig. 6.4
Slide the current position bar up and down the scroll bar for another method of movement.

ScreenTip

Q&A Why does the current record number in the navigation buttons still say 1, although the ScreenTip for the scroll bar says 11?

The ScreenTip of the scroll bar reflects where you are scrolling to, but the current record stays where it is until you have clicked a different record selector or anywhere else in a different record.

Entering information into a datasheet

Now you have seen all the parts of a datasheet and how to move around in it; it's time to enter information.

Adding records

To add a new record into the datasheet, click the New Record navigation button. This places you at the new record at the bottom of the datasheet. Since the table is empty to begin with, you are already in the new record. Rather than clicking the New Record navigation button, you can also choose File, New Record.

Take time now to:

1 Add the 24 records into tblTapes displayed in Figures 6.1 and 6.3. When you want to add the information you can't see, such as the rest of the Description, fake it; add your own description for the movies, as well as other information.

2 Add a few more of your favorite movies.

3 Add some dogs (movies you don't like) that we can delete later.

Editing records

When you first move into a field by pressing the Tab or Enter keys, the whole field appears highlighted. If you type immediately into the field, Access 97 deletes the current information, and the new information appears in its place. Try this now.

Q&A ***What happens when I use a mouse to move into the field?***

The whole field appears highlighted when you move the cursor to the extreme left side of a field. The cursor turns into a white cross. If you click when the cursor is a white cross, the entire field appears highlighted. If you place the cursor anywhere inside the field, then it becomes an insertion point.

In the tblTapes datasheet, click the ID field of the first record; then press the Tab key. The first movie title, *Princess Bride*, appears highlighted, as shown in Figure 6.5.

Fig. 6.5
When first moving into a field with Tab or Enter, all the current information in a field appears highlighted.

ID	Movie Title	Purchase Date	Description	Rati
1	Princess Bride	2/2/94	Cute fantasy story starrin	PG
2	Star Trek I: The Motion Picture	8/1/93	First original Star Trek m(	PG
3	Star Trek II: The Wrath of Khan	8/1/93	Ricardo Montalbon return	PG
4	Star Trek III: The Search for Spock	8/1/93	Kirk and crew become ou	PG
5	Star Wars	5/1/95	Luke Skywalker is introdu	PG
6	Star Wars: Empire Strikes Back	5/1/95	Darth Vader gets revenge	PG
7	Star Wars: Return of the Jedi	5/1/95	Luke becomes a true Jed	PG
8	Twister	10/15/96	Bill Paxton and Linda Hur	PG-1
9	007: Dr. No	9/1/95	First Bond with Sean Cor	PG
10	007: THUNDERBALL	9/1/95	SPECTRE rears it's ugly	PG
11	The Last Boy Scout	10/1/96	Bruce Willis up to his grit	R
12	The Ten Commandments	10/1/95	Moses tells it like it is.	G
13	Monty Python and the Holy Grail	10/1/95	Monty Python tells the st	PG-1
14	Alien	10/1/94	Sigourney Weaver battles	R
15	Alien 2: Aliens	10/1/94	Best of the Alien movies	R
16	Alien 3	10/1/94	Worst of the Alien movies	R

Record: 1 of 30

Q&A *Oops—I tried to type in the ID column, but Access 97 just beeped at me. Why?*

The ID field, if set up like in the example, is an AutoNumber field, which was discussed in Chapter 5. Because Access 97 creates and maintains this field, you can't update the field in any way. If you try to update this field, you will see this message in the status bar: "Control can't be edited; it's bound to AutoNumber field 'ID'".

Type the word Princess in the selected field. Notice that Access 97 replaces the old data with the data you just typed, as in Figure 6.6. Notice the Pencil icon on the record selector for the first record. This indicates Access is editing the current record.

Fig. 6.6
This data replaces the current text.

ID	Movie Title	Purchase Date	Description	Rati
1	Princess	2/2/94	Cute fantasy story starrin	PG
2	Star Trek I: The Motion Picture	8/1/93	First original Star Trek m(	PG
3	Star Trek II: The Wrath of Khan	8/1/93	Ricardo Montalbon return	PG
4	Star Trek III: The Search for Spock	8/1/93	Kirk and crew become ou	PG
5	Star Wars	5/1/95	Luke Skywalker is introdu	PG
6	Star Wars: Empire Strikes Back	5/1/95	Darth Vader gets revenge	PG
7	Star Wars: Return of the Jedi	5/1/95	Luke becomes a true Jed	PG
8	Twister	10/15/96	Bill Paxton and Linda Hur	PG-1
9	007: Dr. No	9/1/95	First Bond with Sean Cor	PG
10	007: THUNDERBALL	9/1/95	SPECTRE rears it's ugly	PG
11	The Last Boy Scout	10/1/96	Bruce Willis up to his grit	R
12	The Ten Commandments	10/1/95	Moses tells it like it is.	G
13	Monty Python and the Holy Grail	10/1/95	Monty Python tells the st	PG-1
14	Alien	10/1/94	Sigourney Weaver battles	R
15	Alien 2: Aliens	10/1/94	Best of the Alien movies	R
16	Alien 3	10/1/94	Worst of the Alien movies	R

Record: 1 of 30

TIP **If you know that you don't ever want to have the entire field** selected when you Tab or Enter to a field, you can change the default behavior for all fields. To do this, choose Tools, Options. The Options dialog box appears and allows you to change various options for your database. Click the Keyboard tab. You can then change the setting for Behavior Entering Field from:, Select Entire Field to:, Go to Start of Field, or Go to End of Field.

You can see other options that affect data entry into fields on the Keyboard page as well. Click OK when you finish setting the options you want.

Here are a few more tips for editing a field:

- To avoid replacing all the data in a field, click the insertion point at the specific position within the field you want to edit. Use Backspace to delete characters to the left of the insertion point. Use Delete to delete characters to the right of the insertion point.

- Once the insertion point is in the field, you can use the Home and End keys to move to the beginning and end of a field.

- Use the right and left arrow keys to move one character at a time.

- Pressing the Insert key will toggle you between overwriting and inserting information. When in overwrite mode, Access displays the text "OVR" in the rightmost panel of the status bar.

- When a field is too long to see it all in the datasheet, but you want to see it to edit it, press Shift+F2. Access 97 opens up the Zoom window dialog box that allows you to see your entire field at once. You can use the Zoom window in a number of different places when working with Access 97.

Keystrokes for moving around the datasheet

When you begin entering data in your database tables, you'll want to know the quickest ways to move around. In this section, I'll show you some ways to move from field to field, record to record, and from the top of the table to the bottom and back. Move from one field to another by using the keyboard and using one of the following:

- **Enter** moves the cursor to the right.

- **Tab** moves the cursor to the right.

- **Shift+Tab** moves the cursor to the left.

- **Right arrow** moves the cursor to the right.

- **Left arrow** moves the cursor to the left.

Moving from record to record is similar to moving between fields. If you press the right arrow, Enter, or Tab keys while you're in the last field of a record, the insertion point moves to the first field of the next record. You can use the up and down arrows to move up or down one record; the insertion point will appear in the same field as the previous record.

 TIP Once you move from one record to another, Access 97 saves the record you leave to the table. We will discuss saving your data later in the "Saving information in a datasheet" section.

Table 6.1 presents a list of key combinations that you can use to move around a datasheet quickly.

Table 6.1 Useful keys for datasheets

Keystrokes	Movement that occurs
Tab, Enter, right arrow	Goes to the next field. At the end of a record, they move to the next record.
Shift+Tab, left arrow	Goes to the previous field. At the beginning of a record, they move to the previous record.
Down arrow	Goes to the next record.
Up arrow	Goes to the previous record.
Home	When editing a field, this key moves the cursor to beginning of the field; otherwise, it moves to the first field of the record.
End	When editing a field, this key moves the cursor to end of the field; otherwise, it moves to the last field of the record.
Ctrl+Home	Goes to the first field in the first record.

continues

Table 6.1 Continued

Keystrokes	Movement that occurs
Ctrl+End	Goes to the last field in the last record.
Page Down	Scrolls the datasheet down a full datasheet page, depending on the size of the datasheet. For example, if the datasheet shows five records at a time, then Page Down moves you down five records. This also is true for Page Up.
Page Up	Scrolls the datasheet up a full datasheet page.

You can always use the mouse to move around the datasheet as well; simply point-and-click in the record or field you want. In fact, once you are comfortable moving around, you will probably use the mouse more than any other method.

Saving information in a datasheet

There are several ways to save your information in datasheets.

- As mentioned in the preceding section, "Keystrokes for moving around the datasheet," when you move to a new record, your information is saved.

- There are times when you work on one record for an extended amount of time, and you don't want to move off of it to save it. To save the record without moving off of it, press Shift+Enter.

- When editing fields in a record, click the pencil button in the record selector (see Figure 6.7) to save the changed fields. The record appears highlighted. To continue editing fields in the same record, click into the next field you want to edit.

Fig. 6.7
The record selector displays a pencil in the record that you are editing.

	ID	Movie Title	Purchase Date	Description
	27	The Last Starfighter	10/1/96	Great space film
	28	Wishing on a Shooting Star	10/1/95	Sad movie
	29	The Tin Star	9/1/93	Cool western
	30	Schindlers List	8/1/96	Very heavy but great mov
	31	Dumb and Dumber	10/2/95	Pretty silly movie
	32	Junior	10/2/96	Arnold comedy
∅	33	Car Wash	10/1/96	Really Dumb movie
*	(AutoNumber)			

tblTapes : Table

Undoing mistakes

I don't know about you, but there are times when I make mistakes when editing my information. I know you probably find it hard to believe but it's true. So thankfully, Access 97 is a very forgiving application.

Access uses a two-level undo. To see what this means, do the following:

1 Edit data in a field.

2 Tab to the next field.

3 Edit the data in the new field, but don't Tab out of the field.

4 Press Esc (Escape key); notice that Access 97 has only undone the current field's data (Level 1).

5 Press Esc again. Now Access 97 restores both fields to the values they were before you edited the record (Level 2).

Q&A **What if I edited more than the two fields mentioned?**
If you edited additional fields in the same record, they would have all been undone at once in step 5.

CAUTION **When you save the record you are working on, use any of the** methods described in the last section. Then type something else; you can't undo the changes you already saved.

Deleting records in a datasheet

When you have records that need to be deleted, take advantage of the record selector.

How to delete one record

Here are the steps for deleting one record in a datasheet:

1 Click the record selector for the record you want to delete. In Figure 6.8, the record for the MovieTitle *Car Wash* appears selected.

Fig. 6.8
This selected record is
ready for deletion.

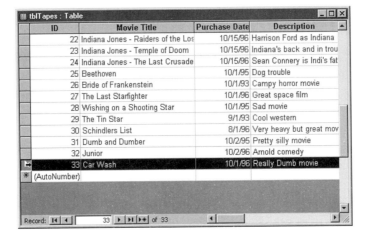

2 Press Delete. The message in Figure 6.9 gives you one last chance to change your mind.

Fig. 6.9
This message is your last
chance before Access
deletes a record.

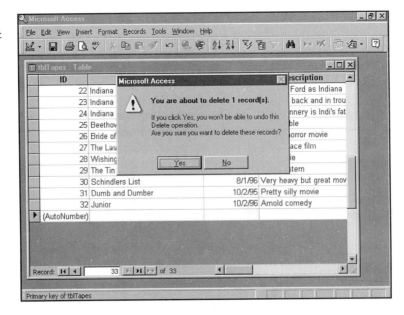

3 Click Yes. Access 97 deletes the record.

Q&A ***After deleting records, why doesn't the AutoNumber field reset back to the next available number?***

Access 97 considers records that have been deleted as used records, and will then skip the incremented number in that field. Access 97 never reuses the ID numbers in a table.

TIP **Having just answered this last question, there is a cool way to** reset the last numbers used by AutoNumber data types. Access 97 has a great feature that lets you **compact** the database you are currently working in. To compact your database, choose <u>T</u>ools, <u>D</u>atabase Utilities. Then choose <u>C</u>ompact Database. You then simply have to reopen your datasheet where you were. The next time you add a record, it will appear consecutive to the last AutoNumber in the datasheet.

Deleting more than one record

It takes a little more work to delete multiple records than it does to delete one record. To delete more than one record, you need to:

1 Click the record selector of the first record you want to delete, holding down the mouse button.

2 Now drag the cursor down over the other records you want to delete. You can see this in Figure 6.10.

3 Press Delete. The message box displayed in Figure 6.9 will be displayed again, telling you three records will be deleted. Press <u>Y</u>es.

Fig. 6.10
These highlighted records are ready for you to delete.

ID	Movie Title	Purchase Date	Description
22	Indiana Jones - Raiders of the Los	10/15/96	Harrison Ford as Indiana
23	Indiana Jones - Temple of Doom	10/15/96	Indiana's back and in trou
24	Indiana Jones - The Last Crusade	10/15/96	Sean Connery is Indi's fat
25	Beethoven	10/1/95	Dog trouble
26	Bride of Frankenstein	10/1/93	Campy horror movie
27	The Last Starfighter	10/1/96	Great space film
28	Wishing on a Shooting Star	10/1/95	Sad movie
29	The Tin Star	9/1/93	Cool western
30	Schindlers List	8/1/96	Very heavy but great mov
31	Dumb and Dumber	10/2/95	Pretty silly movie
32	Junior	10/2/96	Arnold comedy
(AutoNumber)			

tblTapes : Table

Record: 31 of 32

Q&A *Can I delete records that aren't consecutive?*

You can't skip over records in Datasheet view and delete them together. To delete multiple records, you need to use a Delete query, discussed in Chapter 16, "Using Action Queries for Big Changes."

The last type of deletion to look at is deleting all records.

Deleting all records

There are a few ways to delete all the records in a table. One way is to use the method described in the last section to click the first record, and then drag the mouse down to the last record, so that all the records appear highlighted. This is fine if you only have one or two records to delete. But if you have a few thousand records to delete, it could be a pain. So there are alternatives.

In the top-left corner of the datasheet, below the Table icon where row selectors and column headings meet, there is a gray square. If you click the gray square, all the records in the datasheet appear highlighted, as shown in Figure 6.11.

Fig. 6.11
Clicking in the gray box highlights all the records.

ID	Movie Title	Purchase Date	Description	Rati
1	Princess Bride	2/2/94	Cute fantasy story starrin	PG
2	Star Trek I: The Motion Picture	8/1/93	First original Star Trek mc	PG
3	Star Trek II: The Wrath of Khan	8/1/93	Ricardo Montalbon return	PG
4	Star Trek III: The Search for Spock	8/1/93	Kirk and crew become ou	PG
5	Star Wars	5/1/95	Luke Skywalker is introdu	PG
6	Star Wars: Empire Strikes Back	5/1/95	Darth Vader gets revenge	PG
7	Star Wars: Return of the Jedi	5/1/95	Luke becomes a true Jed	PG
8	Twister	10/15/96	Bill Paxton and Linda Hur	PG-1
9	007: Dr. No	9/1/95	First Bond with Sean Cor	PG
10	007: THUNDERBALL	9/1/95	SPECTRE rears it's ugly	PG
11	The Last Boy Scout	10/1/96	Bruce Willis up to his grit	R
12	The Ten Commandments	10/1/95	Moses tells it like it is.	G
13	Monty Python and the Holy Grail	10/1/95	Monty Python tells the st	PG-1
14	Alien	10/1/94	Sigourney Weaver battles	R
15	Alien 2: Aliens	10/1/94	Best of the Alien movies	R
16	Alien 3	10/1/94	Worst of the Alien movies	R

Record: 1 of 30

Primary key of tblTapes

You can also use Ctrl+A, or select the Edit, Select All Records to select all the records in the datasheet.

Now press Delete and you see the message box giving the number of records that you want to delete. At this point, if you clicked Yes, Access 97 would delete all the records. However, you don't want to do this with these records, so click No.

Working with columns

Until now, we have been mostly dealing with individual fields and records at a time. Now we will explore ways to change columns to reflect how you want to work with your information. Some things you can do with columns include:

- Change the size of the columns.
- Move columns around.
- Make selected columns stay on the screen when others scroll off.
- Make columns disappear and reappear.
- Remove columns permanently (be careful).
- Sort information in ascending or descending order.

Changing the size of a column

Often you may want to change the width of a column so you can see more of the text. There are a few methods of resizing columns. You can use Best Fit, resize the columns manually, or set the column width to a specific number.

Using Best Fit to change the size of a column

When you use Best Fit, Access expands the column to the longest length of text in the column, whether in column heading or the field itself. Follow these steps:

1 Place the cursor in the column heading, on the line between the column you want to change and the next column to the right. After placing the cursor correctly, the cursor changes to two arrows pointing away from each other, with a bar in the middle (see Figure 6.12).

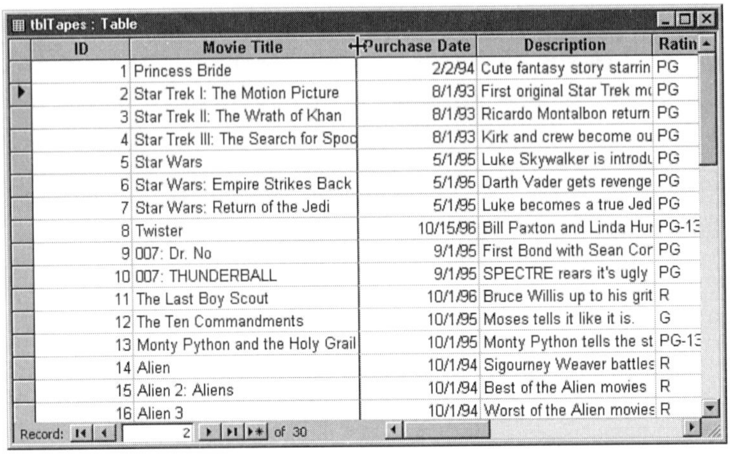

tblTapes : Table

ID	Movie Title	Purchase Date	Description	Ratin
1	Princess Bride	2/2/94	Cute fantasy story starrin	PG
2	Star Trek I: The Motion Picture	8/1/93	First original Star Trek mo	PG
3	Star Trek II: The Wrath of Khan	8/1/93	Ricardo Montalbon return	PG
4	Star Trek III: The Search for Spoc	8/1/93	Kirk and crew become ou	PG
5	Star Wars	5/1/95	Luke Skywalker is introdu	PG
6	Star Wars: Empire Strikes Back	5/1/95	Darth Vader gets revenge	PG
7	Star Wars: Return of the Jedi	5/1/95	Luke becomes a true Jed	PG
8	Twister	10/15/96	Bill Paxton and Linda Hur	PG-13
9	007: Dr. No	9/1/95	First Bond with Sean Cor	PG
10	007: THUNDERBALL	9/1/95	SPECTRE rears it's ugly	PG
11	The Last Boy Scout	10/1/96	Bruce Willis up to his grit	R
12	The Ten Commandments	10/1/95	Moses tells it like it is.	G
13	Monty Python and the Holy Grail	10/1/95	Monty Python tells the st	PG-13
14	Alien	10/1/94	Sigourney Weaver battles	R
15	Alien 2: Aliens	10/1/94	Best of the Alien movies	R
16	Alien 3	10/1/94	Worst of the Alien movies	R

Record: 2 of 30

Fig. 6.12
Changing the column size of the ID column is now only a double-click away.

2 Double-click. The column adjusts to the width of the longest field.

Changing the size of a column manually

To change the column size manually, place the cursor in the column heading row, between the column you want to resize and the next column. When you see the double-headed arrow shown in Figure 6.12, drag the column to the desired width and release the mouse button.

Changing the size of more than one column

The last two methods of sizing columns required you to place the cursor at the end of the column you want to resize. Changing the size of more than one column, however, requires you to first highlight the columns you want to resize. To do this:

1 Place the cursor in the first column heading of the columns you want to size. Hold the mouse button down. The whole column will then be highlighted.

2 Still holding the mouse button down, slide the cursor over to highlight the other columns; then release the mouse button.

3 Choose Format, Column Width. The Column Width dialog box appears (see Figure 6.13). Choose any of the following column widths:

- **Specific Column Width**—Enter a number in the Column Width text box. The number entered indicates the number of characters that will appear.

- **Standard Width**—Sets the width to approximately 1 inch per column.

- **Best Fit**—The column adjusts based upon the longest length of text for each column.

Fig. 6.13
Using the Column Width dialog box, you have various possibilities for sizing multiple columns.

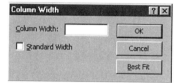

4 Make your selection; then click OK to accept the changes or Cancel to not accept the changes.

Moving columns in the datasheet

There are going to be times when you want to move your columns around in your datasheet, whether permanently or temporarily.

Let's move the PurchaseDate column so that it appears between ID and MovieTitle:

1 Highlight the PurchaseDate column by clicking in the column heading.

2 Click a second time in the column heading and hold down the mouse button. The cursor changes to an arrow with the piece of paper at the tail end of it. You will also see a white line appear along the left side of the column that you want to move.

Q&A *The second time I clicked, the highlighting disappeared from the column. What happened?*

You didn't click in the column heading row the second time. Reposition the cursor and follow steps 1 and 2 again.

3 Drag the column to the left of the MovieTitle column. When a dark line appears on the left side of the MovieTitle column, you know that you have dragged the PurchaseDate column over correctly (see Figure 6.14). Release the mouse button.

Fig. 6.14
This cursor lets you
know you are dragging
a column.

Dragging cursor ──

Highlighted column ──

New location ──

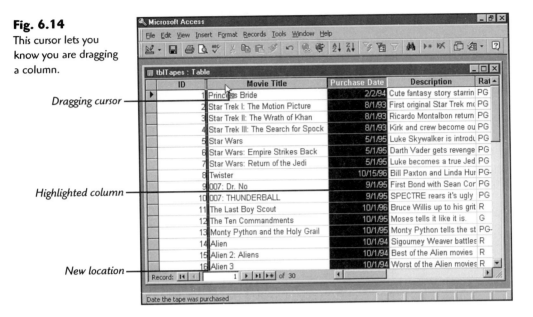

To move multiple columns:

1 Highlight the columns you want to move.

2 Click in the column heading of one of the selected columns.

3 Drag the cursor to the new position and release the mouse button.

Keeping a column on the screen

There are times when you may want a particular column to remain on the
screen while the others scroll off. For an example, I like to keep the
MovieTitle column on the screen so I know which videotape I am working
with.

Keeping a column, or columns, on the screen is *freezing* the column. To
freeze the MovieTitle column:

1 Highlight the MovieTitle column by clicking the right mouse button in
the column heading. This highlights the column and causes the shortcut
menu to appear (see Figure 6.15).

Fig. 6.15
The shortcut menu for datasheets has many useful tools.

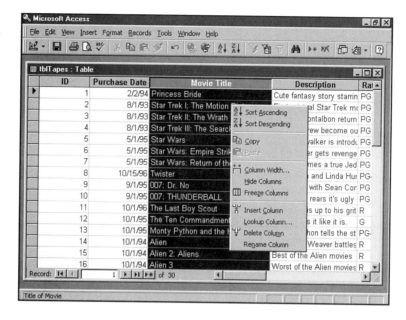

2 Choose Freeze Columns from the shortcut menu. The MovieTitle column moves to the first column and stays there.

To see how the datasheet changes, click the scroll bar at the bottom of the datasheet. You will see the columns scroll off the screen, but the MovieTitle column stays on the left side of the datasheet (see Figure 6.16). Notice that a heavy black line appears to the right of the frozen column.

Fig. 6.16
The MovieTitles column frozen in place.

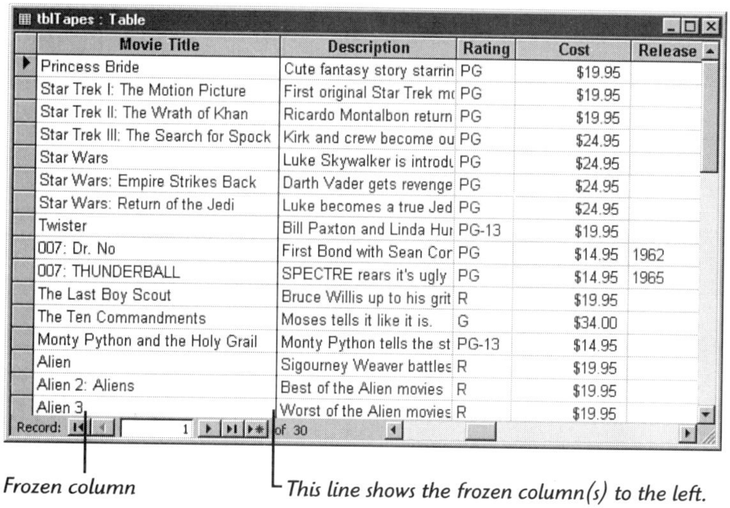

Frozen column   *This line shows the frozen column(s) to the left.*

To freeze multiple columns, highlight the columns to freeze, and then choose Format, Freeze Columns.

To unfreeze a column, choose Format, Unfreeze All Columns. Unfreezing columns is an all or none proposition. You can't unfreeze one of multiple columns.

Hiding columns temporarily

There may be times when you want to temporarily hide a column in a datasheet. For instance, the ID column in the tblTapes table doesn't really do us any good since it is an AutoNumber and can't be updated.

To hide the ID column from the datasheet:

1 Highlight the ID column by clicking in the column heading with the right mouse button; the shortcut menu appears.

2 Choose Hide Columns from the shortcut menu. (You can also select Format, Hide from the Datasheet view menu.)

Q&A ***Does hiding a column get rid of the field permanently?***

You are not affecting the field itself. The field is still in the table. If you switch to Design view, you will see the field name still exists.

If you decide afterward that you need the column back, you can choose Format, Unhide Columns. The Unhide Columns dialog box appears (see Figure 6.17).

Fig. 6.17
The Unhide Columns
dialog box allows you
to change your mind
when hiding columns.

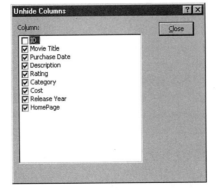

You can then place a check mark by those columns you want to display, in this case ID. When you finish, click Close.

Removing columns permanently

When you have a field in a table that you don't need anymore, you can remove it in Datasheet view.

CAUTION **When you use the method described here for removing a field** in Datasheet view, you are actually removing the field from the table permanently! Make sure you want to remove the field forever. What makes it even more dangerous is that Access doesn't give any warning before deleting the field.

Although it is not recommended you do so at this point in the sample database, to remove a column:

1 Highlight the column by clicking in the column heading with the right mouse button; the shortcut menu appears.

2 Choose Delete Column from the shortcut menu. Access 97 removes the column from the table permanently. You can also choose Edit, Delete Column from the Datasheet view menu to delete a column.

Adding a column while in Datasheet view

You can add a column to the table in Datasheet view by using the following steps:

1 Place the cursor in the column where you want the column to appear.

2 Choose Insert, Column from the Datasheet view menu. Access then creates a new column called Field1 to the left of the column you chose in step 1. Now it's time to change the name.

3 Double-click in the column heading of the new field. You can then type the name you want to use for the field. Remember that this will be the name used in the table structure.

TIP **You may want to switch to Design view and set the Data Type** property of the field, if you need it to be something other than text or number. By default, Access sets the Data Type property to whatever you type into the field the first time you use it. More on data types in Chapter 9.

You have now added a new column to the datasheet.

Another trick you can perform with columns is **sorting**, but I'm going to save that for Chapter 11, "Working with Filters."

Changing the row height

Changing row heights is useful when you have a note or Description field and you want to see more of it without having to use the Zoom dialog box.

As an example, if you look at Figure 6.18, you can see that the description field for all the records is cut off. Wouldn't it be nice to see the whole field?

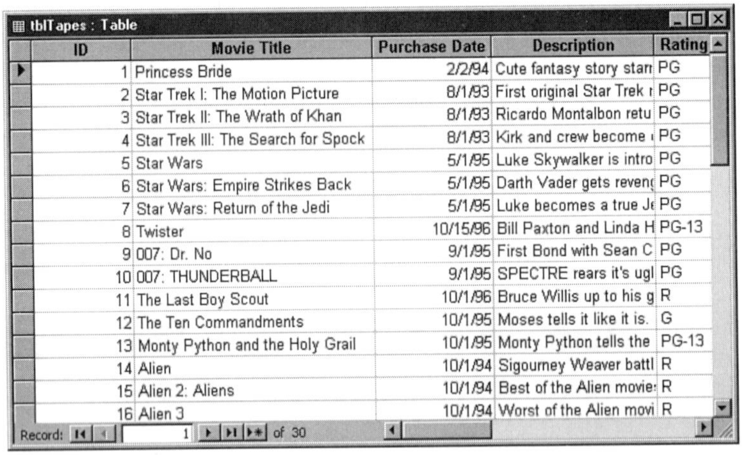

Fig. 6.18
The Description field here only shows part of the information entered.

ID	Movie Title	Purchase Date	Description	Rating
1	Princess Bride	2/2/94	Cute fantasy story star	PG
2	Star Trek I: The Motion Picture	8/1/93	First original Star Trek r	PG
3	Star Trek II: The Wrath of Khan	8/1/93	Ricardo Montalbon retu	PG
4	Star Trek III: The Search for Spock	8/1/93	Kirk and crew become	PG
5	Star Wars	5/1/95	Luke Skywalker is intro	PG
6	Star Wars: Empire Strikes Back	5/1/95	Darth Vader gets reven	PG
7	Star Wars: Return of the Jedi	5/1/95	Luke becomes a true Je	PG
8	Twister	10/15/96	Bill Paxton and Linda H	PG-13
9	007: Dr. No	9/1/95	First Bond with Sean C	PG
10	007: THUNDERBALL	9/1/95	SPECTRE rears it's ugl	PG
11	The Last Boy Scout	10/1/96	Bruce Willis up to his g	R
12	The Ten Commandments	10/1/95	Moses tells it like it is.	G
13	Monty Python and the Holy Grail	10/1/95	Monty Python tells the	PG-13
14	Alien	10/1/94	Sigourney Weaver battl	R
15	Alien 2: Aliens	10/1/94	Best of the Alien movie	R
16	Alien 3	10/1/94	Worst of the Alien movi	R

Record: 1 of 30

To increase the row height of all the rows in the table:

1 Place the cursor between any of the rows in the datasheet, in the record selector area. The cursor changes to a double-headed arrow.

2 Click and hold the mouse button; then drag the cursor up to increase the row's height, or drag it down to decrease the row's height.

You will then see more of the description field, as shown in Figure 6.19.

Fig. 6.19
When the cursor appears, you're ready to increase the height of your rows.

Cursor for adjusting row height

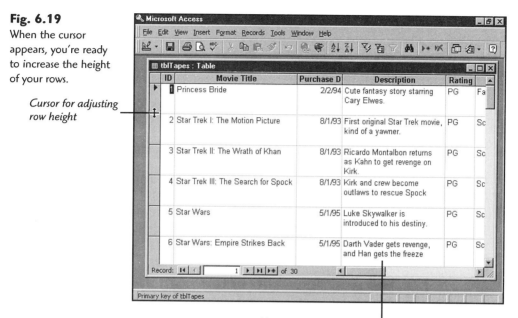

Now you can read everything in the Description field.

You will notice that when you increase the height of your rows, you will see fewer rows at a time in the datasheet.

Changing fonts

When you have a lot of information you have to read and edit, you may want to change the look of the text to make it more readable. To do this, choose Format, Font from the Datasheet view menu. You will then see the Font dialog box, as shown in Figure 6.20.

Here you can play with the settings to select the font you want. When you make changes, you can see them in the Sample boxes and get an idea of what they will look like.

Fig. 6.20
The Font dialog box not only lets you change the style of fonts; you can change the size as well.

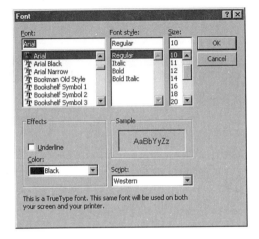

 Q&A *Does changing a font affect only a field, a row, or what?*

When you change the font, you are changing the font for the whole datasheet.

Notice that at the bottom of the Font dialog box, a message tells you whether you are choosing a font on the screen and the printer. If you choose a printer font only, Access tries to match closely but may not match it exactly.

When you have picked the font and size you like, click OK to accept them.

Saving all your changes to the datasheet

 Remember from the discussion in the section called "Saving information in a datasheet" that Access 97 saves the information, or data, as you move from record to record. This is different than saving the layout or format of the datasheet (how the datasheet looks). To save changes to the layout of a datasheet, then continue working, choose File, Save or click the Save button on the toolbar.

Otherwise, when you close the datasheet, you will be given the message box that asks if you want to save your changes to the layout of the table. Click Yes to save the table.

Understanding Relationships Between Tables

● **In this chapter:**

- **How do relationships and Access 97 work together?**

- **How to relate tables in the database**

- **What is Referential Integrity?**

- **What happens if I have to delete a customer's record and he has ordered records?**

How your tables relate to one another can affect the speed with which you can find and report information. If table relationships are incorrect, incomplete, and even wrong, information is more likely to slip into your database. . . . . . ➤

Although the title of this chapter sounds like a marital seminar, setting a relationship in Access 97 is telling two tables in a database they need to work together and get along. Come to think of it, it *is* like a marriage seminar.

What relationships are in Access 97?

Up to this point, you've worked only with one table at a time. Normally, you will be working with at least half a dozen tables, and there are some databases with hundreds. A good example of a database with multiple tables is the Northwind sample database. Start Access 97, and then open Northwind.mdb. Click the Tables tab, if necessary, to bring it to the front (see Figure 7.1).

Fig. 7.1
There are eight tables used in Northwind.mdb.

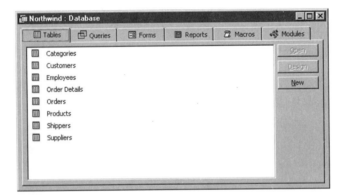

 Looking at the tables in Figure 7.1, you can see the Order Details table is probably related to the Orders table based on the name. To view the details of the relationship, there is a window called the Relationship window. To display this screen, choose Tools, Relationships or click the Relationships toolbar button. If you are in Northwind, as instructed, then you will see something similar to Figure 7.2.

Fig. 7.2
Here are all the
relationships defined
in Northwind.

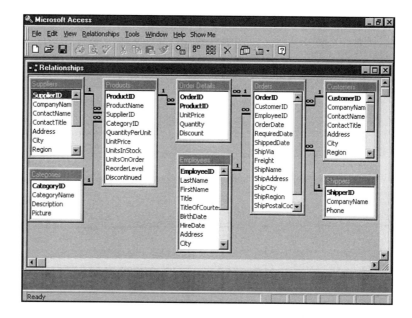

Access 97 uses relationships to relate the tables in your database to one
another. Relationships make sure the integrity of your tables remains intact.
Integrity means maintaining the accuracy of information in your database
tables. Here are a couple of examples of real-life situations that can create
inaccurate information in your database:

- You deleted a customer from a database table; now you find the deleted
  customer still has orders for merchandise. What happens to the orders?
  Do they just sit in their table with no customer to own them?

- You are creating an order for a new customer, but you haven't added
  the new customer in the database ahead of time. Should you just enter a
  "dummy" customer number for the customer?

The answer to both of these questions is no. These questions both have to do
with the *Referential Integrity* of the database. One of the great things about
Access 97 is that it has built-in integrity checks that it will perform on data,
if you want.

Plain English, please!

Referential Integrity makes sure that Access 97 performs only reasonable data and legal operations on the related tables. For instance, with Referential Integrity, you can add order records only for a customer that exists. You can also set it up so Access 97 can't delete a customer that has orders—at least not without deleting the orders, too. Referential integrity is something you must set when working in the Relationships window, and is discussed in the section called "Creating relationships."

We'll work more with the relationship window (shown in Figure 7.2) later in the chapter. However, you first need to understand what kinds of relationships exist between tables and what each relationship provides.

What kind of relationships tables can have

There are three types of relationships you can establish between tables in your Access database:

- One-to-Many
- One-to-One
- Many-to-Many

This all sounds rather complex and a little immoral, but there are good reasons for this flexibility. Let's take a look at each relationship.

One-to-Many relationships

In Figure 7.2, notice that the line beginning at the Customers table has a number 1. At the other end of the line, by the Orders table, there is an infinity symbol. This means that the relationship is a One-to-Many relationship.

Although it sounds like a '60s communal marriage concept, when you say the Customers to Orders table has a One-to-Many relationship, you are saying that one customer can have many orders. The customer-to-order relationship appears in Figure 7.3 by itself.

Fig. 7.3
One-to-Many relationship: One customer can have many orders.

If you look at the line between Orders and OrderDetails in Figure 7.2, you will see the same type of relationship: One order can have many details.

TIP The One-to-Many relationship is the most commonly used relationship.

One-to-One relationship

A One-to-One relationship occurs when there is one record for each side of the relationship, for example, keeping a customer's financial information separate from the customer's information. You would create a separate table, and then create a One-to-One relationship. Figure 7.4 shows an example of what this would look like—although this does not currently exist in Northwind.

Fig. 7.4
A One-to-One relationship: One customer record has one financial record.

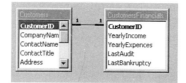

Many-to-Many relationship

The last type of relationship is called Many-to-Many. This is the most confusing of the three.

A good example of a Many-to-Many relationship is a class registration system. In this system, you will have three tables:

- **Classes**—Stores individual class information such as class number, title, and description.

- **Students**—Stores information on the students such as name and student number.

- **Registrations**—Cross-references the two other tables: first, keeping track of which classes the students are in; next, looking at the other side of it—which students are in what classes.

Relating these tables is what a Many-to-Many Relationship is all about, as seen in Figure 7.5.

Fig. 7.5
A Many-to-Many relationship: Class registrations is a classic example of using this type of relationship.

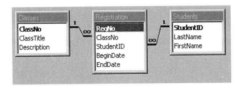

TIP Actually, a Many-to-Many relationship in Access 97 is made up of two One-to-Many relationships.

Using the Relationships window

Just like real life, it takes at least two to make a relationship. Examining all the relationships in Northwind can be overwhelming, so I am going to examine just a few at a time.

Before getting started looking at relationships, let's clear the layout so that we can concentrate on fewer items. Choose Edit, Clear Layout. The relationships themselves still exist; we're just cleaning up the screen.

You will see the Microsoft Access message box.

Click Yes. Access 97 clears the layout for the Relationships window.

Now you are going to add a few tables back into the Relationships window.

Adding a table to the Relationships window

To add a table to the Relationships window, choose Show Table from the Relationships menu.

TIP **When you see an icon beside a menu choice, it usually means** there is an equivalent toolbar button that you can use. Look for the toolbar button for Show Table (the plus sign with a table) on the toolbar for the Relationships window.

Now Access 97 gives you the choice of which tables to display in the Relationships window. Highlight the Orders table (see Figure 7.6) and then click the Add button.

The best way to show the tables to which a table, such as the Orders table, is related is to use the Relationships, Show Direct command. First, though, you need to choose Close in the Show Table dialog box.

Fig. 7.6
You can add individual tables using the Show Table dialog box.

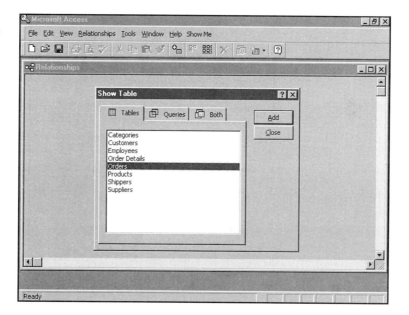

Choose Relationships, Show Direct. Immediately, Access 97 displays those tables that directly relate to the Orders table in this case, the Customers, Order Details, Shippers, and Employees tables (shown in Figure 7.7).

Fig. 7.7
These tables all relate directly to the Orders table.

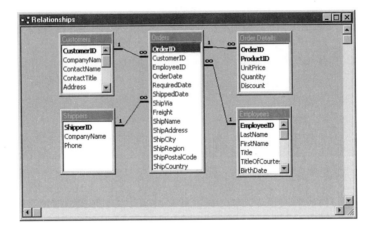

Notice in Figure 7.7 that there is a line between the Orders table and fields in the other four tables. These fields are the related fields.

The fields that make up relationships

If you look again at Figure 7.7, you may notice that the Primary Key fields, the fields that are used to create the relationships between tables, are bolded. For example, the Customers table has a One-to-Many relationship with the Orders table. The CustomerID field in the Customers table is the Primary Key for that table. The OrderID field in the Orders table is the Primary Key for that table. This will always occur when you work with relationships that include Referential Integrity.

 Plain English, please!

Primary Keys are fields that contain information unique in a table. Read Chapter 5, "Learning the Basics About Database Tables," for more details. 💬💬

The field at the other end of a relationship is the Foreign Key. A *Foreign Key* is a field that is used to relate one table to another table. Looking at the relationships for the Northwind Orders table, this time in Figure 7.8, you can see which fields are the Primary Keys, and which are the Foreign Keys.

Fig. 7.8
The relationships for
the Orders table.

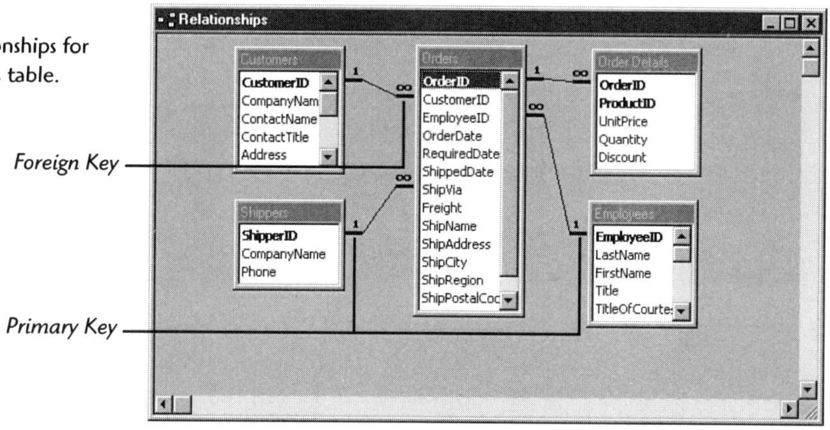

Foreign Key ——

Primary Key ——

TIP **The easiest way to tell which field is the Primary Key, especially** with One-to-Many and Many-to-Many relationships, is that the Primary Key will be on the "One" side of the relationship.

Creating relationships

In order to create a relationship, let's open the VideoLib database, so you can use tables that you created. Let's start from scratch. To do this:

1 Close Access 97 by choosing <u>F</u>ile, E<u>x</u>it.

2 Now start Access 97 again, choosing the VideoLib database at the opening dialog box. You have the three tables created in Chapter 5.

3 Choose <u>T</u>ools, <u>R</u>elationships to open the Relationships window. The Show Table dialog box discussed in the "Adding a table to the Relationships window" section appears.

4 Add both the tblRatings and tblTapes tables by double-clicking each of them. Then click <u>C</u>lose. You will now see the two tables in the Relationships window.

5 Highlight the Rating field in the tblRatings table.

6 Press the mouse button; then drag the cursor over to the Rating field in the tblTapes tables. A new dialog box called the Relationships dialog box appears, as seen in Figure 7.9.

Fig. 7.9
Create relationships
in the Relationships
dialog box.

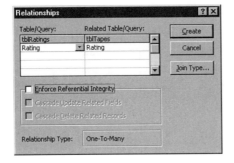

Before clicking the Create button, you need to set up Referential Integrity. Click the box next to the Enforce Referential Integrity option to add a check mark. Click Create to create the relationship. You'll see the newly created One-to-Many relationship between the tblRatings and tblTapes tables.

TIP In Figure 7.9, notice that the Rating field is both a Primary Key (in the tblRatings table) and a Foreign Key (in the tblTapes table).

Now if you try to delete a record in the tblTapes table or to change the Rating in the tblRatings table, you would get the error message displayed in Figure 7.10.

Fig. 7.10
Referential Integrity
in action.

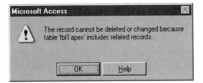

On the other side, if you try to place a Rating in a record in the tblTapes table, and the rating isn't in the tblRatings table, Access 97 lets you know about that, too (see Figure 7.11).

Fig. 7.11
Referential Integrity
prevents you from
creating errors in your
database.

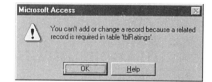

Editing and deleting relationships

One last topic for the Relationships window is editing and deleting relationships. To do this:

1 In the Relationships window, place the cursor over the relationship line between the tblRatings and tblTapes tables.

2 Press the mouse button. The line should appear highlighted.

3 Press the right mouse button. The shortcut menu for the Relationships menu appears, shown in Figure 7.12. You can now select Edit Relationship or Delete (a relationship).

Using Cascade Update and Cascade Delete

There may be some cases when you want to delete all records relating to a record being deleted. For example, back in Northwind, if a customer was deleted by mistake, you may want to delete all that customer's orders as well. Use this approach carefully so you don't delete any records you really need!

In the Relationships dialog box, there is an option for this called Cascade Delete.

The other option, Cascade Update Related Fields, will cascade changes made to the Primary Key field to all the related Foreign Keys. For example, if you change the PG-13 rating to PG-14 in the tblRatings table, then all the Rating entries in the tblTapes table that were PG-13 also change to PG-14.

Cascade Deletes is good only if you don't mind leaving the deleting up to whoever is using the system. Use Cascade Updates only on those Primary Key fields that are *not* AutoNumber, because you can't change AutoNumbers.

Fig. 7.12
You can either delete
or edit a relationship
from this menu.

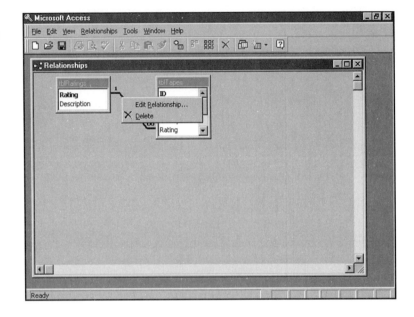

There are options you can change when editing relationships. One example is deciding whether to turn on or off the following features: Referential Integrity, Cascade Deletes, and Cascade Updates. You can also change the fields used for the relationship if necessary.

Always use caution when changing relationships; remember that they can affect how performance and how data can be entered, as well as how the tables work with one another.

Saving Time with Table Wizards

● **In this chapter:**

- **A quick way to create tables using the Table Wizard**

- **Using the Field builder to create fields**

You've learned how to create tables the hard way and relate them to each other. Now check out the quick way to create tables! . . . . ●

You have created a number of tables for the VideoLib database. In this chapter, you will create the last two tables that will be used for VideoLib. Take a look at the tables listed in Table 8.1, remembering that the tblBorrowedTapes and tblBorrowers will be created in this chapter.

Table 8.1   Tables used in VideoLib.mdb

Table Name	Description
tblBorrowers	People who borrow movies.
tblBorrowedTapes	History of movies that each person has borrowed.
tblCategories	Categories for the different movies such as Adventure, Action, and so on.
tblRatings	Ratings for the different movies such as G, PG, PG13, and so on.
tblTapes	Stores the information for each movie in the collection.

There are times when you have to create a table that contains common fields. For example, in the VideoLib database, we want to create a new table called tblBorrowers. The tblBorrowers table is going to keep track of people you lend videos to. As you might suspect, some of the fields in this table will be unique to the borrowers of video tapes. However, some of the fields are very common and appear in just about any table that houses information on people—LastName, FirstName, Address, and so on. One way to take advantage of these common fields when creating tables is to use the Table Wizard.

 Q&A *What's the difference between the Table Wizard and the Database Wizard, which we talked about earlier in the book?*

You should use the Database Wizard to create a complete database application and use the Table Wizard to create an individual table in your database. You will inevitably use the Table Wizard much more than you will the Database Wizard.

Before creating the tblBorrowers table with the Table Wizard, we need to create another table to use with the new tblBorrowers table.

Creating the tblBorrowedTapes table with Design view first

Besides wanting to keep a record of people who are borrowing tapes, we want to know how long they have had the tapes. To do this, we will create a tblBorrowedTapes table. This table is unique, in that the fields used in the table are particular to that table. We will use the Design view method described in Chapter 5 to create it. With the VideoLib database opened in Access 97:

1 Click the Tables tab and then <u>N</u>ew. The New Table dialog box opens.

2 Highlight Design View and click OK.

3 Create the fields as displayed in Figure 8.1. This figure shows how the table will look after it has been saved. Be sure to use the Data Types displayed as well.

Fig. 8.1
Fields used in the tblBorrowedTapes table.

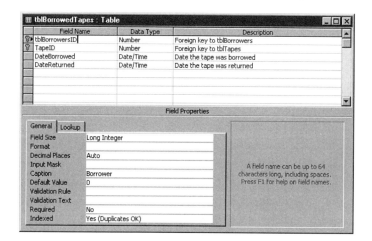

4 Highlight both the tblBorrowersID and TapeID fields by clicking the gray bar on the left side of tblBorrowersID, then dragging the cursor down over TapeID.

5 Click the Primary Key button. Figure 8.1 shows the two fields used for the Primary Key.

6 Close and save the table with the tblBorrowedTapes name.

We will be using this table later in the "Creating relationships with the Table Wizard" section.

Using the Table Wizard

In the Tables tab in the Database window, click <u>N</u>ew. In the New Table dialog box, select Table Wizard and click OK. You will see the first screen of the Table Wizard (see Figure 8.2).

Fig. 8.2
Using the Table Wizard for common fields saves you a lot of time.

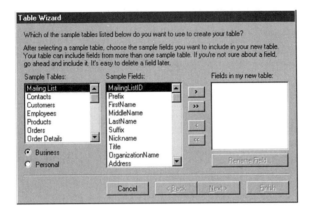

Choosing a sample table format

In Figure 8.2, you can see three lists:

- **Sample Tables**—This list provides several sample tables for either business or personal use. When you choose either the Business or Personal option, Sample Tables lists all the tables appropriate to that choice.

- **Sample Fields**—When you select a table template from the Sample Tables list, a list of field names appropriate to that table appear in the Sample Fields list.

- **Fields in my new Table**—You can choose any of the fields from the Sample Fields list and insert them into the table you're creating.

For the Borrowers table, click the Business option. Then select the Mailing List sample table, which is the table selected by default.

Selecting the fields for the new table

Once you select the sample table you want to use, you can start moving the fields over into your table.

 TIP **If the sample table you selected doesn't contain all the fields you** need, you can then pick fields from another sample table. Simply choose a different table from the Sample Tables list; then select fields from the Sample Fields list and move them into your table.

There are four buttons (see Table 8.2) located between the Sample Fields and Fields in my new table list. Use these for choosing fields for your table.

Table 8.2   Creating fields in your table

This button	Is called...	...and allows you to
>	Select Current Field	Move the selected field from the Sample Fields list to the Fields in my new table list.
>>	Select All Fields	Move all the fields in the Sample Fields list to the Fields in my new table list.
<	Unselect Current Field	Move the selected field in the Fields in my new Table list back to the Sample Fields list.
<<	Unselect All Fields	Move all the fields in the Fields in my new Table list back to the Sample Fields list.

Select a field from the Sample Fields list, and click the > button to move it into the Fields in my new table list. For our example, select the FirstName field and click the > button. The FirstName field moves to the Fields in my new table list.

 TIP **A quicker way to move fields is to double-click the field. If** you double-click a field that is in the Sample Fields list, it will move over to the other list, and vice versa.

To complete our example, move all the fields in Figure 8.3 into the Fields in my new table list.

Fig. 8.3
The fields in the last column will appear in the new table.

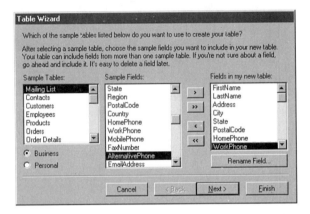

Here are the fields to be used: FirstName, LastName, Address, City, State, PostalCode, HomePhone, and WorkPhone.

After you move all the fields over, click the Next button, located at the bottom of the Table Wizard.

Specifying a name for the new table

The next screen in the wizard (see Figure 8.4) asks you to type a name for the new table. Type tblBorrowers.

Fig. 8.4
Name your table using this page of the Table Wizard.

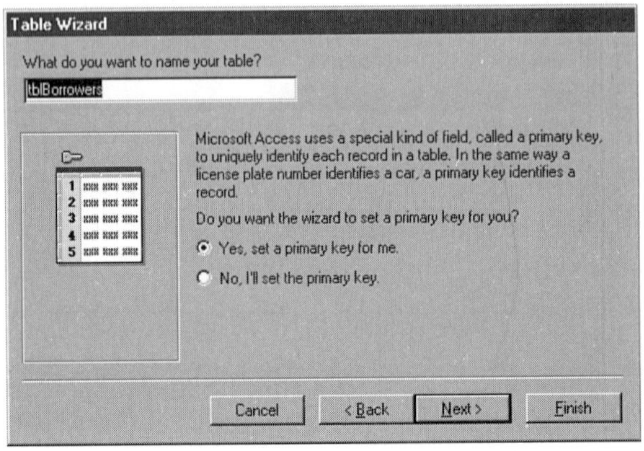

Q&A *I forget, why is there a tbl at the beginning of tblBorrowers?*

It is always a good idea to have a standard when you are naming various objects (such as tables, forms, and reports) in the database. The most common ones are tbl in front of table names and qry in front of query names. This is helpful when the standards appear in the same folder; it makes it easy to identify your objects.

Accept the default response to the question, "Do you want the wizard to set a primary key for you?" Access 97 creates the Primary Key for you.

Click <u>N</u>ext when you have typed in the table name. The next page of the Table Wizard (see Figure 8.5) displays the relationships that exist or don't exist between the new table and others in the database. We will now create the relationships for our new table.

Fig. 8.5
You can see whether or not the current table relates to other tables.

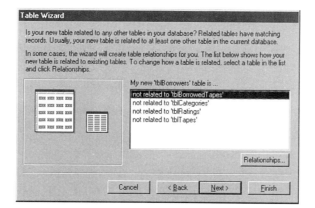

Creating relationships with the Table Wizard

To create a relationship between the new tblBorrowers table and tblBorrowedTapes:

1 Click the Relationships button. Access 97 opens the Relationships dialog box for the Table Wizard. There are two choices available: "The tables aren't related" and "One record in the 'tblBorrowers' table will match many records in the 'tblBorrowedTapes' table."

2 Click the second choice as shown in Figure 8.6 and then click OK. You are now back at the Table Wizard screen that lists relationships. This time it says: "related to 'tblBorrowedTapes'" (see Figure 8.7).

Fig. 8.6
Here you choose to relate the table to tblBorrowedTapes.

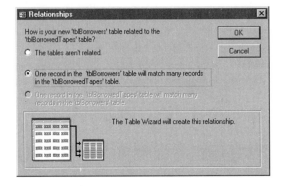

Fig. 8.7
The relation has now been specified between the new table and tblBorrowedTapes.

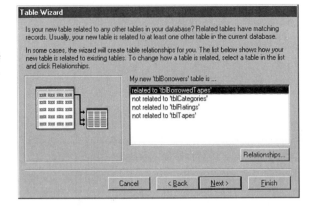

Q&A ***Why didn't Access 97 ask me which fields to use for the relationship?***

In the first section of this chapter, we created the tblBorrowedTapes table, which contains a tblBorrowersID field. This is the name of the Primary Key field that the Table Wizard just created in the new table, tblBorrowers. The Table Wizard takes the name of the table, in this case tblBorrowers, and puts ID on the end. It then assumes you want to create a relationship between the matching field names.

TIP **Although the Table Wizard sets up the initial relationship for you,** you *still* have to tell Access 97 to use Referential Integrity. When you have finished with the Table Wizard, you have to edit the relationship by choosing Tools, Relationships in the Database window. Then follow the directions in Chapter 7, "Understanding Relationships Between Tables."

Click Next. The last screen in the Table Wizard appears. The last screen gives you three options:

- Modify the table design.

- Enter data directly into the table.

- Enter data into the table using a form the wizard creates for me.

Select the Modify the Table Design option (see Figure 8.8); this will open the table in Design View, allowing you to see the completed table structure.

Fig. 8.8
You can choose any of these options to occur after the wizard does its work.

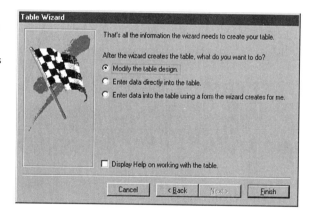

Before clicking the Finish button, use the Back button to make sure you have completed everything correctly. Once you click Finish with this wizard, you will have to make corrections manually.

Click Finish. Access 97 will then open the new table in Table Design view, as shown Figure 8.9.

Fig. 8.9
This table was created
using the Table Wizard.

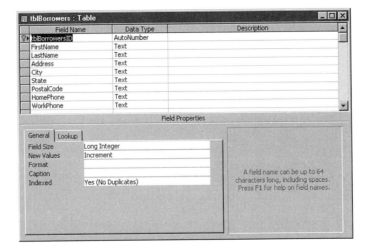

When you use the Table Wizard, Access 97 makes a "best guess" as to the
properties (data type, field size, and so on) and it usually does a good job.
However, you should double-check the properties to make sure they're what
you want. Changing the properties after entering data can cause problems.
We will discuss Properties in the next chapter.

Creating a table using the Table Wizard was easy. It's also easy to add fields
to the table later by using the Field Builder.

Using the Field Builder to add a field to your table

Besides giving you a tool in the Table Wizard to create a complete table,
Access also gives you a method to add a field to an existing table, picking
from common fields. This will be done using the Field Builder, a subset of the
Table Wizard. Adding a field to a table, in this case a FaxNumber field, is
straightforward. While in the tblBorrowers table in Design view:

1 Place the cursor in the empty Name property below the last field,
WorkPhone.

2 Click the <u>B</u>uild button and the Field Builder dialog box appears. This
dialog box is part of the Table Wizard.

3 Make sure to select the Business option button and the Mailing List table in the Sample Tables list.

4 Scroll down the Sample Fields list until you find FaxNumber, as shown in Figure 8.10.

Fig. 8.10
Look familiar? The Field Builder is a subset of the Table Wizard.

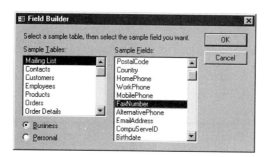

5 Select the FaxNumber field in the Sample Fields list and Click OK. Access 97 then copies the field and all its properties into the tblBorrowers table.

6 Choose File, Close, and save the table.

A Closer Look at Field Properties

● **In this chapter:**

● **Examining some table field properties**

● **What does propagate mean in Access 97?**

● **Looking at indexes**

● **Modifying table structures**

Setting up tables correctly the first time will save you a lot of time later when you begin working with queries, forms, and reports . . . . ➤

It's time to take a closer look at how Access 97 sets up tables. You have created tables manually and you've seen how to do it using the wizards. Remember that tables contain fields. In this chapter, I explain more about how to work with field properties and set up indexes.

 Plain English, please!

Access 97 uses an **index** to enhance performance in searching and sorting data for fields. Just as an index in a book helps you to search for words throughout the book's text, an Access 97 index enhances Access 97's capability to locate information, among other tasks. Part III, "Finding Information in Your Database," discusses searching and sorting data in detail. "

There are a number of field properties you can use that add safeguards for data entry. I will give you some examples of these, as well as other properties that you can use for various purposes.

 Plain English, please!

Properties in Access 97 describe how an object looks or acts. Examples of properties are Width, Height, and Name. Field properties describe details about fields. Examples of field properties are Data Type, Caption, and Default Values. We will discuss these and other properties as we go through the chapter. "

Working with field properties

Field properties are no different than other properties. In Figure 9.1, you can see the Field Properties pane in the bottom half of the Table Design window, which appears when you're in Design view. In the upper pane, you can see the other properties: Name, Data Type, and Description.

Fig. 9.1
You can see field
properties in the Tabl
Design view.

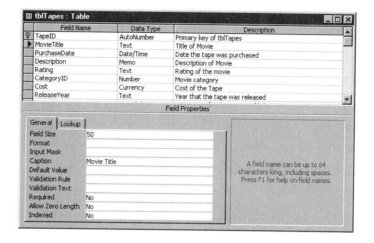

Specifying the data type for fields in your database

In my opinion, Data Type is probably the most important field property. You set this property to specify the type of data you can enter in a particular field; the data type you choose determines other field properties used in the bottom pane. You can see various examples of the Data Type field in Figure 9.1.

Table 9.1 lists all the settings that the DataType property can use and explains what they provide.

Table 9.1 Available data types

This Data Type	Provides
Text	(Default) Text or combinations of text and numbers. Numbers that don't require calculations are also used.
Memo	Up to 65,535 characters.
Number	Numeric data used in mathematical calculations.
Date/Time	Date and time values. Can use different formats.
Currency	Currency values and numeric data used in mathematical calculations involving data with one to four decimal places.

continues

Table 9.1   Continued

This Data Type	Provides
AutoNumber	A unique sequential (incremented by 1) number or random number assigned by Access 97 whenever you add a new record to a table. You can't update AutoNumber fields.
Yes/No	Values and fields that contain only one of two values (Yes/No, True/False, or On/Off).
OLE Object	An object (such as a Microsoft Word document, graphics, sounds, and so on) linked to or embedded in a Microsoft Access 97 table. For more information on OLE Objects, see Chapter 25.
Hyperlink	Text or combinations of text and numbers stored as text and used as a hyperlink address.
Lookup Wizard	Creates a field that allows you to choose a value from another table or from a list of values by using a list box or combo box. You will see more on this later in the chapter.

 TIP   **As mentioned in Table 9.1, Text is the default for the Data Type** property. If you want to change this default, choose Tools, Options. Then click the Tables/Queries tab. You see the setting Default Field Type. You may want to change this default, for example, if your work includes more Number data than Text.

You can also change Default Field Sizes for Text and Number. The next section discusses the Field Size property. A good reason to change the text field size default would be if you tend to use longer text strings. You can change the field from 50 to 75, for example.

Setting the Field Size

How you use the Field Size property depends on the Data Type. For Text, use 0 to 254 (characters). When Number is the Data Type, Access 97 gives you a number of different sizes that store values of various lengths such as Integer values.

To see an example of Field Size, click in the CategoryID field. You will see the field size is Long Integer. Long Integer is the default Field Size for Number data types.

Plain English, please!

You can use **Long Integer** to store larger values than Integer values can; this is the default for the data type of Number. 99

When creating relationships between tables, you must set Foreign Keys to the Field Size of Long Integer.

TIP **When thinking of field sizes for text fields, always specify the** largest size the field will require. Unlike some other database systems, Access 97 only uses space for text that is entered (called using variable length fields). Some database systems pad fields with spaces, thus wasting disk space (called fixed length fields).

Formatting the data

When you set the Format of the field, you are telling Access 97 how you want the field to look when viewed on the screen or in a report. Just like the Field Size Property, this one will depend on the Data Type of the field. For example:

1 Click in the PurchaseDate field.

2 Set the Data Type property to Date/Time.

3 Click in the Format field in the lower pane on the down arrow of the list. You see a list of Date/Time settings for the Format field.

You can see these settings in Figure 9.2.

Fig. 9.2
When you set the Data Type property to Date/Time, you can choose from these formats.

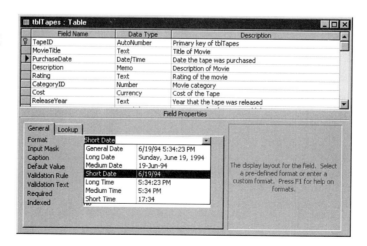

For other settings such as Text and Numbers, you can set custom Format property settings using symbols. You will combine the symbols in Table 9.2 with text, as displayed in Table 9.3 in the Format property. Which symbols you choose depends on the Data Type you use. For example, if you use the Data Type of Text, then use these symbols.

Table 9.2   Format property symbols

Symbol	Description
@	Requires a Text character (either a character or a space).
&	Doesn't require a Text character.
<	Forces all characters to lowercase.
>	Forces all characters to uppercase.

You can then combine the symbols to get the following examples, which show both combined symbols and text.

Table 9.3   Format property examples

Example	Format	Result
Phone Number	(@@@) @@@-@@@@	(555) 782-2222
Force to Uppercase	>	WA
Force to Lowercase	<	wa

To see the symbols used for other data types, place the cursor in the Format property in the lower pane of the Design view and press F1. You can then choose from the data types listed under the Setting section.

To set Format property, follow these steps:

1 Open the tblBorrowers table in Design view.

2 Click in the State field.

3 Type > in the Format property.

Now when you save the change to the table structure, and open the table in Datasheet view, the State field will be forced to uppercase.

Controlling how you enter information

While it's useful to alter the appearance of information after it is entered, it's even nicer if you can control how you enter it. To do this, use the Input Mask property. The Input Mask property helps control accuracy and save data entry time by forcing the user to input the data as specified by the mask.

The best way to learn how to use the Input Mask property is to use the Input Mask Wizard. To create a mask for the HomePhone field in the tblBorrowers table:

1 Open the tblBorrowers table in Design view.

2 Place the cursor in the HomePhone field. Looking at the HomePhone field, you see this already has an input mask that says:

!\(999") "000\-0000;;_

This already has an input mask because when we created this table using the Table Wizard in the last chapter, the Input Mask is one of the properties it supplied with the fields you chose. Ignore this for now.

3 Click the Builder button beside the Input Mask property as shown in Figure 9.3. Access 97 asks you to save the table, and the Input Mask Wizard begins.

Fig. 9.3
There are quite a few places in Access 97 where you can use Builder buttons to open builders and wizards.

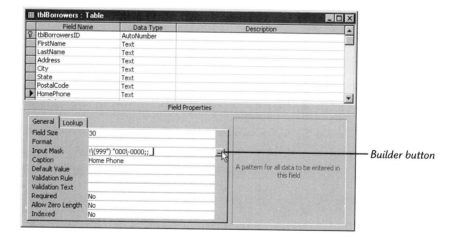

Builder button

4 Highlight the Phone Number input mask (see Figure 9.4).

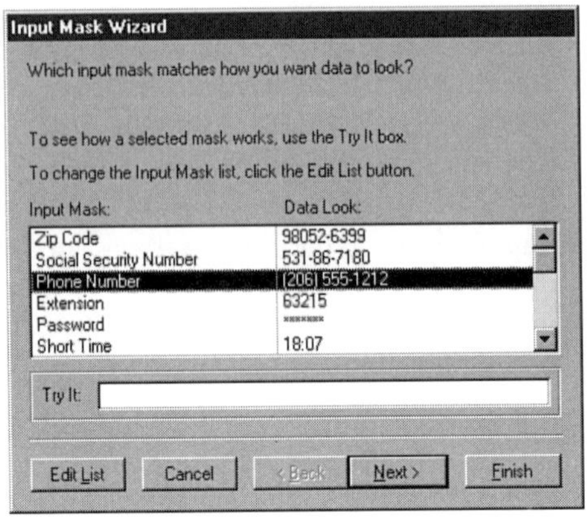

Fig. 9.4
The Input Mask Wizard
helps to create
common input masks.

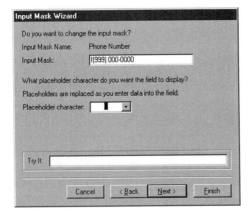

5 Click the Next button. A screen appears showing the input mask with current settings. This screen also lets you make changes to the mask or choose a placeholder (see Figure 9.5).

Fig. 9.5
Choose your desired
input mask in the
Input Mask Wizard.

66 *Plain English, please!*

A **placeholder** is a character that appears where text will go in a string. For instance, the underscore character appears for each of the 10 available spots for typing input in a phone number (where you type the numbers). This occurs both on forms and with the table in Datasheet view. 99

6 Click the Finish button. Once you click the Finish button, the Input Mask Wizard is complete and the Input Mask property is filled in.

To get a complete listing of the characters used for the Input Mask, press F1 while in the Input Mask property.

When you use an input mask on a field, the information you enter into the field must conform with the way you set up the mask. For example, to check out the HomePhone Input Mask you added, open the tblBorrowers table in Datasheet view. Then try to enter a wrong phone number into the Home-Phone, such as using letters instead of numbers. Access 97 won't let you.

Here are a few things to keep in mind when you are thinking of using input masks:

- Make sure you are comfortable with input masks before you place them on important fields in tables.

- Use the Input Mask Wizard whenever possible.

- Use the default input mask supplied when you create a field using the Field Builder or Table Wizard.

Take some time to add an input mask to a couple of other fields in the tblBorrowers table.

Showing a different face using the Caption property

The Caption property lets you display column headings for your fields that are different than the actual field name. This is useful since it is better not to use spaces when you name your fields in Design view; it is easier to read field names when they have spaces between the words in the name.

For instance, you can set the Caption property to Last Name for the LastName field. To do this, with the tblBorrowers table open in Design view:

1 Place the cursor in the LastName field.

2 Type Last Name in the Caption property.

3 Save and switch the table to Datasheet view.

Datasheets will then display Last Name for the column heading. When you use this field on reports and forms, Access 97 also uses the field's Caption property for the label. Read more about using fields on forms in Chapter 19, "Working with Controls on Forms."

Save time by setting Default Values for your fields

When you enter a new record into a table, the value you (or Access 97) sets in the Default Value property automatically supplies the data in a field. The user can then overwrite the data if he wants to. To get a better idea of how this works, let's set the Default Value property for a couple of fields in the tblBorrowers table.

Open the table tblBorrowers in Design view, if you aren't already there. The first example places a default of WA in the State field. To do this:

1 Place the cursor in the State field.

2 In the Field Properties pane, click in the Default Value property.

3 Type WA and press Enter. Access 97 then places quotes (" ") around the text you just entered, as in Figure 9.6.

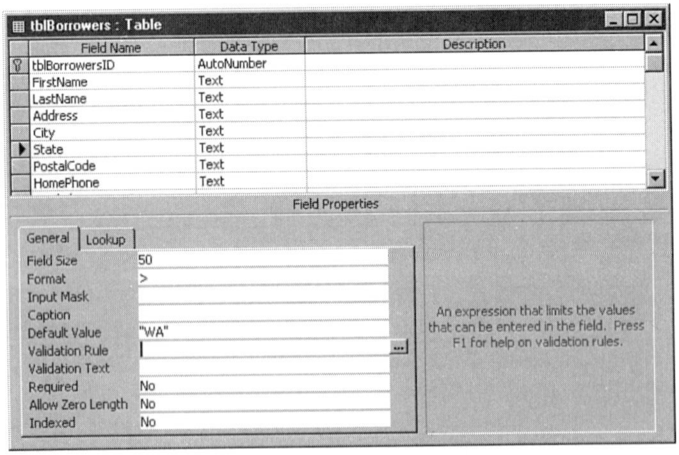

Fig. 9.6
Access 97 places the quotes and text in the Default Value property.

4 Save and switch the table into Datasheet view.

You see WA in the State field for any records created after you set the default value (see Figure 9.7). You can still overwrite the value in the new record, and the Default Value property does not affect values already in the table.

The reason I said, "you or Access 97," is that by default, Access 97 sets the Default Value to 0 for Number and Currency data types. You can then change it if you want.

Fig. 9.7
Notice WA in the State field in the new record.

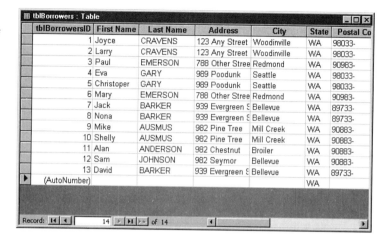

tblBorrowersID	First Name	Last Name	Address	City	State	Postal Co
1	Joyce	CRAVENS	123 Any Street	Woodinville	WA	98033-
2	Larry	CRAVENS	123 Any Street	Woodinville	WA	98033-
3	Paul	EMERSON	788 Other Stree	Redmond	WA	90983-
4	Eva	GARY	989 Poodunk	Seattle	WA	98033-
5	Christoper	GARY	989 Poodunk	Seattle	WA	98033-
6	Mary	EMERSON	788 Other Stree	Redmond	WA	90983-
7	Jack	BARKER	939 Evergreen S	Bellevue	WA	89733-
8	Nona	BARKER	939 Evergreen S	Bellevue	WA	89733-
9	Mike	AUSMUS	982 Pine Tree	Mill Creek	WA	90883-
10	Shelly	AUSMUS	982 Pine Tree	Mill Creek	WA	90883-
11	Alan	ANDERSON	982 Chestnut	Broiler	WA	90883-
12	Sam	JOHNSON	982 Seymor	Bellevue	WA	90883-
13	David	BARKER	939 Evergreen S	Bellevue	WA	89733-
(AutoNumber)					WA	

Record: 14 of 14

Another good example for using the Default Value property is placing a default date into a Date/Time type property. In this case, we are going to set the default value to display the current date.

> ### 66 *Plain English, please!*
>
> When you call a function, you are calling a routine that will return a value. In the case of Date(), it is one of the many built-in Access 97 functions available. One way to learn what functions are available is to use the Expression Builder. I will be discussing the Expression Builder to view and use Access 97 functions in the next section. 99

Using the Expression Builder to set the Default Value property

There are various places in Access 97 that you can use the Expression Builder to supply expressions for you. One of them is the Default Value property. I mentioned that we would like to have today's date placed in a field by default. That field is the PurchaseDate field in the tblTapes table.

To have today's date as the default for the PurchaseDate field:

1 Open the tblTapes table in Design view.

2 Click in the PurchaseDate field.

3 Place the cursor in the Default Value property. You will see a Builder button next to the property, as you did with the Input Mask property.

4 Click the Builder button. The Expression builder opens, as shown in Figure 9.8. One of the choices in the bottom-left list is Functions.

Fig. 9.8
Let Access 97 help you create your expressions that go into the Default Value property.

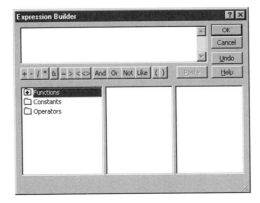

5 Double-click the plus sign (+) next to Functions. You will see another folder that says Built-In Functions.

6 Click the Built-in Functions folder. The middle and right columns fill in with choices. The first list contains logical groupings of the functions; the second contains the functions themselves.

7 Click the Date/Time grouping listed in the middle list. You will then see the Date function listed with other functions in the right list.

8 Double-click the Date function in the right list. The Date() expression will be filled into the top text box (see Figure 9.9). The Date() function returns today's date. If you want the current date and time of entry, use the Now() function.

Fig. 9.9
The Expression Builder has now created the expression needed to store today's date.

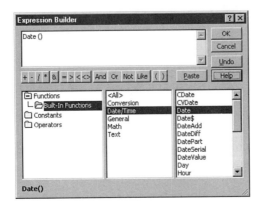

Q&A **What are the parentheses used for?**

Sometimes functions require you to pass values to them that they will use. You insert these values in the parentheses. When you have more than one value to pass to a function, you need to separate them with a comma.

9 Click OK. Access 97 then copies Date( ) into the Default Value property.

You can now save and open the tblTapes table in Datasheet view; then look at the new record to see today's date in the PurchaseDate field. This function will retrieve the current date as you add new records.

Validating information when entered into a field

The Validation Rule property places rules on the way the data is entered. For example, look at the PurchaseDate field again. It does not make sense to allow a future date to be entered in the PurchaseDate field.

The way to keep people from doing this is to place the validation rule <=Date( ) in the Validation Rule property. The expression <=Date( ) rule says that the PurchaseDate must be less than or equal to today's date. (Remember the Date( ) function from the last section.) The <= operator is one of many you can use for comparing data, as shown in Table 9.4.

Table 9.4 Comparison operators

Operator	Description
=	Equal to
>	Greater than
<	Less than
<=	Less than or equal to
>=	Greater than or equal to

To create a validation rule:

1 Type the expression you want to use as the rule into the Validation Rule property. In this case, type <=Date( ).

2 Save the table; then switch to Datasheet view.

3 Try to place a value that does not fall into the range specified by the rule. Again, in this example, it would be a future date in the field. Access 97 displays the message box shown in Figure 9.10.

Fig. 9.10
This is Access 97's validation message. While it does the job, it is not very user-friendly.

Another example of a Validation Rule is if you don't want the state NY placed in the State field. You can place the <>"NY" expression in the Validation Rule property.

To get a friendlier message in the message box, as in Figure 9.10, type the following string into the Validation Text property: Please enter a date on or before today! You can see the settings for the Validation Rule and Validation Text in Figure 9.11.

Fig. 9.11
Here is an example that does a good job of validating data and telling the user what is wrong.

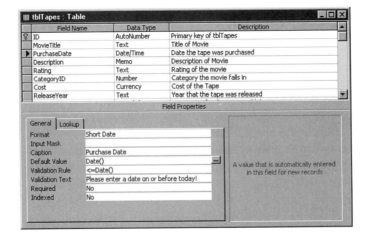

 Q&A *When I switched to Datasheet view, why did I get a message box telling me: Data integrity Rules have been changed?*

This message appears whenever you set or change Validation Rules (and other validating properties) on fields that already contain data. This message lets you know that Access 97 will check all the existing data to make sure it complies with the new rule(s).

Requiring people to enter information into a field

When you have a field that must have data in it, set the Required Field to Yes. By setting the Required Field to Yes, you are saying that a field can't be Null.

CAUTION **Null is very important, and dangerous, in Access 97. To have a** field that is Null means that a field is unknown and has no value. This can really mess up calculations used in queries, forms, and reports. You can find more information on how to handle Null values in queries in Chapter 13, "Using Calculated Fields in Your Query."

Since you should have a title for all your movies, let's make the MovieTitle field a required field.

1 Open the tblTapes table in Design view. Then place the cursor in the MovieTitle field.

2 In the Field Properties pane, pick Yes from the Required property drop-down list (see Figure 9.12).

Fig. 9.12
The MovieTitle is now a required field.

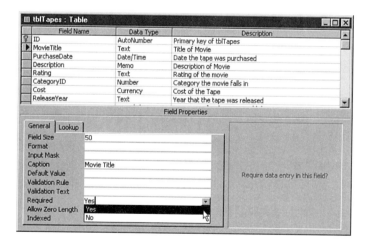

3 Switch to Datasheet view. Access 97 asks you to save the changes and notifies you that the data integrity rules noted in the last Q&A occurred. Click Yes to check the data against the new rule.

Now if you delete all the text from the MovieTitle field in a record and try to save it, you will see an error message.

Try setting the Required property for a couple of other fields.

Using the Lookup Wizard

If you set the Data Type property to Lookup Wizard, Access 97 takes you into the Lookup Wizard. Here's what the Lookup Wizard will do for you:

- Set the Lookup properties for a field. This enables Access 97 to show you a combo box (drop-down) or list box. This box contains all the choices available for this field, and you can choose them either in Datasheet view of the table or on a form. By using the Lookup properties, Access 97 limits the choices that the user can use, thereby helping to keep the information correct.

- Create any necessary relationships between the Lookup table and the table you are currently modifying.

To learn how to use the Lookup Wizard, we will use the table created in Chapter 5 called tblCategories. This table contains the movie categories that you will use for the CategoryID field (see Figure 9.13). Enter the categories into the tblCategories table, if you haven't already.

Fig. 9.13
Here are the Categories used in Videolib.mdb.

To create the Lookup field:

1 Open the tblTapes table in Design view.

2 Place the cursor in the Data Type property of the CategoryID field.

3 Now choose Lookup Wizard from the list of Data Types. Access 97 starts the Lookup Wizard.

4 In the first screen, choose whether you want Access 97 to look up the values in a table or query, or create your own list (see Figure 9.14). We want Access 97 to use a table, so select the first option.

Fig. 9.14
Decide whether to use
a record source (table
or query) or create
your own list.

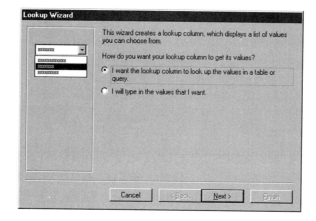

5 Click <u>N</u>ext to go to the next screen. This screen asks you to specify which table you want to use for the lookup source.

6 Choose tblCategories (see Figure 9.15); then click <u>N</u>ext.

Fig. 9.15
We will use
tblCategories for the
Lookup table.

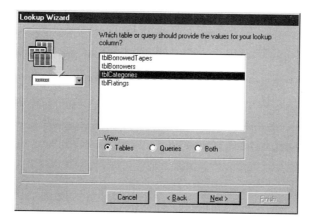

The next screen asks you to specify which fields you want to include in the lookup field. Access 97 uses these fields in the Combo Box controls when you are using the datasheets and forms.

7 Click the Move All Right (>>) button (see Figure 9.16). The CategoryID will be the bound column in the Combo Box, and Description will appear.

Fig. 9.16
Select all the fields you want to use in the Combo Box.

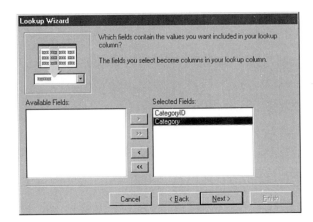

66 *Plain English, please!*

The **bound column** is the field in the Lookup table (tblCategories) that Access 97 stores in the field in the current table (tblTapes). Access 97 does this whenever data is entered into the field, whether through a datasheet or a form. 99

8 Click <u>N</u>ext to go to the next screen. This screen lets you specify how wide you want the columns, and whether you want to hide the key (bound) column. Access 97 does this by default (see Figure 9.17).

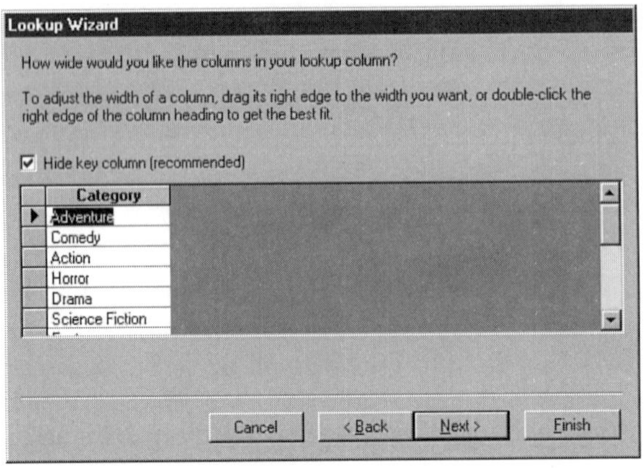

Fig. 9.17
Specify how wide you want the displayed field(s).

9 Click <u>N</u>ext to go to the last screen. This screen lets you specify what you want the top of the lookup column to say.

10 Type Category for the label of the lookup column (see Figure 9.18), and then click Finish. You will see a message box that tells you to save the table before Access 97 can create Relationships. Click Yes.

Fig. 9.18
Finishing your lookup field.

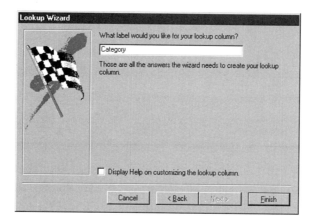

11 You return to the Design view of the tblTapes table. While in the CategoryID field, if you click the Lookup tab in the field properties, you will see the lookup properties now filled in (see Figure 9.19). Save and then close the table.

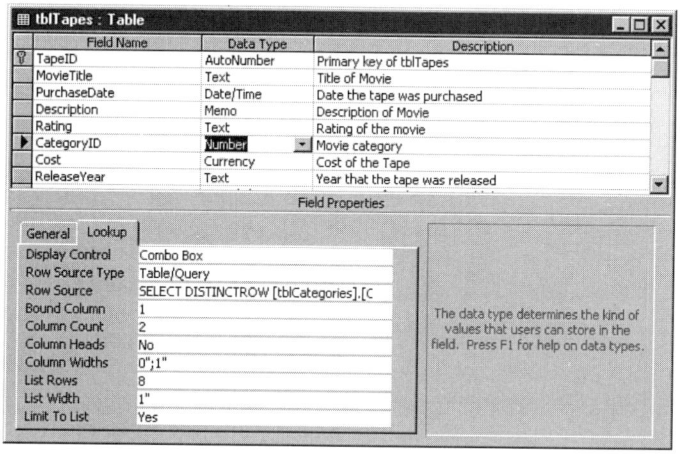

Fig. 9.19
The lookup properties are now set up for you.

12 Open the table in Database view. Then select the category you want to use from the list (see Figure 9.20).

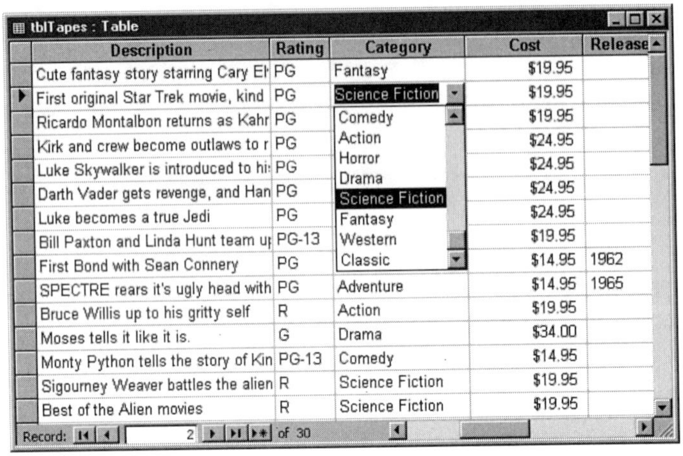

Fig. 9.20
Now pick and choose your categories from a list.

Description	Rating	Category	Cost	Release
Cute fantasy story starring Cary El	PG	Fantasy	$19.95	
First original Star Trek movie, kind	PG	Science Fiction	$19.95	
Ricardo Montalbon returns as Kahr	PG	Comedy	$19.95	
Kirk and crew become outlaws to r	PG	Action	$24.95	
Luke Skywalker is introduced to hi	PG	Horror	$24.95	
Darth Vader gets revenge, and Han	PG	Drama / Science Fiction	$24.95	
Luke becomes a true Jedi	PG	Fantasy	$24.95	
Bill Paxton and Linda Hunt team up	PG-13	Western	$19.95	
First Bond with Sean Connery	PG	Classic	$14.95	1962
SPECTRE rears it's ugly head with	PG	Adventure	$14.95	1965
Bruce Willis up to his gritty self	R	Action	$19.95	
Moses tells it like it is.	G	Drama	$34.00	
Monty Python tells the story of Kin	PG-13	Comedy	$14.95	
Sigourney Weaver battles the alien	R	Science Fiction	$19.95	
Best of the Alien movies	R	Science Fiction	$19.95	

Record: 2 of 30

You have set your first Lookup properties for your database. These types of field properties are quite common and are used throughout database applications.

We can also set up the Rating field Lookup properties, but we will be working with it later in the book.

Working with indexes

Let's go back to the tblBorrowers table in Design view to work with indexes. Indexes play a very important role in Access 97; they can help you increase performance when creating and running queries. In talking about performance, I mean the speed in which Access 97 performs lookups, sorting, and reports. You will want to set up indexes on any fields used for sorting, criteria, or joins—topics discussed in later chapters.

There are two choices for indexes: Duplicates OK and No Duplicates. Duplicates OK allows you to add information into a field with repeating data, such as Ratings in the tblTapes table. No Duplicates means the values entered must be unique, such as ID, also in tblTapes.

You can set up an index on an individual field simply by choosing Yes (Duplicates OK) in the Indexed property in the Field Properties pane of the Design view.

CAUTION **You have to set up indexes carefully. If you set up an index with** Yes (No Duplicates) and then try to add two records with the same value, you will get an error.

There are times when you want to create indexes for multiple fields. This type of index is a composite index. An example of a common composite index would be last name and first name together. This combination is used often for sorting tables, and an index would help performance. To view the composite index:

1 Choose <u>V</u>iew, <u>I</u>ndexes from the menu. Access 97 opens the Indexes dialog box (see Figure 9.21). Note that the indexes that appear in the tblBorrowers table were created by the Table Wizard.

Fig. 9.21
Indexes already created by the Table Wizard.

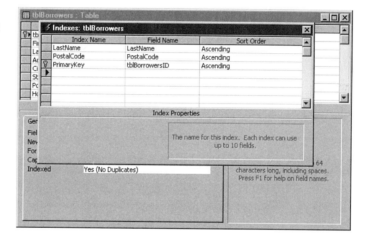

2 Type FullName in the blank row of the Index column following the PrimaryKey index.

3 Move into the Field Name in the same row, and type LastName. When you move into the column, you can also pick LastName from the list of fields presented. Leave the Sort Order as Ascending.

4 Move into the row below the LastName field. Leave the Index Name field blank, and type FirstName into the Field Name column. Again, you can pick from the list of fields presented. Your indexes should now look like Figure 9.22.

Fig. 9.22
The FullName composite index consists of the LastName and FirstName fields.

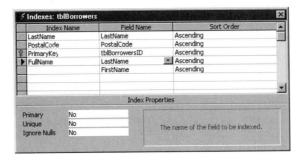

5 Close the Indexes dialog box. Then save and close the tblBorrowers table.

Access 97 will use the FullName index automatically wherever the LastName and FirstName fields are used for searching and sorting purposes.

Part III: Finding Information in Your Database

10

Locating and Sorting Information

● In this chapter:

- Sorting columns of information

- Using the Find dialog box to locate information in a datasheet

- Using the Find/Replace dialog box for replacing information

Order information anyway you want it with two clicks of the mouse! . . . . ▶

When you have a lot of information you are trying to sift through, you may become frustrated, unless you know how to use a few very nice Access 97 features.

The first time-saver is the sort feature. Sorting your data in a set order makes it easier to read your information.

The second feature is the ability to find information, as well as replace it with very little effort.

Taking advantage of the Sort feature

Access 97 lets you sort information simply by placing the cursor in a column and choosing the Sort command.

To see how to use the Sort feature, open the VideoLib.mdb. Next, open the tblTapes table in Datasheet view. You will see the tblTapes table ordered by the Primary Key, in this case ID (see Figure 10.1).

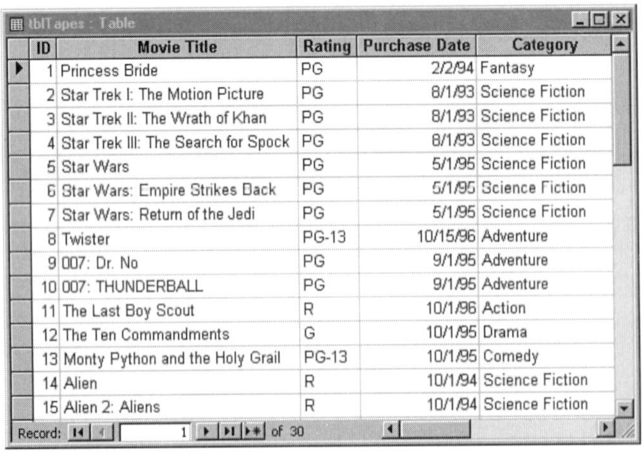

Fig. 10.1
The tblTapes in Datasheet view, sorted by the ID field.

ID	Movie Title	Rating	Purchase Date	Category
1	Princess Bride	PG	2/2/94	Fantasy
2	Star Trek I: The Motion Picture	PG	8/1/93	Science Fiction
3	Star Trek II: The Wrath of Khan	PG	8/1/93	Science Fiction
4	Star Trek III: The Search for Spock	PG	8/1/93	Science Fiction
5	Star Wars	PG	5/1/95	Science Fiction
6	Star Wars: Empire Strikes Back	PG	5/1/95	Science Fiction
7	Star Wars: Return of the Jedi	PG	5/1/95	Science Fiction
8	Twister	PG-13	10/15/96	Adventure
9	007: Dr. No	PG	9/1/95	Adventure
10	007: THUNDERBALL	PG	9/1/95	Adventure
11	The Last Boy Scout	R	10/1/96	Action
12	The Ten Commandments	G	10/1/95	Drama
13	Monty Python and the Holy Grail	PG-13	10/1/95	Comedy
14	Alien	R	10/1/94	Science Fiction
15	Alien 2: Aliens	R	10/1/94	Science Fiction

Record: 1 of 30

There are a couple of ways to sort text, number, or date/time information. You can sort one or more columns at a time, using ascending (A–Z alphabetically for text) or descending (Z–A alphabetically for text) order.

Sorting a single column on your table

To sort the tblTapes table based on the Category column, place the cursor *anywhere* in the Category column. This includes the column heading. Click either the Sort Ascending or Sort Descending toolbar buttons. You can also right-click and choose Sort Ascending or Sort Descending from the shortcut menu (see Figure 10.2).

Fig. 10.2

Notice the icons beside the Sort Ascending and Sort Descending commands and locate them on the toolbar.

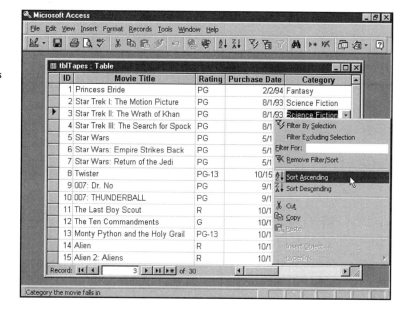

If you choose Sort Ascending, as selected in Figure 10.2, then the records in the table appear in alphabetical order, based on entries in the category column. You can see the result of the sort in Figure 10.3.

Q&A   *Did the actual data get sorted in the table?*

The actual order in the table is, in fact, NOT affected. Notice that I said that Access 97 displays the table in the order of the Category column. This is just like other layout changes mentioned in Chapter 6, "Maintaining Your Information with Datasheets."

Fig. 10.3
The tblTapes table
sorted by Category.

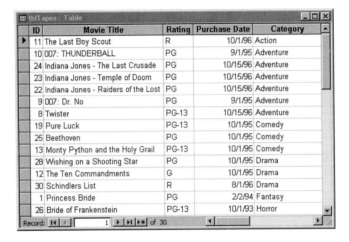

ID	Movie Title	Rating	Purchase Date	Category
11	The Last Boy Scout	R	10/1/96	Action
10	007: THUNDERBALL	PG	9/1/95	Adventure
24	Indiana Jones - The Last Crusade	PG	10/15/96	Adventure
23	Indiana Jones - Temple of Doom	PG	10/15/96	Adventure
22	Indiana Jones - Raiders of the Lost	PG	10/15/96	Adventure
9	007: Dr. No	PG	9/1/95	Adventure
8	Twister	PG-13	10/15/96	Adventure
19	Pure Luck	PG-13	10/1/95	Comedy
25	Beethoven	PG	10/1/95	Comedy
13	Monty Python and the Holy Grail	PG-13	10/1/95	Comedy
28	Wishing on a Shooting Star	PG	10/1/95	Drama
12	The Ten Commandments	G	10/1/95	Drama
30	Schindlers List	R	8/1/96	Drama
1	Princess Bride	PG	2/2/94	Fantasy
26	Bride of Frankenstein	PG-13	10/1/93	Horror

Any time you want to change the sort order, you can simply place the cursor
in another column and then choose the Sort command you want to perform.

Sorting multiple columns

When you want to sort more than one column, you need to do a little more
work. The two columns you want to sort by must be adjacent to each other;
the column that you want to sort by first must be to the left of the other
column. For instance, try sorting by Rating and then Category. First you have
to move the Category column to the right side of the Rating column. Here are
the steps:

1 Highlight the Category column by clicking the Category column heading. The entire column appears highlighted.

2 Let go of the mouse button and then press it again, holding it this time.
   You will see an arrow with the outline of a page for a cursor.

3 Now drag the Category column over the Rating column (see Figure
   10.4). When you get just to the right of the Rating column, let up on the
   mouse button. Now you will have the Rating and Category columns side
   by side.

4 Click the mouse button on the Rating column header, highlighting the
   column. Holding the mouse button down, drag it over the Category
   column so that both the Rating and Category columns appear highlighted.

5 Click the Sort Ascending button. Your datasheet changes to look like
   Figure 10.5.

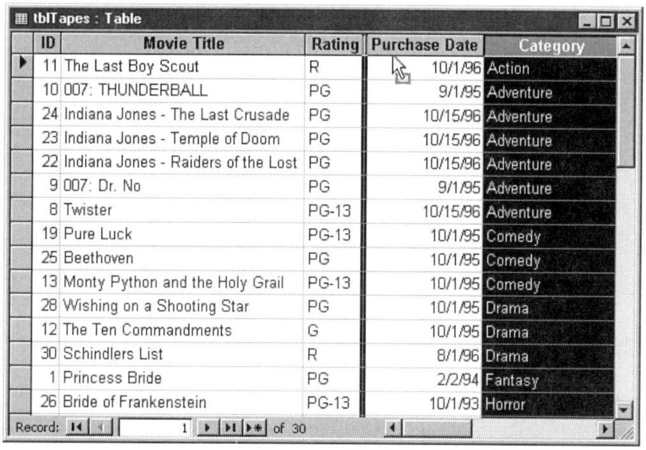

Fig. 10.4
Moving the Category
column to the right of
the Rating column.

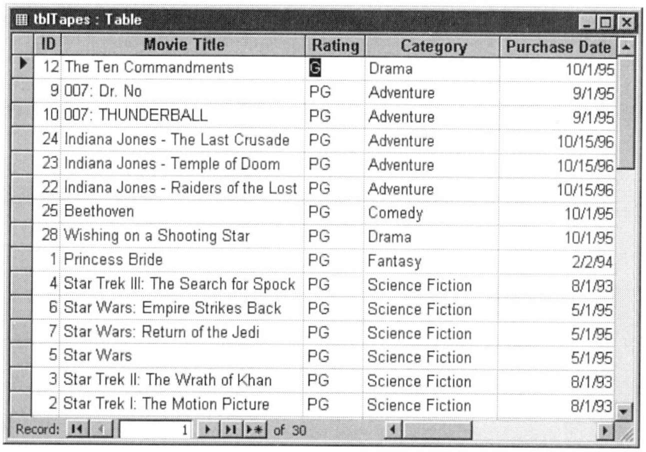

ID	Movie Title	Rating	Purchase Date	Category
11	The Last Boy Scout	R	10/1/96	Action
10	007: THUNDERBALL	PG	9/1/95	Adventure
24	Indiana Jones - The Last Crusade	PG	10/15/96	Adventure
23	Indiana Jones - Temple of Doom	PG	10/15/96	Adventure
22	Indiana Jones - Raiders of the Lost	PG	10/15/96	Adventure
9	007: Dr. No	PG	9/1/95	Adventure
8	Twister	PG-13	10/15/96	Adventure
19	Pure Luck	PG-13	10/1/95	Comedy
25	Beethoven	PG	10/1/95	Comedy
13	Monty Python and the Holy Grail	PG-13	10/1/95	Comedy
28	Wishing on a Shooting Star	PG	10/1/95	Drama
12	The Ten Commandments	G	10/1/95	Drama
30	Schindlers List	R	8/1/96	Drama
1	Princess Bride	PG	2/2/94	Fantasy
26	Bride of Frankenstein	PG-13	10/1/93	Horror

Record: 1 of 30

Fig. 10.5
New sort order of
Ratings and Categories.

ID	Movie Title	Rating	Category	Purchase Date
12	The Ten Commandments	G	Drama	10/1/95
9	007: Dr. No	PG	Adventure	9/1/95
10	007: THUNDERBALL	PG	Adventure	9/1/95
24	Indiana Jones - The Last Crusade	PG	Adventure	10/15/96
23	Indiana Jones - Temple of Doom	PG	Adventure	10/15/96
22	Indiana Jones - Raiders of the Lost	PG	Adventure	10/15/96
25	Beethoven	PG	Comedy	10/1/95
28	Wishing on a Shooting Star	PG	Drama	10/1/95
1	Princess Bride	PG	Fantasy	2/2/94
4	Star Trek III: The Search for Spock	PG	Science Fiction	8/1/93
6	Star Wars: Empire Strikes Back	PG	Science Fiction	5/1/95
7	Star Wars: Return of the Jedi	PG	Science Fiction	5/1/95
5	Star Wars	PG	Science Fiction	5/1/95
3	Star Trek II: The Wrath of Khan	PG	Science Fiction	8/1/93
2	Star Trek I: The Motion Picture	PG	Science Fiction	8/1/93

Record: 1 of 30

TIP   **Although you have to have the columns next to each other to sort**
them, you can rearrange the columns again after you sort them.

Let's see how to find one record that has a piece of information you are
looking for, using the Find dialog box. To begin, sort the datasheet on the ID
field to set it in its original order.

Locating information using the Find dialog box

Although you probably haven't put that much data into the tblTapes table, it's a good time to learn how to find data in your tables when you need to. To do this, look up a Movie Title using the Find dialog box.

1 Place the cursor in the first row of the Movie Title column, but not in the column header.

2 Click the Find toolbar button. The Find dialog box appears, displayed in Figure 10.6. The first field in this dialog box is the Fi<u>n</u>d What field, where you enter the text you are looking for.

Fig. 10.6
The Find dialog box allows you to locate information in your tables.

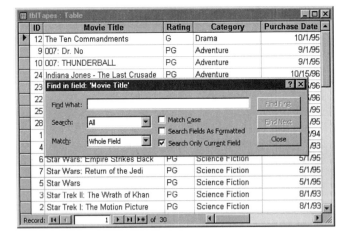

3 Type "Star Wars" in the Fi<u>n</u>d What field. In the Search field, enter one of the following options to specify which direction in the table you want to search:

• Up from the current location

• Down from the current location

• All directions from the current location

Leave All selected for this example.

4 In the Match text box, decide how much of the field you want to compare the search word to. Click the drop-down list and choose one of the following options: Any Part of Field, Whole Field, or Start of Field. For this example, set this to Start of Field, since there are multiple entries of Star Wars. You can use <u>F</u>ind Next to locate more than one record.

5 You can decide whether or not to search for an exact match with regard to case. For example, if you check Match <u>C</u>ase, then "twister" you won't find anything since the title is "Twister." For this example, don't check this option, since you don't care about case.

6 The Search Fields As F<u>o</u>rmatted option allows you to find formatted information that has its Format property set a certain way. To find more information about the Format property, see Chapter 9. For this example, don't check this option.

7 The Search Only Curr<u>e</u>nt Field option allows you to search based on the current field or on all the fields in the table. Since you are already in the field you want to search, leave this option checked.

8 Click Find Fir<u>s</u>t. Access 97 then finds the first of the Star Wars tapes (see Figure 10.7).

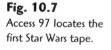

Fig. 10.7
Access 97 locates the
first Star Wars tape.

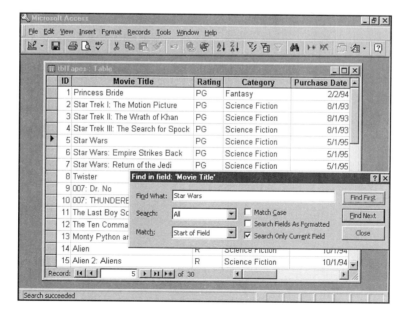

TIP **A few suggestions for better performance:**

- If you know the direction you want to search, specify it. For instance, since you know you are at the beginning of the table, select the Use Down for the Search setting to save Access 97 from having to look all directions.

- Don't select the Search Fields As Formatted option.

- Check the Search Only Current Field option if you know the information you need is in the current column.

Use the Find First button to locate the first occurrence of the text entered in the Find What field. The Find Next button continues the search in the same direction you set using the Search option.

To find the next tape in the series, click the Find Next button. Access 97 finds the next record in the table that starts with "Star Wars." When you run out of Star Wars videos, you will see a "not found" message as shown in Figure 10.8.

Fig. 10.8
This message means it's the end of the road for the current search text.

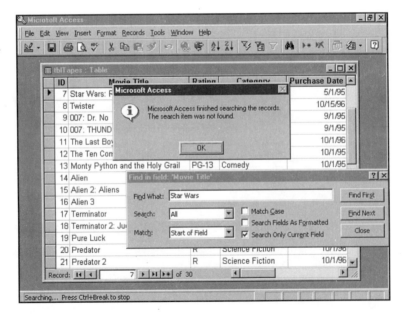

Locating text in the middle of a field

Say you want to find a movie that has some anger in it. Locating a title with "Wrath" in it should be no problem. This time:

1 Set the Find What field to "Wrath."

2 Change the Search option to Up, since you are at the end of the table.

3 Set the Match option to Any Part of Field, since you don't know where the text may be.

4 Click Find First. Figure 10.9 shows the record found.

Fig. 10.9
Locating text in the middle of a field.

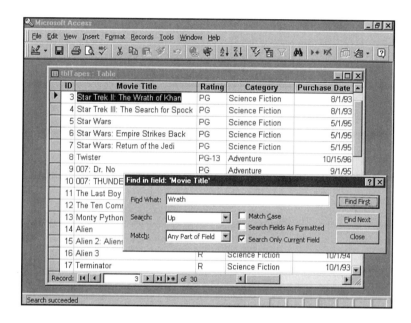

This is a very useful feature for finding the information located anywhere in your table. But what if you want to replace some text?

Replacing information using the Replace dialog box

Say you made a mistake typing in one of the titles. What if instead of typing "Star Trek III: The Search for Spock," you typed in "Star Trek III: The Search for Smock." Ouch, Leonard Nimoy wouldn't appreciate that at all.

You can use the Find dialog box to move to the record that has Smock in the middle of the MovieTitle column and then modify the text. But why not have Access 97 do it in one step?

Click the Close button if you are still in the Find dialog box.

Now, with the cursor still in the MovieTitle column, choose Edit, Replace. You will then notice a dialog box that looks vaguely familiar (see Figure 10.9). Actually quite familiar, since it is the Find dialog box from Figure 10.9 with an extra field called Replace With and a couple of changes to the options.

In Figure 10.10, you can also see the misspelled field title "Smock" in the fourth record.

Fig. 10.10
The Replace dialog box is very similar to the Find dialog box.

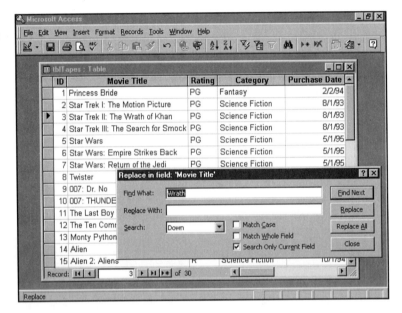

Q&A *Why is "Wrath" in the Find What field?*

The two dialog boxes, Find and Replace, are so similar that each will show the Find What field last used in either dialog box.

The Match option has been changed to the Match Whole Field check box option, and the Search Fields As Formatted option has been dropped altogether.

To perform this Search and Replace:

1 Type in the text "Smock" in the Find What field.

2 Type in the text "Spock" in the Replace With field.

3 Set the Search option to All, since you don't know where the record will be. Everything else is fine as it is.

4 Click Replace All. A warning appears stating you can't undo the replace operation.

5 Click Yes. Now the entry changes. See Figure 10.11, which shows the Replace dialog box with the options set and the word replaced.

CAUTION When you use the Replace All button, all occurrences change in the field (or in the table if you didn't check the Search Only Current Field option). Be sure you want every occurrence replaced when using the Replace All command. If you're not sure, use Find Next and Replace to review each entry individually.

Fig. 10.11
Using the Replace dialog box is a great way to change mistakes in your information.

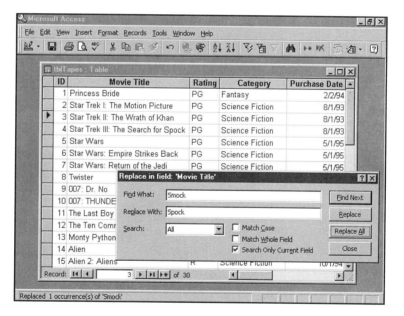

6 Click Close.

11

Working with Filters

● In this chapter:

- **Temporarily reduce the number of records you deal with using filters**

- **Using Filter by Selection is a click away**

- **What you see is what you get, using Filter by Form**

- **Saving filters for another session**

Filters allow you to manipulate your information into something more manageable. . . . . ❯

This chapter will help you to work more easily with large sets of records. In order to make a set of records more manageable, you can "filter out" data that isn't pertinent for that session. Notice I said for that session. Anything you do using filters is not permanent; you can reset the records so you can see all the data. To start, open the tblTapes table in Datasheet view. Figure 11.1 shows the tblTapes table opened in the Datasheet view and sorted by Movie Title.

Fig. 11.1
Notice the Filter toolbar commands you can use.

Movie Title	Rating	Category	Purchase Date	Cost
007: Dr. No	PG	Adventure	9/1/95	$14.95
007: THUNDERBALL	PG	Adventure	9/1/95	$14.95
Alien	R	Science Fiction	10/1/94	$19.95
Alien 2: Aliens	R	Science Fiction	10/1/94	$19.95
Alien 3	R	Science Fiction	10/1/94	$19.95
Beethoven	PG	Comedy	10/1/95	$9.95
Bride of Frankenstein	PG-13	Horror	10/1/93	$9.95
Indiana Jones - Raiders of the Lost	PG	Adventure	10/15/96	$24.95
Indiana Jones - Temple of Doom	PG	Adventure	10/15/96	$24.95
Indiana Jones - The Last Crusade	PG	Adventure	10/15/96	$24.95
Monty Python and the Holy Grail	PG-13	Comedy	10/1/95	$14.95
Predator	R	Science Fiction	10/1/96	$19.95
Predator 2	R	Science Fiction	10/1/96	$19.95
Princess Bride	PG	Fantasy	2/2/94	$19.95
Pure Luck	PG-13	Comedy	10/1/95	$9.95
Schindlers List	R	Drama	8/1/96	$24.95
Star Trek I: The Motion Picture	PG	Science Fiction	8/1/93	$19.95
Star Trek II: The Wrath of Khan	PG	Science Fiction	8/1/93	$19.95

Apply/Remove Filter

Filter by Form

Filter by Selection

Number of records in the table

Pay close attention to the number of records that are in the table. This appears in the navigation buttons at the bottom of the datasheet. In this example, there are 30 records.

Filter by Selection

By using Filter by Selection, you tell Access 97 that you want to see only certain records, based on the value in the field in which the cursor currently resides. For example, say I want to take a look at those movies that have the Adventure Category. To do this:

1 In the Category column, click a field that has Adventure for the Category (see Figure 11.2).

Fig. 11.2
The Adventure category is ready for Filter by Selection.

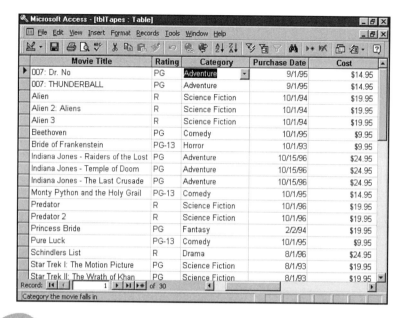

 Q&A ***Do I need to highlight the whole field to use it as the filter?***

No. If you are filtering on the whole field, all you have to do is have the cursor in the field itself. If you highlight a portion of a field, Access 97 filters records based on the highlighted text.

2 Click the Filter by Selection button. Only those records that have Adventure for their Category appear, as in Figure 11.3.

Fig. 11.3
Now, Access 97 only displays the Adventure flicks.

Notice that the word *(Filtered)* now appears on the status bar in Figure 11.3 This tells you there is a filter set.

Looking at a subset of your filtered information

As you look at the adventure movies, you may decide that you want to look at only the Indiana Jones movies. Instead of removing the filter by clicking the Remove Filter button (located on the toolbar), you can further filter out information in the current set of data by selecting another field that will narrow your search further.

TIP **You can remove filters by using the Apply/Remove Filter** command. This is a toggle button, used throughout this chapter. It allows you to apply a filter if there's not one currently applied, or remove a filter that you are currently using.

To filter your information even more, click the first word in the field that you want to filter. For example, highlight Indiana in the tblTapes table.

With Indiana highlighted, click the Filter by Selection toolbar button. Now only the Indiana Jones series appears.

Types of filter values you can use

When you specify the value you want to look for, there are various ways to do it that give you different results. Table 11.1 defines the different ways to apply filters and provides examples of the results you get when you use a particular filter method.

Table 11.1 Ways of specifying information for filter by selection

Selected	Where selected	Filtered	Example
Entire Value	Entire Field	Exact Matches	The Last Starfighter returns The Last Starfighter
Part of a Value	Start of a Field	Only records starting with the selected	Star in Star Trek returns characters in all Star Trek and Star Wars movies

Selected	Where selected	Filtered	Example
Part of a Value	After the first character but before the last	Any record containing those characters	Star in The Last Star Fighter returns all Star Trek and Star Wars movies, plus The Last Starfighter, The Tin Star, and Wishing on a Shooting Star
Part of a Value	Last of a Field	Only records ending with the selected characters	Star in The Tin Star returns The Tin Star and Wishing on a Shooting Star

You can see from Table 11.1 that even though there are only four ways to select data, by using them correctly, you can narrow the information you have to work with.

Excluding records based on selection

There are times when you want to display information based on what the data isn't rather than what it is. For instance, we have a lot of Science Fiction movies in this table. What if you want to display all the tapes that are NOT Science Fiction. This is the way you do it:

1 Click the Remove Filter button to make sure Access 97 removes all filters.

2 Place the cursor in the Category column in a field that has Science Fiction for the category. Make sure you either have the whole field highlighted or none of it.

3 Click the right mouse button in the field. A shortcut menu appears (see Figure 11.4).

Fig. 11.4
This shortcut menu contains all the commands you need for Filter by Selection.

Choose the Filter Excluding Selection command.

TIP   **The third command, Filter For, allows you to enter a value when** you're not necessarily on the value needed. For example, if you really want Adventure, but didn't see any records handy with Adventure to highlight, you can type it in the Filter For, and Access 97 filters on that category. Great Stuff!

4 Click the Filter Excluding Selection. You will see all categories except Science Fiction, as shown in Figure 11.5.

Fig. 11.5
This filter shows every category except Science Fiction.

Movie Title	Rating	Category	Purchase Date	Cost	
007: Dr. No	PG	Adventure	9/1/95	$14.95	Fi
007: THUNDERBALL	PG	Adventure	9/1/95	$14.95	SF
Beethoven	PG	Comedy	10/1/95	$9.95	Dc
Bride of Frankenstein	PG-13	Horror	10/1/93	$9.95	Ca
Indiana Jones - Raiders of the Lost	PG	Adventure	10/15/96	$24.95	Ha
Indiana Jones - Temple of Doom	PG	Adventure	10/15/96	$24.95	Inc
Indiana Jones - The Last Crusade	PG	Adventure	10/15/96	$24.95	Se
Monty Python and the Holy Grail	PG-13	Comedy	10/1/95	$14.95	Mc
Princess Bride	PG	Fantasy	2/2/94	$19.95	Cu
Pure Luck	PG-13	Comedy	10/1/95	$9.95	Th
Schindlers List	R	Drama	8/1/96	$24.95	Ve
The Last Boy Scout	R	Action	10/1/96	$19.95	Br
The Ten Commandments	G	Drama	10/1/95	$34.00	Mc
The Tin Star	PG	Western	9/1/93	$19.95	Cc
Twister	PG-13	Adventure	10/15/96	$19.95	Bi
Wishing on a Shooting Star	PG	Drama	10/1/95	$19.95	Sa
*		0	12/17/96	$0.00	

Record: ◄ ◄   1 ► ►I ►* of 16 (Filtered)
Category the movie falls in   FLTR

Using Filter by Selection is a great, quick way to filter your information, but there is a more powerful way—Filter by Form.

Using Filter by Form to select information

With Filter by Selection, you were filtering records based on a field you selected in the datasheet, and then selected another field in the subset to narrow it further. When using Filter by Form, Access 97 takes you to a different screen to specify the criteria you want to filter with. Using Filter by Form, although more complicated, allows you to be more specific and filter your data based on a combination of selected values from multiple fields.

To see what this looks like, remove any filters you may have by clicking the Remove Filter button, and check the total records displayed at the bottom of the datasheet. You want to make sure all the records are there. Click the Filter by Form button. The datasheet will suddenly look as if you deleted all the records (see Figure 11.6).

Fig. 11.6
Don't panic if it seems like all your records are gone; this is Filter by Form.

Clear Grid ──────

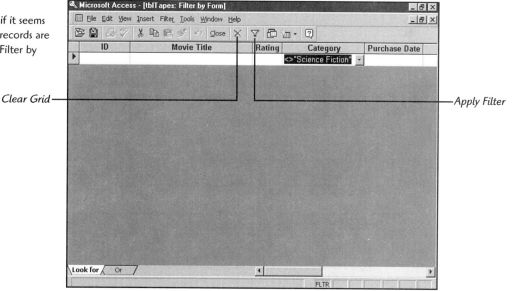

────── Apply Filter

 Q&A *What is the text in the Category column?*

Remember that in the last section you looked for all the categories other than Science Fiction. Hence the string: <> "Science Fiction". To clear this entry, click the Clear Grid button.

Now you can pick the fields you want to filter and display your information. Click Categories to see the drop-down list, as in Figure 11.7.

 Plain English, please!

Criteria are the values you want to compare to the information, thus creating the filter. Access 97 uses this term a lot when dealing with Access 97 queries, which I will talk about in the next chapter.

Fig. 11.7
Pick and choose your criteria for displaying information.

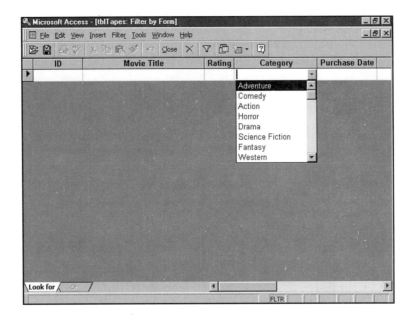

 Now pick Adventure from the list. Then click the Apply Filter button. You will now see the tapes in the Adventure category.

Using more than one filter criterion

There are many cases where you want to combine criteria together and use Complex criteria. An operator compares a field to an expression. Table 11.2 shows some of the operators used in criteria.

Table 11.2   Criterion operators

Operator	Description
=	Equal to
>	Greater than
<	Less than
<=	Less than or equal to
>=	Greater than or equal to

Q&A ***Do you have to type AND and OR in uppercase?***

The use of uppercase for AND and OR is simply to make it clear that I am using these as operators. In fact, when Access 97 presents them, it generally uses proper lowercase (combination of upper- and lowercase).

ANDing criteria together in a filter

The AND operator allows you to filter records based on two or more criteria. When you apply a filter using the AND operator, only those records that meet *both* (or all) criteria appear. To show how to use the AND operator, we'll choose all movies that are in the Science Fiction category *and* are rated R. To do this:

1 Click the Filter by Form button to return to the Filter by Form screen. Your screen should be blank as shown in Figure 11.7. Click the Rating criteria and select R.

2 Click the Category criteria and select Science Fiction.

3 Click the Apply Filter button. Now those movies rated R that are Science Fiction appear. By using these two criteria together, you can perform an AND of these two criteria, as mentioned in step 3.

ORing criteria together in a filter

There are many times when I feel like seeing either an Action or a Science Fiction movie. When that is the case, then you need to use the Look For and Or (currently disabled) tabs displayed at the bottom of the Filter by Form.

1 Click the Filter by Form button.

2 Click the Clear Grid button.

3 Choose Science Fiction for the Category. As soon as you enter the first criteria, Access 97 enables an Or tab at the bottom of the Filter by Form (see Figure 11.8).

4 Click the Or tab at the bottom of the Filter by Form screen.

TIP **When you want to go back to the first screen in Filter by Form,** click the Look For tab.

Fig. 11.8
Using more than one
criterion by ORing
them together.

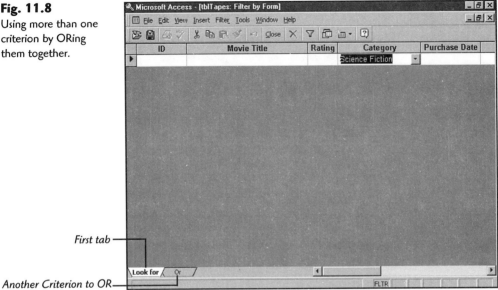

First tab

Another Criterion to OR

5 Choose Action for the second Category.

6 Click the Apply Filter button. You will see only movies with the
   Categories of Science Fiction OR Action (see Figure 11.9).

Fig. 11.9
Results with the criteria
set to Categories that
are Science Fiction or
Action.

ID	Movie Title	Rating	Category	Purchase Date	
2	Star Trek I: The Motion Picture	PG	Science Fiction	8/1/93	First orig
3	Star Trek II: The Wrath of Khan	PG	Science Fiction	8/1/93	Ricardo
4	Star Trek III: The Search for Spock	PG	Science Fiction	8/1/93	Kirk and
5	Star Wars	PG	Science Fiction	5/1/95	Luke Sk
6	Star Wars: Empire Strikes Back	PG	Science Fiction	5/1/95	Darth Va
7	Star Wars: Return of the Jedi	PG	Science Fiction	5/1/95	Luke be
11	The Last Boy Scout	R	Action	10/1/96	Bruce W
14	Alien	R	Science Fiction	10/1/94	Sigourne
15	Alien 2: Aliens	R	Science Fiction	10/1/94	Best of
16	Alien 3	R	Science Fiction	10/1/94	Worst o
17	Terminator	R	Science Fiction	10/1/93	First of t
18	Terminator 2: Judgment Day	R	Science Fiction	10/1/93	Arnold's
20	Predator	R	Science Fiction	10/1/96	Arnold n
21	Predator 2	R	Science Fiction	10/1/96	Danny G
27	The Last Starfighter	PG-13	Science Fiction	10/1/96	Great sp
* (AutoNumber)			0	1/21/97	

Record: I◄ ◄ 1 ► ►I ►* of 15 (Filtered)

Primary key of tblTapes   FLTR

Combining ANDs and ORs criteria

When you want to combine ANDs and ORs, you simply add another criterion to one that you already set. If you want to see any action flick but want to see only R-rated science fiction movies, you need to add the R for Rating criteria to the criteria screen with Science Fiction for the Category.

Using the current criteria set for the OR filter to add the R rating:

1 Click the Filter by Form button. Access 97 takes you to the first tab of the Filter by Form, which is Science Fiction in Category.

2 Type R in the Rating column, next to the Category Field that says Science Fiction. In Access 97, the criterion displays the records where the Rating is set to R and the Category field is set to Science Fiction, or where the Category field is set to Action and we don't care about the Rating.

Note that with any of the filters you set, if no records match the criteria, Access 97 presents you with a blank datasheet with a new record.

Saving your filters

You can save filters with your datasheet like other Layout changes described in Chapter 6, simply by clicking the Save button on the toolbar. If you exit the datasheet without saving, Access 97 will ask if you want to save your filter.

The next time you open the datasheet, the filter is available if you click the Apply Filter button.

You cannot save more than one filter at a time, but if you find that you use one filter a lot, you can save it as a query. You will then use the datasheet off the query (discussed in the next chapter).

Part IV: Viewing Your Data with Queries

12

Query Basics 101

● **In this chapter:**

- **What are queries?**

- **How do you create a query?**

- **Specifying criteria in a query**

- **Selecting fields for a query**

- **Looking at the different types of queries**

You can use queries to perform monotonous database functions and to look at your data from many views. . . . .

O nce you create your tables and enter your data, you will want to poll information in various sort orders based on criteria that you set. Queries help you do just that. Queries play a big role in Access 97 by giving you the ability to view data the way you want to for a specific purpose.

Where does Access 97 uses queries?

In the last chapter, you saw how to use filters in a datasheet. Remember that filters are only temporary; you can't save and reuse a filter the next time you want to look at a subset of your information. If you have a subset of your data that you want to use more than once, or a combination of data from various tables, then a query is your answer.

You can use queries in a number of places in Access 97. Here are just a few of the ways:

- Limiting the fields that a form is based on.
- Creating a report that displays information from more than one table.
- Generate mailing labels for a specific ZIP Code.
- Performing bulk update operations such as deleting all the archived invoices.

Introducing Query Design

Queries are based on the tables that store your data. So when you want to create a query, you have to pick which tables you want to include in the query. You can also base queries on more than one table (or query). For now, let's create a query using one table, tblTapes. (Chapter 14, "Working with Multiple Tables, Parameters, and Complex Criteria," discusses using more than one table.)

Some of the tasks performed in creating a query are specifying:

- Fields to include in the query
- How we want the data sorted
- Criteria used in the query

When creating queries, the best place to start is in the Query Design view:

1 Open the VideoLib database.

2 Click the Query tab. At this point, there are no queries listed because we haven't created any queries yet.

3 Click the <u>N</u>ew button located on the right side of the Database window. The New Query dialog box appears (see Figure 12.1).

Fig. 12.1
You can go directly into a new query with Query Design view.

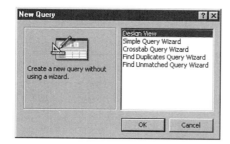

4 Click OK to continue. Before you get into the Query Design view, the Show Table dialog box appears (see Figure 12.2).

Fig. 12.2
The first task when designing a query is to decide which table(s) to use.

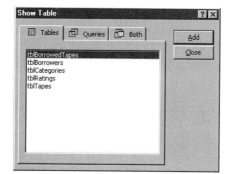

Q&A *If the name of the dialog box is Show Table, how come I see a Queries tab?*

The name of the Show Table dialog box is kind of a misnomer, since you can see the Queries tab here as well. You can, in fact, base queries off of other queries, but we won't get into that right now.

5 Highlight the tblTapes table, and click <u>A</u>dd. Access 97 then adds the table to the Query Design view. Click the <u>C</u>lose button. The Query Design view displays the tblTapes table at the top of the screen (see Figure 12.3).

Fig. 12.3
The Query Design view is the main headquarters for your query needs.

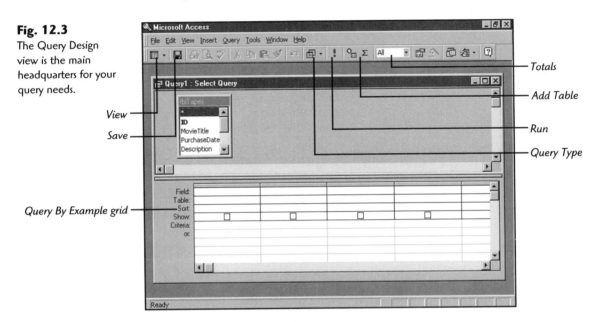

Examining the parts of the Query Design view screen

On the menu bar (in Figure 12.3), notice that the only new menu selection is Query. This menu contains commands, most of which are reflected on the toolbar that is directly below it. We will visit this menu later.

The Query Design view toolbar contains a number of the same commands that other toolbars have, but there are a few new ones (refer to Figure 12.3).

Just below the toolbar, you can see the tblTapes table outlined with its fields displayed; this is the Query Design area. The Field List is different depending upon the table on which you base your query.

You can add tables or queries as needed by clicking the Add Table button on the toolbar. The Add Table button calls up the Show Table dialog box discussed in the previous section (refer to Figure 12.2).

You will use the fields listed in the Field List in the QBE (Query By Example) grid, located below the Query Design area. You will create most of the design in this area. The columns contain fields from the fields of the selected table, in our example this is tblTapes. These are the tasks that each row performs for the fields:

- **Field**   This row contains the field (from the Field List) that you want to include in the query. This can also contain an expression (a temporary field that you made). Chapter 13 discusses expressions.

- **Table**   Displays the name of the table that the field is in. This is useful if you are basing your query on more than one table, especially if you have fields in the different tables that have the same name.

- **Sort**   Allows you to specify which field(s) to base the sort order on.

- **Show**   Determines whether or not to display the field in the datasheet that displays. Use this when you have a field used as a criterion but don't want it to show.

- **Criteria**   As discussed in the last chapter, criteria allows you to include, or not include, records based on individual or combined field values. Just like Filters, you can combine criteria by using ANDs and ORs.

More rows may appear based on which type of query you create. Let's continue creating the query.

Specifying fields to include in the query

The next step is to grab a couple of the fields from the Query Design area and bring them down to the QBE grid. There are a few ways to do this, but for now, I will show you a nice, quick way.

Double-click the MovieTitle field in the tblTapes Field List. Access 97 moves the field down to the QBE grid in the first column (see Figure 12.4). The table in which the field exists appears in the second row, Table.

Once you include one field in the query, you have the minimum you need to make a query. Let's see what it looks like.

Fig. 12.4
You can choose a field to include simply by double-clicking the field.

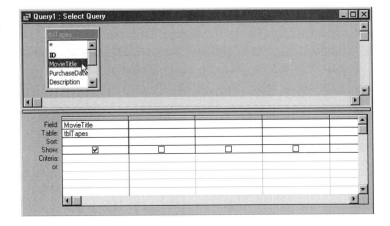

Looking at the different views of a query

You are currently in Query Design view. There are two other views for queries: Datasheet, which you are familiar with from working with tables, and SQL view. To check out the current query in Datasheet view, click the View button. You will then see the information for all records using MovieTitle field. By clicking the down arrow next to the View button, you can see all three views available mentioned earlier in this paragraph (see Figure 12.5).

Fig. 12.5
The Datasheet results of your first query.

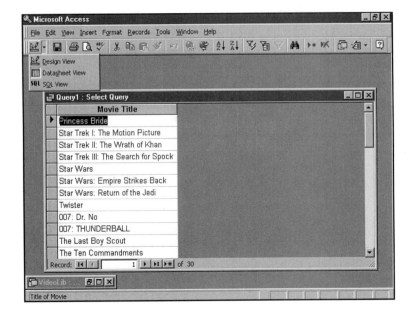

The other view mentioned earlier is the SQL View. SQL (Structured Query Language) is the language in which Access 97 stores queries. It is a standard language for querying data used in many databases. Using SQL is beyond the scope of this book.

Sorting data in a query

The information presented in Figure 12.5 was nice, but it would be even nicer if the titles were in alphabetical order. Let's go back to Query Design view and see how to do this. To specify the sort order of a field:

1 In the Query By Example grid, place the cursor in the Sort row of the field to sort by. When you do this, you will notice that the sort field is actually a drop-down list.

2 Click the down arrow. You will then see three choices: Ascending, Descending, and (not sorted).

3 Choose Ascending for the MovieTitle sort entry (see Figure 12.6).

Fig. 12.6
Sorting is straightforward in the QBE grid.

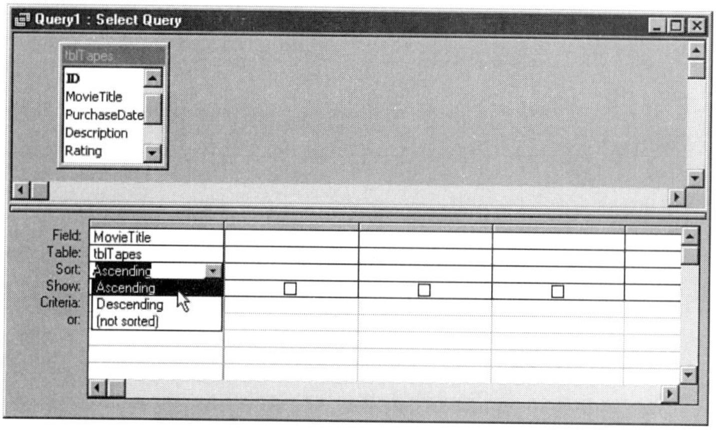

4 Click the Datasheet View button to view the results (see Figure 12.7).

When you finish looking at the results, click the Design View button to return to the Query Design view. It's now time to specify criteria for your query.

Fig. 12.7
This datasheet now
sorted alphabetically
by MovieTitle.

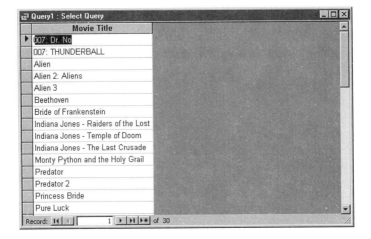

Specifying criteria for your query

One benefit that queries provide is the ability to limit your data in many
different ways. Before going overboard, though, I want to show you how to
do it the easy way.

To see all the movies that start with the word Star:

    1 Click the Design View button to return to the Query Design view (see
Figure 12.6). In the QBE grid, type the following in the first row of the
criteria for the MovieTitle field: Like Star*.

    2 Press Enter. Access 97 then converts it to: Like "Star*" placing quotes
around Star*. You can see this criterion in Figure 12.8.

Isn't it nice that Access 97 adds the quotes for you? "Like" and a wild-card
character such as the asterisk (*) tells Access 97 that you want all the
MovieTitles that start with the word "Star." Click the Datasheet View button
to see the results (see Figure 12.9).

You will see additional wild cards and ways to specify criteria in Chapter 14,
"Working with Multiple Tables, Parameters, and Complex Criteria."

There you have it. You have created your first query. Now take a look at how
to save what you created for later use.

Fig. 12.8
Setting the criteria for
MovieTitles starting
with Star.

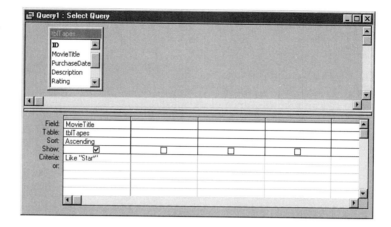

Fig. 12.9
This datasheet now
shows all MovieTitles
starting with Star.

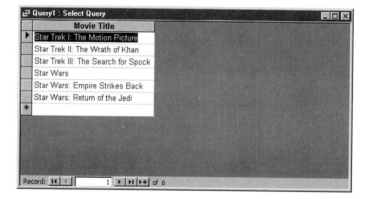

Saving the query

Whereas filters are temporary, you usually design queries for later use in
various areas of Access 97. To save your query, you can either click the Save
button or choose File, Close from the menu. You will then be asked to enter
the name of the new query. In this example, enter: qryMovieTitles and then
click OK. If you closed your query, you will now see your new query under
the Query tab in the Database window.

Q&A *Why did you put the qry in the front of the query
name?*

It is always good to use a standard when naming your objects such as tables
and queries. Sometimes, Access 97 displays both queries and tables in the
same list, so it's good to distinguish between the two.

Selecting additional fields for your query

I'm almost done showing you the query basics. Now, let's look at the different ways to add fields to the QBE grid.

When you want to include all the fields in a table (or query), you can double-click (or drag and drop) the asterisk in the Fields list to place all the fields in the QBE grid. (see Figure 12.10).

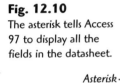

Fig. 12.10
The asterisk tells Access 97 to display all the fields in the datasheet.

Asterisk —

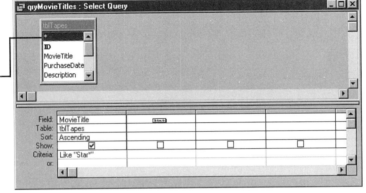

Now click the Datasheet View button.

When you run this query, you will see that MovieTitle appears twice in the datasheet. The reason you have MovieTitle in the datasheet twice is that it was first specified with the criteria and then included again when you brought the asterisk down. To get rid of one of them, remove the check from the Show property in the MovieTitle column in the QBE grid (see Figure 12.11).

Fig. 12.11
Use the Show property to control fields displayed in the Datasheet.

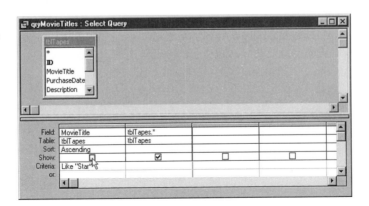

Now when you click the Datasheet View button, Access 97 only shows the MovieTitle column from the asterisk but uses the original criterion set.

Other methods of adding fields are:

- Drag and drop individual fields from the Field list into the QBE grid.

- Double-click the title of the Field List. This highlights all the fields. You can then drag them down to the QBE grid and delete those fields you are not interested in.

Moving or deleting fields in the QBE grid

Moving fields around the QBE grid is similar to moving columns in the datasheet. Click the field you want to move, release the mouse button, and then click and drag the field to where you want it.

To delete the field, simply highlight the column, and press the Delete key.

Now that you have seen how to create a simple query, it's a good time to discuss different types of queries.

Looking at the different types of queries

 Access 97 queries come in a variety of flavors. You can see some flavors by clicking the down arrow next to the Query Type button (see Figure 12.12).

The first type of query, Select Query, has been mentioned a number of times. Select queries allow you to view your data in various ways and then base reports and forms from them.

Fig. 12.12
Queries can do much
more than just display
information.

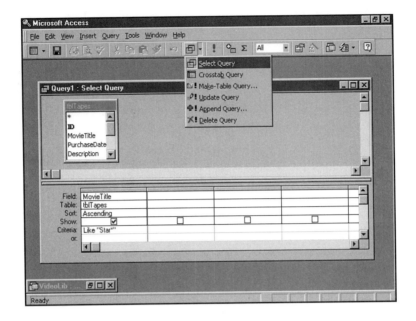

Other types of Queries are SQL Server specific queries (which I won't get into in this book) and Action queries. Here is a list of the different types of Action queries and their purpose:

- **Make-Table**   Creates a new table based on the fields included in the QBE grid.

- **Update**   Updates fields in the specific table, or tables with values provided.

- **Append**   Adds new records to a table.

- **Delete**   Deletes records in the requested table(s).

There is also a type of query called a Crosstab query. This query gives you a cross-tabulation of data such as the total of a customer's invoices over a 12-month period.

13

Using Calculated Fields in Your Query

● **In this chapter:**

- **Create calculated fields to enhance queries**

- **Give names to calculated fields in queries**

- **Set properties for fields in queries**

- **Use built-in Access 97 functions in calculated fields**

Calculated fields allow you to combine fields and include outside elements in your queries. . . . . ➤

You were introduced to queries in the last chapter and shown how to display fields. Calculated fields allow you to create expressions from existing fields to use for display. Here are some examples of actions you can perform using calculated fields:

- Combine LastName and FirstName fields, separated by a comma, into an expression for display purposes, such as Barker, Diana.

- Add days, weeks, or months to the current date to display a future date.

- Multiply one field such as a Quantity field times a Cost field to display the total cost of an item.

Access 97 bases calculated fields off of other fields, literal values, and functions. Before creating some calculated fields, let's take a look at the syntax that Access 97 requires us to use when creating them.

 Plain English, please!

When using a **literal value,** you are using a text or number value itself, rather than a field or a variable (for example, "Star Wars" instead of MovieTitle). You need to include the quotes in the case of text.

Calculated fields syntax

When you calculate fields, you need to use a certain syntax. After you learn this syntax, you can create any calculated field you need in a query. Taking one of the examples previously mentioned, combining LastName and FirstName fields with a comma, the syntax for that calculated field is: Expr1: [LastName] & ", " & [FirstName]. I will walk you through actually using this example in a moment. First, let's look at the syntax piece by piece.

 Plain English, please!

Syntax is the structure for the command you use, or the way you will type it out. In calculated fields, this includes standard operators and ways of supplying fields for them to work correctly.

First, the name of the new expression

The first part of the calculated field shown, Expr1, is the name of the new field. Access 97 supplies this if you don't. This is the name you will refer to later when you use this field in a form, report, or another expression. You will want to use a more meaningful name, depending on the calculated field's purpose. I will go into further detail about changing this name to something more meaningful in the "Naming calculated fields" section later in this chapter.

Using brackets around field names

When you use fields from tables in your query, you must use square brackets around the field names. If you don't have any spaces in the names of your fields, Access 97 will put the square brackets around the fields for you. [LastName] and [FirstName] are good examples of this.

Using operators in a calculated field

There are a number of operators that you can use in calculated fields. Some are for performing mathematical calculations such as those seen in Table 13.1.

Table 13.1   Mathematical operators for calculated fields

Operator	Description
+	Addition
-	Subtraction
*	Multiplication
/	Division
^	nth Power

An example for using a mathematical operator would be multiplying Quantity and Cost fields for a new total cost field. It would look like this: TotalCost: [Quantity] * [Cost].

You saw another operator used—the ampersand (&). This was used to combine two strings with a literal into a single new string: Expr1: [LastName] & ", " & [FirstName].

Another popular calculated field combines the fields City, State, and Zip code with punctuation into a single field. The syntax for this would look like: CityStateZip: [City] & ", " & [State] & " " & {ZipCode], and the result would look like: Indianapolis, IN 46207.

In this address example, we added spaces and commas between the City, State, and Zip code by placing them between double quotes, thus using them as literals.

Some examples of calculated fields

The following list contains some additional calculated fields that are very useful:

SubTotal: [Quantity]*[Amount]

TotalAmount: [SubTotal]+([SubTotal]*[TaxRate])

30Days: [InvoiceDate]+30

AreaCode: Left([Phone],3)

Q&A   **Do all fields in the calculated field have to be down in the QBE grid?**

No, as long as the fields are in the Field List in the query design area, you can use them in the QBE grid. It also doesn't matter which order the fields or calculated fields are in.

Creating a query with a calculated field

Creating calculated fields is easy if you know the syntax for the calculated field you want to create, which we just covered.

Creating the base query for calculated fields

In order to show you how to create calculated fields, we need to make a query to work with. We will continue to build on the query for the remainder of the chapter.

1 Open the VideoLib database.

2 Create a New query by clicking the Queries tab in the database window; then click the New button. The New Query dialog box appears.

3 In the New Query dialog box, click the OK button, since you will be going into Query Design view. You will see the Show Table dialog box.

4 In the Show Table dialog box, select the tblBorrowers table, and then click Add. Access 97 adds the tblBorrowers table to the query design area. Click Close to close the Show Table dialog box.

5 Double-click the LastName and FirstName fields (in that order) from the tblBorrower field list.

6 Set the Sort order of LastName to Ascending. Your query should then look like Figure 13.1.

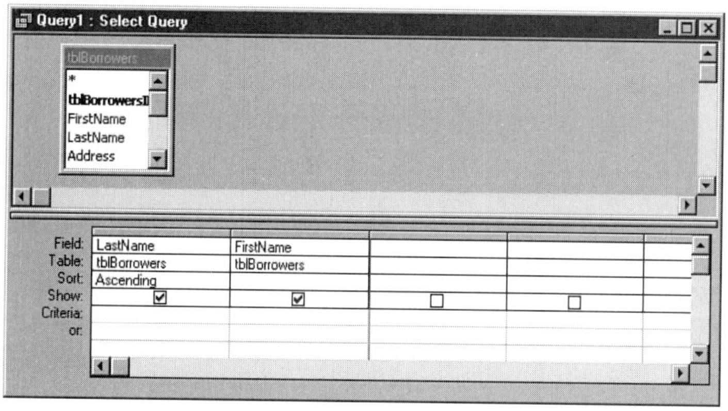

Fig. 13.1
The query in Design view.

7 Now click the Datasheet view button to see the datasheet results (see Figure 13.2).

Fig. 13.2
Same query in
Datasheet view.

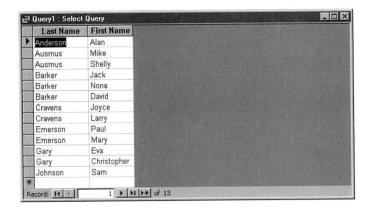

Now you're ready to continue with a calculated field.

Creating a simple calculated field

One of the simplest and most useful examples of a calculated field is to add
two fields of the Text data type together. It is useful because there are a
number of times when you want to take last names and first names and
combine them in different ways on mailing labels, reports, and forms.

1   Change to the Query Design view. Then, in the QBE grid, place the
    cursor in the empty column to the right of the FirstName field.

2   Press Shift+F2. The Zoom dialog appears, as shown in Figure 13.3.

Fig. 13.3
Use the Zoom dialog
box to see all the text
you're editing.

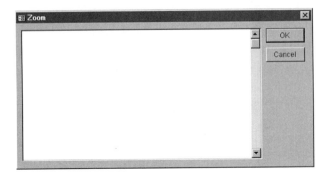

TIP **The Zoom feature is a great tool for entering information when** you want to see the whole entry. You can use it with fields, properties, and in other places in Access 97 where you enter data.

3 Type the string: LastName & ", " & FirstName and then click OK. After you click OK, Access 97 converts the field to read Expr1: [LastName] & ", " & [FirstName].

Access 97 created the name Expr1. Now when you press the Datasheet view button, you see another field displayed in the datasheet (see Figure 13.4).

Fig. 13.4
Expr1 now displays the First and Last Name together.

Last Name	First Name	Expr1
▶ Anderson	Alan	Anderson, Alan
Ausmus	Mike	Ausmus, Mike
Ausmus	Shelly	Ausmus, Shelly
Barker	Jack	Barker, Jack
Barker	Nona	Barker, Nona
Barker	David	Barker, David
Cravens	Joyce	Cravens, Joyce
Cravens	Larry	Cravens, Larry
Emerson	Paul	Emerson, Paul
Emerson	Mary	Emerson, Mary
Gary	Eva	Gary, Eva
Gary	Christopher	Gary, Christopher
Johnson	Sam	Johnson, Sam

Query1 : Select Query

Record: ◄◄ ◄ 1 ► ►► ►* of 13

Naming calculated fields

While the name Expr1 is very expressive (pun intended), you can use your own name instead. For instance, we would like the calculated field just created to look like this: FullName: [LastName] & ", " & [FirstName]. In this example in the calculated field, simply replace the text Expr1 with FullName.

You just created a calculated field called FullName. Because you have named the calculated field as you should, with no spaces, you will want to set the Caption property of the calculated field.

Setting the Caption property of a calculated field

As with table fields, you can set the Caption property of a field in a query to display text other than what the field name is. This is useful with fields that are calculated fields, in that you can display a space in the caption, but not have one in the name of the field. The reason this is not useful in fields from a table is that the Caption property of the field itself is already used.

To set the Caption property for the FullName calculated field you created:

1 Place the cursor in the FullName column in the query.

2 Choose <u>V</u>iew, <u>P</u>roperties from the menu. You will then see a property sheet similar to the properties in a text field.

3 In the Caption property, type Full Name (see Figure 13.5).

Fig. 13.5
Set these properties in your queries for calculated fields.

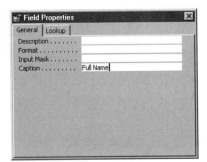

Using a built-in Access 97 function in a calculated field

Access 97 functions greatly increase your ability to display the data in your tables in meaningful ways. With these functions, you can either:

- Display portions of the data.

- Combine the data with new information supplied by Access 97 functions.

- Combine Access 97 functions to display totally new information.

In Table 13.2, there was a calculated field called AreaCode. The expression used was Left([Phone],3). This falls into the first category of types of information provided by Access functions.

Left() is a built-in Access 97 function as discussed in Chapter 9, where the Date() function was used. The Left() function, along with the two arguments, [Phone] and 3, tell Access 97 to take the three leftmost characters of the Phone field and return them. The return value (again, the three leftmost characters of the Phone field) is used for the calculated field and called AreaCode.

 Q&A **What are Arguments?**

Sometimes, functions require you to pass values to them, called Arguments. The function will use the arguments to perform its task. When you have more than one argument to pass to a function, you separate them with a comma. In this instance, the current arguments are the [Phone] field and the 3.

Another example of using an Access 97 function in a calculated field would be getting the initials of the first and the last names. This is performed by also using the Left() function. Here is the calculated field:

Initials: Left([FirstName],1) & Left([LastName],1)

Handling Null values in calculated fields

One of the problems that can occur when using fields in calculated fields is that one of the fields may contain a Null value.

The Null value will spread, or propagate, throughout the query results.

 Plain English, please!

A **Null value** occurs when no value has been entered into a field, and no default value exists. When a field contains a Null value, it means that the value is unknown, and Access 97 doesn't know how to deal with it. **99**

To show you how to deal with Null values, a temporary table has been created that contains the necessary fields. The fields, in this case, are Quantity and Amounts. Look at the datasheet with Quantity and Amounts, and the TotalAmount calculated field in Figure 13.6. This query has not done anything special with Null values. Figure 13.7 displays the results of quantity where Null values are not handled.

Fig. 13.6

The query design before Null propagation is accounted for.

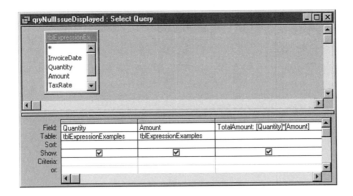

Fig. 13.7

Notice that TotalAmount fields are Null (blank) because of Null propagation.

Null values ——

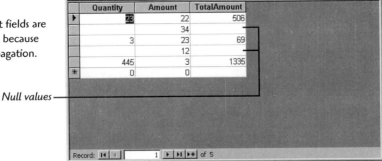

In order to prepare for Null values, there is an Access 97 function called IsNull(). The syntax for the IsNull() function is:

IsNull(expression)

Expression can be a field or calculated value. IsNull() then returns whether the expression is a Null value (True) or not (False).

This is going to be used along with another function called IIF(), pronounced Immediate If. The syntax for the IIF() function is:

IIf(criteria, value1, value2)

By calling the IIF() function if the *criteria* evaluates to True, then IIF() returns *value1*; otherwise, if *criteria* evaluates to False, *value2* is returned.

To fix the query shown in Figure 13.6, we will create a calculated field called FixedQty. The IIf() function with the IsNull(Quantity) as its criteria (which returns True or False) will be used. Here is the expression to use:

FixedQty: IIf(IsNull([Quantity]),0,[Quantity])

If the IsNull() function (*criteria*) returns True, then 0 (*value1*) is used in place of the Quantity. If IsNull() returns False, the Quantity field itself (*value2*) is used. You can see this calculated field in Figure 13.8 where the query appears in design mode; the resulting datasheet appears in Figure 13.9.

Fig. 13.8
The query design with Null propagation accounted for.

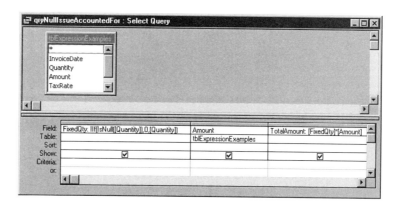

Fig. 13.9
Query results with the Null issue taken care of.

Null values are now replaced with zeroes.

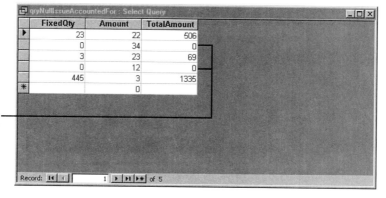

Notice that the TotalAmount calculated field now uses the FixedQty calculated field instead of the Quantity field.

 TIP **You will probably want to create another calculated field on the** Amount field if you had to worry about that field being Null as well.

14

Working with Multiple Tables, Parameters, and Complex Criteria

● In this chapter:

- Using multiple tables in queries

- Taking parameters in queries

- Using expressions in criteria

- Working with AND and OR in query criteria

Using expressions and complex criteria enables you to pull the information you need out of multiple tables. . . . . ❯

By now, you should be comfortable finding information in your database using a filter or query with one table. You have learned that using calculated fields and criteria in your query allows you to do even more sophisticated searches in a table. In this chapter, we take a step further by introducing you to queries using multiple tables, expressions, and complex criteria. This greatly increases your ability to find and use information in your database.

In order to show you how to use the new features in this chapter, I want to revisit a couple of tables that we created in the VideoLib database. These tables are: tblCategories, which contains all the categories possible for your tapes; and tblBorrowedTapes, which keeps track of which tapes the borrowers have. You can see these two tables in Design view in Figure 14.1 and Datasheet view in Figure 14.2.

Fig. 14.1
Notice the descriptions to see what each field does.

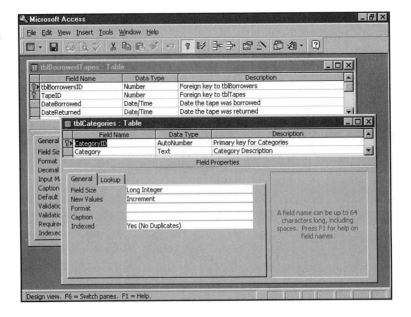

Now that you can see the design and sample data used in the tables, take a look at the relationships that exist between all the tables in the VideoLib database and, in particular, the tblBorrowedTapes table, shown in Figure 14.3.

Fig. 14.2
Sample data in the tblCategories and tblBorrowedTapes tables.

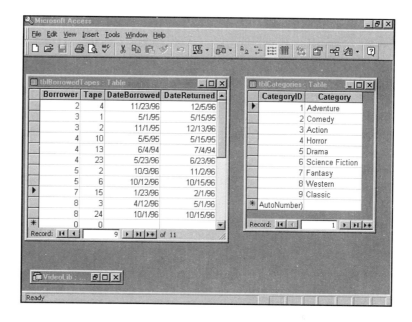

Fig. 14.3
A many-to-many relationship in the tblBorrowedTapes table.

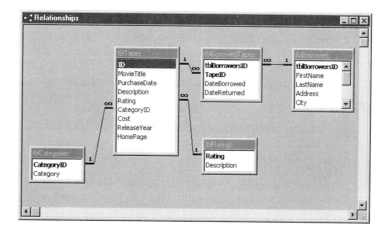

Notice the join lines between the tables. For a refresher on relationships, see Chapter 7, "Understanding Relationships Between Tables."

Using multiple tables in a query

In order to use a query with multiple tables, we need to create a query:

1 Choose the Queries tab, and click <u>N</u>ew.

2 In the New Queries dialog box, create the query using the Design view by clicking OK.

3 In the Show Table dialog box (still a ridiculous dialog box since you can see both tables AND queries), hold down the Ctrl key. Then select both the tblCategories and tblTapes tables.

4 Click the <u>A</u>dd button. Both tables appear behind the Show Table dialog box in the query design area.

5 Click <u>C</u>lose. You will now see the Query Design view with the two tables displayed (see Figure 14.4).

Fig. 14.4
Access creates the join lines for you based on relationships.

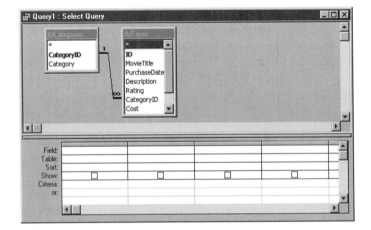

Q&A ***How come I don't see the Table row in the Query by Example grid as shown in Figure 14.4?***

If you don't see the Table row, you need to choose <u>V</u>iew, Table <u>N</u>ames. If you want to have all your new queries display the Table row, which I recommend, choose <u>T</u>ools and <u>O</u>ptions. Then click the Tables/Queries tab. On this tab, you can click the <u>S</u>how Table Names check box. Click OK to close the Options dialog box.

6 Pull down the Category field from tblCategories and the MovieTitle field from tblTapes tables into Field in the QBE grid using your favorite technique.

7 Set the Sort row in the MovieTitles column to Ascending.

8 Click the Datasheet view button. You will now see the Categories field beside the MovieTitles field.

You might be saying to yourself, "So what, I can already display the CategoryID and MovieTitles fields located in the tblTapes table in Datasheet view." (Remember that the CategoryID field has its Lookup tab set to the tblCategories table, as described in Chapter 9, "A Closer Look at Field Properties.")

This is preparation for the following sections. Next, you will see how to solve a real-world problem while learning about joins.

 Plain English, please!

> A **join** is the connection between two tables based on one or more fields within the table, just as Relationships use joins but not to specify referential integrity. You will understand more as we go on. **"**

Using the different types of joins

Access 97 has three different types of joins that can exist. But first, take a look at a problem that you need to solve.

The problem defined

Say you want to see all the Categories in which you don't own a movie. How would you go about it? When you run the query as we created it previously, you only see categories in which there *are* movies. This is a problem.

By working with the join line, you can affect how you get information in your queries. To see how you can affect the joins in a query, double-click the join line between the two tables: tblCategories and tblTapes. When you successfully double-click the join line, the Join Properties dialog box appears, as in Figure 14.5.

Fig. 14.5

Access gives you three types of joins to affect your queries.

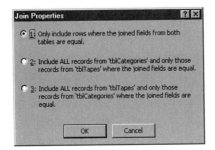

Take a look at the three types of joins shown in the Join Properties dialog box.

Inner joins: Joined fields in both tables must be equal

The first choice, known as an Inner join says that in order for records to appear in the resulting datasheet, there has to be a record on each side of the join.

At this point, you can't tell which categories aren't showing up, unless you open tblCategories and manually check. The reason the Inner join won't work in this case is because an inner join only shows records where the same CategoryID exists in both tblCategories and tblTapes. If a category existed in tblCategories, but no record was in tblTapes that used it, you wouldn't see it anyway. Checking by hand would be mundane and would defeat the purpose of this example, so don't check. Instead, take a look at the next type of join.

Left Outer joins: All of one, and some of the other (the solution)

As the description says for the second type of join, "Include All Records from 'tblCategories' and only those records from 'tblTapes' where the joined fields are equal." Eureka! This is the join you want to start with.

This type of join, called a Left Outer join, tells you to include all the records for the table on the one side of a One-To-Many relationship, and only those that match on the Many side. By choosing this join, you are on the correct path to solving the problem.

Right Outer joins: Some of one, and all of the other

Yes, as you probably can guess, this is the opposite of the Left Outer join. This is useful when you have records in a table on many sides of a One-To-Many relationship, for which there isn't a record on the one side, as described in Chapter 7, "Understanding Relationships Between Tables."

An example of this is having entries in the Orders table (many) for a customer (one) that doesn't exist. If you have set your relationships up correctly though, with referential integrity, you should not have to use this join type.

The complete solution

Choose the Left Outer join (2) and click OK. When you do, you will see an arrow pointing to the tblTapes table at the end of the join line (see Figure 14.6).

Fig. 14.6
This query uses a Left
Outer join.

Join Type Arrow ——

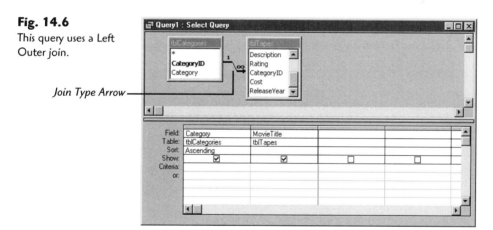

You can tell what type the join line is by observing if there is an arrow, and if there is, which direction it points.

Even though you specify what type of join you use, you aren't done yet. Remember, the question was, "How do you find out what movie categories aren't being used yet?" To complete this, you need to assign a simple criteria. Type the expression Is Null in the criteria line for the MovieTitle. Your query will then look like Figure 14.7.

Fig. 14.7
The completed query
to find Categories not
used, displayed in
Design view.

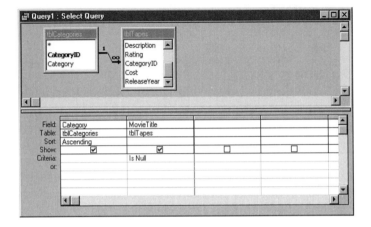

When you click the Datasheet view button, you should see the categories that
haven't been chosen. In Figure 14.8, the Classic category hasn't been used.

Fig. 14.8
The completed query
to find Categories not
used, displayed in
Datasheet view.

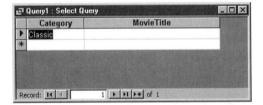

Choose File, Close and save this query as qryUnusedCategories.

You have now learned how to use two tables in a query, as well as how to use
the join lines. Now let's take a look at how to use three tables with a Many-
To-Many relationship.

Displaying a Many-To-Many relationship in a query

In order to display a Many-To-Many relationship in a query, you simply add the
tables you want, and pull down the fields into the QBE grid. For this example,
look at the names of the people you have loaned tapes to. To create the query:

1 Choose New in the Queries tab of the Database window. Then click OK
to accept creating the query with the Design view.

2 In the Show Table dialog box, hold the Ctrl key down and click the tblBorrowers, tblTapesBorrowed, and tblTapes table. Then click <u>A</u>dd.

3 Click <u>C</u>lose. You will then see the three tables in the query design area.

4 Bring down the following fields into the QBE grid from their Field Lists:

- LastName, FirstName, and HomePhone fields from the tblBorrowers table.

- MovieTitle field from the tblTapes table.

- DateBorrowed from the tblBorrowedTapes table.

Your query will then look like Figure 14.9 in Design view and something like Figure 14.10 in Datasheet view.

Fig. 14.9
The completed query in Design view showing who borrowed which tape.

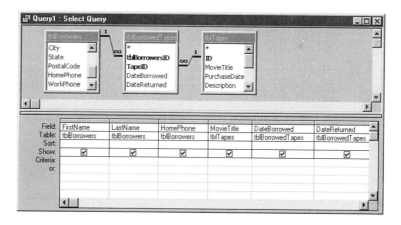

You have to admit, this is a useful query!

TIP **To zero in on those who still haven't returned movies, place the** Is Null expression in the first criteria row of the DateReturned field.

Another thing you can do is to specify a criteria based on the tapes you want to find. For example, say you want to find out who borrowed the *Princess Bride* tape (great movie for families!). To find it, type Princess Bride in the first row of the criteria of the MovieTitles field. Then click the Datasheet View button. Access shows you who borrowed the *Princess Bride* movie (see Figure 14.11).

Query1 : Select Query

First Name	Last Name	Home Phone	Movie Title	DateBorrowed	DateReturned
Larry	Cravens	(555) 344-3344	Star Trek III: The Search for Spock	11/23/96	12/5/96
Paul	Emerson	(555) 533-4443	Princess Bride	5/1/95	5/15/95
Paul	Emerson	(555) 533-4443	Star Trek I: The Motion Picture	11/1/95	12/13/96
Eva	Gary	(555) 334-4333	007: THUNDERBALL	5/5/95	5/15/95
Eva	Gary	(555) 334-4333	Monty Python and the Holy Grail	6/4/94	7/4/94
Eva	Gary	(555) 334-4333	Indiana Jones - Temple of Doom	5/23/96	6/23/96
Christopher	Gary	(555) 555-3344	Star Trek I: The Motion Picture	10/3/96	
Christopher	Gary	(555) 555-3344	Star Wars: Empire Strikes Back	10/12/96	
Jack	Barker	(555) 534-4443	Alien 2: Aliens	1/23/96	2/1/96

Record: 1 of 11

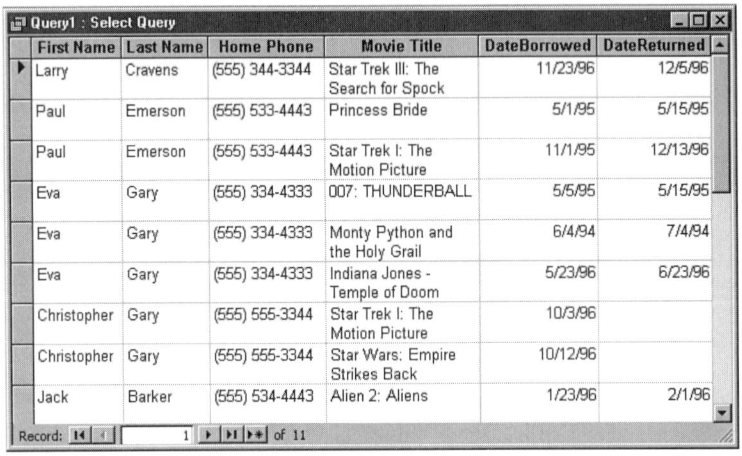

Fig. 14.10
Wouldn't it be nice if people returned tapes in a timely manner?

Query1 : Select Query

First Name	Last Name	Home Phone	Movie Title	DateBorrowed	DateReturned
Paul	Emerson	(555) 533-4443	Princess Bride	5/1/95	5/15/95

Record: 1 of 1

Fig. 14.11
Using a query to find who borrowed the *Princess Bride* tape.

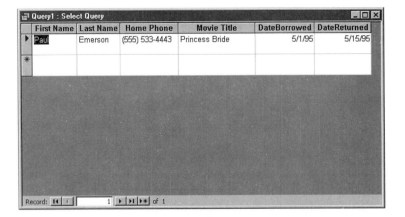

It is great that you can use criteria to specify a piece of information you are interested in; but it is kind of a pain to have to open the query in Design view and type the name in the criteria row. Wouldn't it be great to be able to run the query and have it ask you for the name of the tape you are interested in? You can.

Using parameters and expressions

It may sound difficult to achieve the kind of friendly query that I was just talking about, but it isn't. For starters, you are going to create your first parameter.

Plain English, please!

Parameters allow Access to use outside (of the query) information in the query. You can use parameters as part of the criteria portion of the query, or as part of calculated fields.

Creating a query to answer your specific questions (parameterized)

To tell your query to answer your questions on-the-fly:

1 Click the Design View button of the query you just created to locate the *Princess Bride* tape.

2 In the criteria where you have Princess Bride, type in the following: [Enter the title you are looking for:]

 Q&A *What are the square things at the beginning and end of the text?*

Those things are square brackets. You use the left square bracket (just to the right of the P key) at the beginning of the text, and the right square bracket (to the right of the left square bracket) at the end of the text.

 TIP **Don't forget you can use Shift+F2 and the Zoom dialog box** appears. Here you can see the entire text you type.

3 Choose File, Close from the menu and save the query with the name qryFindABorrowedTape.

4 Double-click the qryFindABorrowedTape query in the list of queries in the Database window. Before displaying the datasheet, Access gives you the Enter Parameter Value dialog box shown in Figure 14.12.

Fig. 14.12
By typing in the name of tape, Access will show who borrowed it.

5 Type in the name of a tape you know someone borrowed. For instance, I know that someone borrowed the *007: THUNDERBALL* tape, so I can type that title in to get the information on who has it. If you aren't quite sure how to spell a title, read the "Using the Like command" section found later in this chapter.

Close the query and run it again typing the names of various tapes you are interested in. As you can see, it's a lot more convenient being able to specify titles with the Parameter dialog box than going into the Design view. Try creating parameters for other queries you created.

Q&A   ***Can you use more than one parameter in a query?***

Definitely. You can use as many as you want. When you use more than one parameter in criteria, you use Complex criteria, discussed later in the "Getting more complex" section.

One thing is still not right about the qryFindABorrowedTape query. Being the lazy guy I am, I like to type as little as possible to get my result. In order to do that, I have to show you how to use expressions in your queries, along with parameters.

An expression is worth a thousand words (a few anyway)

Before going further, I would like to explain what expressions are. Expressions allow you to use criteria that include more than only a value or parameter to compare against. There are also some commands that you can include to help build your expression. The command we will discuss is Like.

The Like command lets you use wild cards in your criteria. Here are some examples of using the Like command in the MovieTitles criteria (see Table 14.1).

Table 14.1   Using wild cards with Like

Expression	Results
"Star*"	Star Wars and Star Trek movies
"*Star*"	Star Wars, Star Trek movies, and any other movies with Star in it, such as *Last Star*

Expression	Results
	Fighter
"*Star"	*The Tin Star* and *Wishing on a Star*
"L?st"	*Last Star Fighter* and *Schindler's List*

Plain English, please!

Wild cards allow you to specify parts of text that you want to locate, having Access fill in the blanks, using symbols. Use the question mark (?) for one character and the asterisk (*) for groups of characters.

Are these parameters case-sensitive?

No, you can use "Star*" as well "star*" and Access still provides the same results.

You can also use parameters with the Like command, which is what we will do. We will enhance the query you just created, so you first need to make a copy of it. To do this:

1 Highlight the qryFindABorrowedTape query in the list of queries.

2 Choose Edit, Copy.

3 Choose Edit, Paste.

4 Type qryFindBorrowedTapes for the new Query Name, and then click OK.

5 Highlight qryFindBorrowedTapes, and click Design.

6 Place the cursor in the first criteria row for the MovieTitle field.

7 Now press Shift+F2 to bring up the Zoom dialog box.

8 In the Zoom dialog box, place the cursor immediately before the left square bracket and type Like, with a space after it.

9 Place the cursor immediately after the right square bracket. Type &*.

10 Click OK. If you press Shift+F2 again, you see that Access placed quotes around the asterisk and spaced out the expression. The final expression should look like Figure 14.13.

Fig. 14.13
The final expression for the criteria.

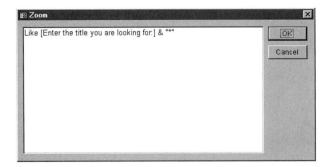

11 Choose File, Close and save the query.

Now when you run the query, you can type Star and all the borrowed titles beginning with Star appear.

It's time to use multiple fields in criteria. To do this, you will revisit the OR and AND operators, first introduced in Chapter 11. When you combine fields for criteria, you create complex criteria.

Combining AND and OR for complex criteria

Create a new query with tblTapes and tblCategories tables. Pull down the MovieTitle and Rating fields from the tblTapes table and Category field from the tblCategories, all into the QBE grid.

Now you can look at the titles rated "R" OR "PG". To do this, type "R" in the first criteria row of the Rating field, "PG" in the OR row, again in the Rating field. The query will then look like Figure 14.14.

Fig. 14.14
Creating an OR
complex criteria.

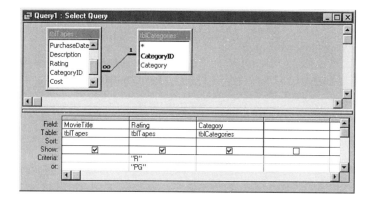

To narrow down the titles to those that are rated R or PG and have the category of Action, you must use the AND operator. To add an AND to an expression, type Action in the first row of the criteria for the Category field. If you leave only the one entry of Action, then the criteria will read: (Rating = "R" And Category = "Action") Or (Rating = "PG"). Notice the placement of the parentheses (I put them here for your benefit).

To see the movies that are either R Action or PG Action movies only, you can do one of the following:

- Type Action on both lines of criteria for the Category field with each Rating, as in Figure 14.15.

Fig. 14.15
One way to signify
Action R Or PG
movies.

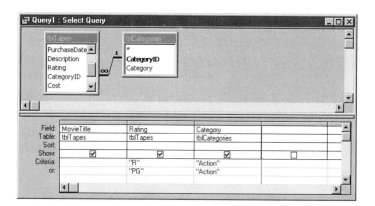

- Type Action in the first line of criteria for the Category field. Type the expression: R Or PG in the first line of criteria for the Rating field (see Figure 14.16).

Fig. 14.16
Combine the R and P movies with an OR statement in one line of criteria.

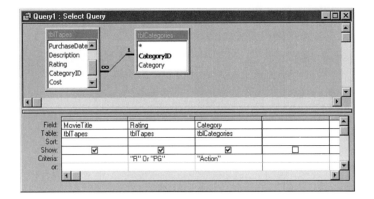

Try working with these expressions and with others until you feel comfortable creating complex criteria. Try using parameters with them, as in Figure 14.17, where two dialog boxes will now appear when you run this query: one for the [Enter Rating] parameter, the other for the [Enter Category] parameter.

Fig. 14.17
You can have any number of parameters in complex criteria.

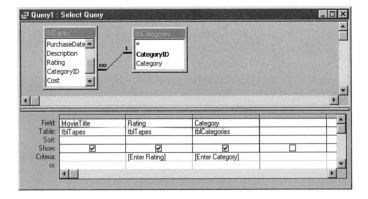

Don't forget to place brackets around your parameters. Otherwise, Access 97 places quotes around them and assumes they are literals.

15

Looking at Totals Queries

● **In this chapter:**

● Take a look at various examples of Totals queries

● Learn Access 97's various capabilities using the Total row in the QBE grid

● Create Totals queries to summarize information

Access 97 Totals queries can add a new dimension to your information . . . . ➤

This may sound like something out of the Twilight Zone, but you can see new aspects of your data by using the queries featured in this chapter.

Getting the total picture

Totals queries are great when you want to summarize your data. Before going into detail about how to create them, I want to take a moment to show you some examples.

Some examples of Totals queries

Here are just a few examples of what you can do. Note that these queries have not been built and are just displayed here for examples:

- Using the Northwind database, you can take three tables from that database, Customers, Orders, and Order Details, and create a Totals query to see the total dollar amounts of the invoices for each company (see Figure 15.1).

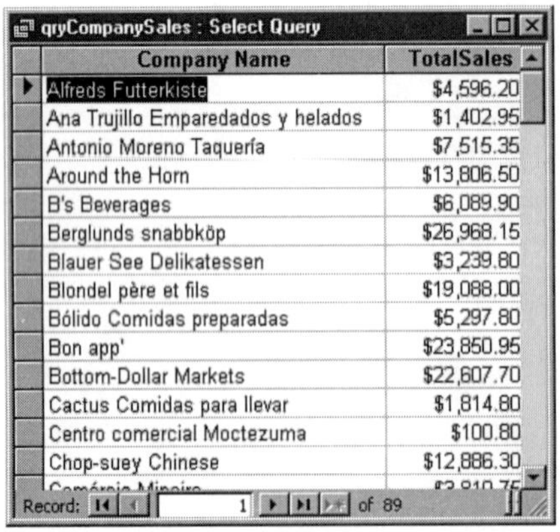
qryCompanySales : Select Query

Company Name	TotalSales
Alfreds Futterkiste	$4,596.20
Ana Trujillo Emparedados y helados	$1,402.95
Antonio Moreno Taquería	$7,515.35
Around the Horn	$13,806.50
B's Beverages	$6,089.90
Berglunds snabbköp	$26,968.15
Blauer See Delikatessen	$3,239.80
Blondel père et fils	$19,088.00
Bólido Comidas preparadas	$5,297.80
Bon app'	$23,850.95
Bottom-Dollar Markets	$22,607.70
Cactus Comidas para llevar	$1,814.80
Centro comercial Moctezuma	$100.80
Chop-suey Chinese	$12,886.30

Record: 1 of 89

Fig. 15.1
Adding up the sales for each company.

- Using Northwind's customer table again, you can find the number of customers located in each country, as in Figure 15.2.

Fig. 15.2
Counting the number of customers in each country.

qryCustomerCountryCount : Select Query

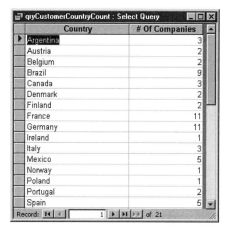

Country	# Of Companies
Argentina	3
Austria	2
Belgium	2
Brazil	9
Canada	3
Denmark	2
Finland	2
France	11
Germany	11
Ireland	1
Italy	3
Mexico	5
Norway	1
Poland	1
Portugal	2
Spain	5

Record: 1 of 21

- Looking back at the VideoLib database, you can use a Totals query to count the number of tapes in each category (see Figure 15.3).

Fig. 15.3
Bringing it home to the VideoLib database by counting the number of tapes in each category.

qryCategoryTapeCount : Select Query

Category	# of Tapes
Action	1
Adventure	6
Comedy	3
Drama	3
Fantasy	1
Horror	1
Science Fiction	14
Western	1

Record: 1 of 8

- Lastly, here's another example using the VideoLib database. You can get a total cost of tapes per category (see Figure 15.4). Believe it or not, I know people who are that interested in their collections. (Not me, of course.)

Fig. 15.4
As you can see from this query, Science Fiction is popular in this collection.

qryCategoryTapeCost : Select Query

Category	Cost of Tapes
Action	$19.95
Adventure	$124.70
Comedy	$34.85
Drama	$78.90
Fantasy	$19.95
Horror	$9.95
Science Fiction	$289.30
Western	$19.95

Record: 1 of 8

Now that you have a flavor for the kind of results you can get from Totals queries, take a look at how to create the queries.

Creating a base query for a Totals query

As you can see by looking at the title bar for the query in Figure 15.4, Totals queries are, in fact, Select queries. What this means is that you need to create a simple Select query and then tell Access 97 to make it a Totals query. Let's start with the last example (see Figure 15.4) in which we displayed the total cost of tapes for the various categories.

To start:

1 Create a new query using the Design view.

2 In the Show Table dialog box, select the tblCategories and tblTapes tables to use in the query.

3 Once in the Query Design view, double-click the Category field in the tblCategories field list and the Cost field in the tblTapes table. Remember that by double-clicking the fields, Access 97 places them in the QBE grid.

4 Set the Sort row to Ascending in the Category field.

5 Click the Save button and name the query qryCategoryTapeCost. At this point, your query should look somewhat like Figure 15.5 in Design view, and like Figure 15.6 in Datasheet view. Note that your data may be different.

Fig. 15.5
Here is your Select query in Design view for listing categories and tape costs.

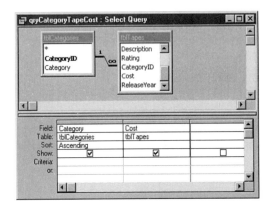

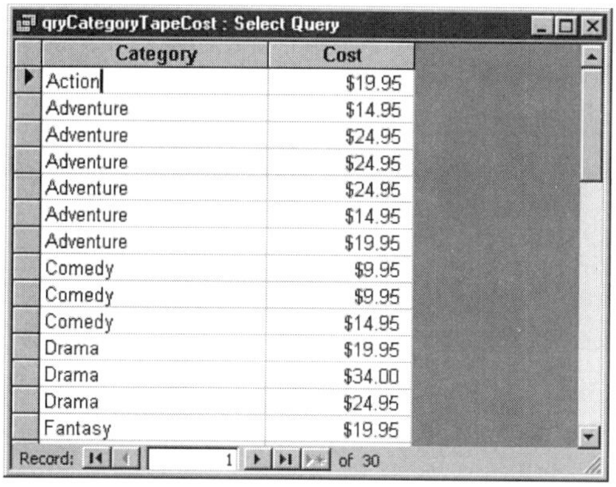

Fig. 15.6
This query in Datasheet
view is not where you
want to be for
summarizing the data.

Category	Cost
▶ Action	$19.95
Adventure	$14.95
Adventure	$24.95
Adventure	$24.95
Adventure	$24.95
Adventure	$14.95
Adventure	$19.95
Comedy	$9.95
Comedy	$9.95
Comedy	$14.95
Drama	$19.95
Drama	$34.00
Drama	$24.95
Fantasy	$19.95

qryCategoryTapeCost : Select Query

Record: 1 of 30

Q&A *Why do you save your queries so much, even before you do anything significant with them?*

Call it a habit, but you never know when you're going to accidentally hit the wrong button and end up losing your query, perhaps by hitting the Close button and then clicking No instead of Yes when the Save dialog box appears. Develop a good habit for all your queries, forms, reports, and so on by saving often.

Working with the Total row

Σ

You are now ready to create the totals portion of the query. To do this, click the Totals button (the button with the Sigma sign on it). When you do this, a new row titled Total appears just above the Sort row. Each field now displays Group By in the Total row (see Figure 15.7.)

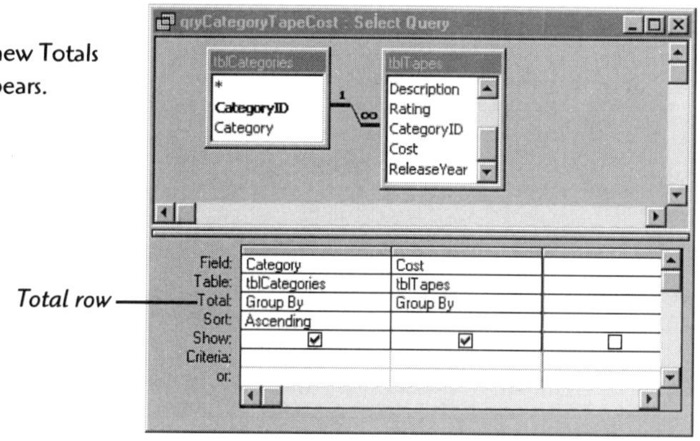

Fig. 15.7
Notice the new Totals
row that appears.

Total row ———

qryCategoryTapeCost : Select Query

tblCategories: *, CategoryID, Category
tblTapes: Description, Rating, CategoryID, Cost, ReleaseYear

Field:	Category	Cost	
Table:	tblCategories	tblTapes	
Total:	Group By	Group By	
Sort:	Ascending		
Show:	☑	☑	☐
Criteria:			
or:			

Click the Total row in the Cost field; a drop-down list appears. When you click this drop-down list, you see the various aggregate functions and options available.

 Plain English, please!

An **aggregate function** returns an accumulated value for a given set of records. In this case, the aggregate function is a set of records in the qryCategoryTapeCost query. You can have aggregate functions return different types of calculations, as seen in Table 15.1.

Table 15.1   Aggregate functions available in the Total row

Select function	Returns	Data types the function works with
Sum	Sum of values in the field	Number, Date/Time, Currency, and AutoNumber
Avg	Average of values in the field	Number, Date/Time, Currency, and AutoNumber
Min	Lowest value in the field	Text, Number, Date/Time, Currency, and AutoNumber
Max	Highest value in the field	Text, Number, Date/Time, Currency, and AutoNumber
Count	Number of values in the field, excluding those that are Null	Text, Memo, Number, Date/Time, Currency, AutoNumber, Yes/No, and OLE Object
StDev	Standard deviation of the values in the field	Number, Date/Time, Currency, and AutoNumber
Var	Variance of the values in the field	Number, Date/Time, Currency, and AutoNumber

Table 15.2 shows other available options in the Total row.

Table 15.2   Other options available in the Total row

Select option	In order to
Group By	Specify that you want to Group the query by this field.
Expression	Create a calculated field that includes aggregate function(s) in its expression.
Where	Specify criteria for a field and don't show the field.

As you can see, there are a number of tasks you can accomplish using the Total row. For now, choose the Sum function (see Figure 15.8).

Fig. 15.8
You can accomplish a number of tasks using the Total row.

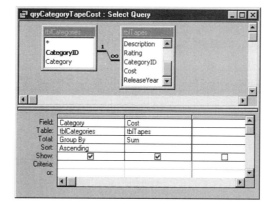

You have now created a Totals query. Click the Run button on the toolbar. When you run the query as it is, it should look like Figure 15.9.

Fig. 15.9
Here is the Totals query you just created in Datasheet view.

Category	SumOfCost
Action	$19.95
Adventure	$124.70
Comedy	$34.85
Drama	$78.90
Fantasy	$19.95
Horror	$9.95
Science Fiction	$289.30
Western	$19.95

Record: 1 of 8

Giving an alternate name to the totaled field(s)

You may notice in Figure 15.9 that the title of the totaled field is SumOfCost. Access 97 assigns this name to the field if you don't assign your own name. To assign your own name to the field, click the Design View button to bring the query back into Design view. Now, in the Cost field, just before the field name, type: Total Cost: including the colon. The field now says: Total Cost: Cost.

Q&A *I thought you said DON'T use spaces or special characters in field names?*

This is true. The only time I allow this for myself is when I am displaying only the information in a query. If I were using this query for a form or report, then I would use a standard name such as SumOfCost. Then I would set the Caption property of the field to Total Cost, as discussed in Chapter 13, "Using Calculated Fields in Your Query."

Adding another field to the Totals query

Say you want to count the number of tapes you have in each category. You can do this with the query you just created.

Taking the qryCategoryTapeCost query that you have been working on:

1 Open the query in Design view.

2 Drag the ID field from the tblTapes Field List down to the QBE grid.

3 In the Total row of the ID field, choose Count from the drop-down list. Then in the Field, type Tape Counts: just before the ID. Now your query will look like Figure 15.10 in Design view, and like Figure 15.11 when you change to Datasheet view.

Fig. 15.10
Check out the new field for counting tapes added to this query in each category.

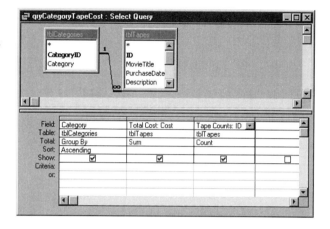

Fig. 15.11
It's great when you can create queries that perform multiple tasks.

CAUTION **Remember from Table 15.1 that the Count function counts all** values that are non-Null. This means that when you pick a field to count, make sure it is a field that will always have a value in it. Otherwise, you will get some wacky counts and won't know why! That is why I chose the ID field, since it is an AutoNumber field and sure to have a value.

TIP **Now you can enhance this query by adding a parameter that lets** you input the specific criteria that interest you. Type in: Like [Enter Category] & "*" into the criteria.

Then when you run the query, if you press Enter without specifying a category, Access 97 returns all categories or lets you enter a specific category. Try it!

Changing the name of the query

Since you added to the query and changed its purpose, you may want to change the name also. To change the name of any of the objects in the Database window:

1 Highlight the object (in this example, the qryCategoryTapeCost query).

2 Click the right mouse button to bring up the shortcut menu, and choose Rename.

3 Type in the new name for the object: qryCategoryTapeSummary.

4 Press Enter.

Renaming objects to something more meaningful is always a good idea. Just be careful if you have based a form or report on the query, because you will have to change it there as well. But I will discuss that later when I talk about the form and report objects.

Well, there you have it. You can now create Totals queries to perform your summarizing tasks, including parameters and multiple fields. Now it's time to take a look at some of the available action-type queries.

16

Using Action Queries for Big Changes

● **In this chapter:**

- **Why do you need Action queries?**

- **Looking at the different types of Action queries**

- **Creating each of the different types of Action queries**

Action queries allow you to make changes throughout your tables with very little effort . . . . **>**

While you use a Select query to look at your information in various ways, in order to make any changes to the data, you have to do it by hand. This is not a big deal when you contend with a small amount of data, as with the VideoLib database.

What if you have hundreds or thousands of records to deal with? Then it would be kind of a pain to have to go record by record to change a value. (But hey, that's job security, right?)

When I say Action queries, I am talking about those queries that perform specific actions against your data. In order for you to see how this works with a medium amount of data, we are going to use the Northwind database for this chapter. Open up that database now; then create a new query. In the Show Table dialog box, choose the Customers table, click <u>A</u>dd, and then click Close.

Now you are in the Query Design view. Click the Query Type button, and then focus on the Action query buttons on the subtoolbar (see Figure 16.1). The Action query buttons are the ones with the exclamation points (!) in the icons.

Fig. 16.1
The Action query buttons.

Action queries

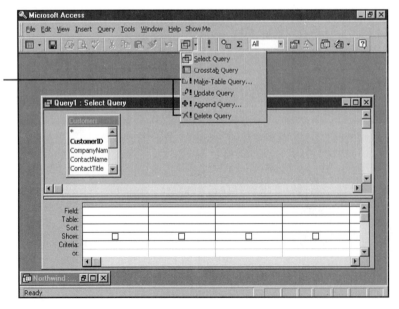

What are the different types of Action queries?

As you can see, there are four types of Action queries. You will find a use for each of the different types at one time or another. Here is a list of each, with a description and examples of where you would use them.

- **Make-Table**   This query allows you to create a new table from fields you specify (even from multiple tables). One example of a Make-Table query is a situation where you need to perform some temporary changes to a set of records. (You do this with the Customers table.) That way you can mess around with the new table without having to worry about trashing the original data. You can also use this for big reports to narrow down the data.

- **Update**   When you want to update many records at a time, for instance, when all employees get a five percent raise to their salary, just because. (For some reason, I always get an "Oh yeah, right" from all my students when I suggest that example.)

- **Append**   There are times when you need to convert data from other systems. Then you can add the data to a table that already exists in the database.

- **Delete**   At the end of month, you may want to create history files to store invoices that are over a year old. After you copy the invoice into the history table, probably using an Append query, you can then use a Delete query to remove the records from the current invoices table.

Suggestions for creating Action queries

Here are a few suggestions to help make your life a lot easier when you deal with Action queries.

- **If you are unsure of yourself, make a copy**   Until you are comfortable creating the various type of Action queries, it is a good idea to copy your tables and save them with a different name. This ensures that you won't lose important information.

- **Create a select query first**   Always create a Select query before you try to create an Action query to perform a task. You then can make sure your query behaves as it should (contains the correct fields, has the right records based on the criteria, and so forth).

- **Datasheet View versus the Run Command**   Before, when we created Select queries, we dealt mainly with the Datasheet view to execute the queries. Now you have the Run button as well. Use the Datasheet View button when you want to check out the affected records. Then use the Run button when you want to actually execute the query.

Creating a Make-Table query

The first query to create is a Make-Table query. Since this type of query creates a new table, it's perfect for helping you create a table to use for the rest of the Action query examples.

Starting the Make-Table query

First, you need to create a Select query that displays all the customers in the U.S.A. So you have started creating the query; now continue:

1 Drag down the asterisk (*) from the Customers field list, and place it in the QBE grid.

2 Drag down the Country field.

3 In the Country field of the QBE grid: type USA in the Criteria row; then remove the check from the Show check box. Your query should look like the one in Figure 16.2.

Click the Run button on the toolbar. When you run it, it returns the 13 records displayed in Figure 16.3. You're now ready to make this query into a Make-Table query.

4 Switch back to Query Design view.

Query1 : Select Query
Customers
Region
PostalCode
Country
Phone
Fax
Field: Customers.* Country
Table: Customers Customers
Sort:
Show:
Criteria: "USA"
or:

Fig. 16.2
Select query for basing the Make-Table query on.

Query1 : Select Query
Customer ID Company Name Contact Name Contact T
GREAL Great Lakes Food Market Howard Snyder Marketing Manager
HUNGC Hungry Coyote Import Store Yoshi Latimer Sales Representati
LAZYK Lazy K Kountry Store John Steel Marketing Manager
LETSS Let's Stop N Shop Jaime Yorres Owner
LONEP Lonesome Pine Restaurant Fran Wilson Sales Manager
OLDWO Old World Delicatessen Rene Phillips Sales Representati
RATTC Rattlesnake Canyon Grocery Paula Wilson Assistant Sales Re
SAVEA Save-a-lot Markets Jose Pavarotti Sales Representati
SPLIR Split Rail Beer & Ale Art Braunschweiger Sales Manager
THEBI The Big Cheese Liz Nixon Marketing Manager
THECR The Cracker Box Liu Wong Marketing Assistan
TRAIH Trail's Head Gourmet Provisioners Helvetius Nagy Sales Associate
Record: 1 of 13

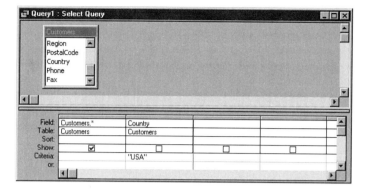

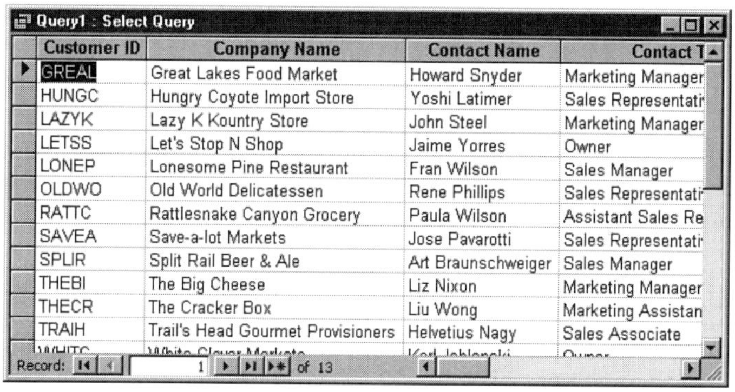

Fig. 16.3
These are the customers based in the U.S.A.

5 Choose Query, Make-Table Query from the menu. You then see the Make Table dialog box. You are asked for a Table Name to put the data into; and if you want to create the new table in the Current Database or Another Database.

6 Type “NewCustomers” in the Table Name (see Figure 16.4). Then click OK.

Make Table
Make New Table
Table Name: NewCustomers
OK
Cancel
Current Database
Another Database:
File Name:

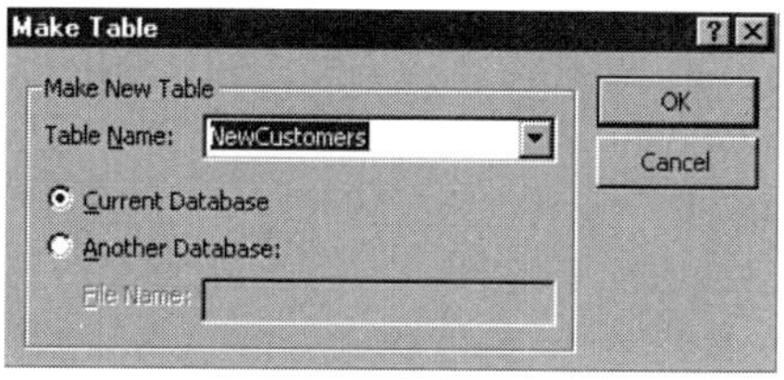

Fig. 16.4
Naming your new table.

The query window basically looks the same as a Select query, except in the title bar. You will now see Make Table Query instead of Select Query.

Before running this query, you need to add a TaxRate field to the table.

Adding another field to a table with Make-Table

Adding a new field to the new table in a Make-Table query is no harder than creating a calculated field in a query. Follow these steps:

1 Place the cursor in the column after the Country field in the QBE grid.

2 Type "TaxRate: .07" to create a new field called TaxRate and to place the value .07 in the field for each of the records. Take a look at the final query in Figure 16.5.

Fig. 16.5
The new TaxRate field.

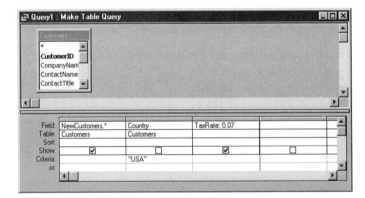

Executing the Make-Table query

Since you have already viewed this query in Datasheet view, click the Run button. Access 97 lets you know that you are about to paste the records (also called rows) into the new table (see Figure 16.6). The good news is that the number of records (13) matches what you had in the Select query.

Fig. 16.6
Last chance to cancel
the query.

 TIP The message tells you that once you click **Y**es, **creating your table is irreversible..** This is not a big deal with a Make-Table query since you can just delete the created table if necessary.

 Q&A *How did I get the dialog box from Figure 16.7 rather than the one from 16.6?*

If you got the dialog box shown in Figure 16.7, then you already ran the query once accidentally and created the NewCustomers table. Just answer **Y**es to continue, and the dialog box seen in Figure 16.6 appears.

Fig. 16.7
This dialog means you
already ran the query
once and created the
table.

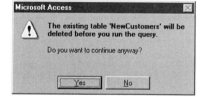

Click **Y**es to execute the query.

When you go to the Database window, you see a NewCustomers table in the list of tables. Congratulations on your first Make-Table query. Now close and save the query with the qryMakeNewCustomers name.

 TIP Whenever you create an Action query, Access 97 places an icon beside the query in the Database window. This is the same icon used on the submenu in the Query Design. For instance, the Make-Table query has a starburst with an exclamation point by it. This makes it easier to identify the types of queries.

Creating an Update query

For the Update query example, I want to update the TaxRate field for those customers that are in the Region (State) of WA.

1 Create a new Select query and pick NewCustomers in the Show Table dialog box.

2 In the Query Design view, drag the Region and TaxRate fields into the QBE grid.

3 In the first Criteria row of the Region field, type WA.

If you run the query now, you would see that three records appear with the TaxRate of 0.07.

4 Choose Query, Update Query from the menu or click the Update Query button. The title bar of the query changes to reflect that this is now an Update query.

The other change is that a new row appears in the QBE grid called Update To. Here you place the new value for updating the current field.

5 In the Update To row of the TaxRate field, type .085.

Now the query reflects the change you want to make in the table (see Figure 16.8).

Fig. 16.8
This Update query changes the TaxRate field to .085 for those customers in the Region WA.

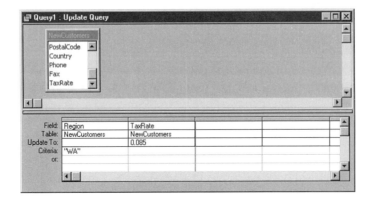

Q&A *What about the Region field? Do I do anything with that field?*

No, by leaving that field empty and just using the criteria row, you tell Access 97 that you don't want to do anything to the Region field except use it for criteria. It's like clicking the Show check box off when creating a Select query.

6 Click the Datasheet View button to see the affected fields. You should see something like Figure 16.9.

Fig. 16.9
Access 97 will update these three records.

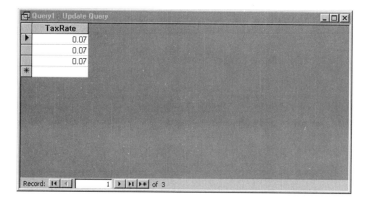

Q&A *Wait a minute! I thought you said the Datasheet view showed me the records that are going to be affected. Why do I just see three records with the TaxRate showing .07?*

This is the field that is going to be affected. Datasheet view shows you the fields as they currently are. Since the Region field is just for criteria, it will not show up in this view. From here, you can see that Access 97 will update three records.

7 After switching back to the Design view, click the Run button. You see the same dialog box used when you ran the Make-Table query, telling you that you are about to update three rows.

8 Click <u>Y</u>es. Then close and save this query as qryUpdateTaxRate.

When you open the NewCustomers table in Datasheet view, you see that the customers in WA have a different TaxRate field value than the others (see Figure 16.10).

Fig. 16.10
The successfully
updated TaxRate fields
in records with WA for
Region.

CustomerID	CompanyName	Region	TaxRate
GREAL	Great Lakes Food Market	OR	0.07
HUNGC	Hungry Coyote Import Store	OR	0.07
LAZYK	Lazy K Kountry Store	WA	0.085
LETSS	Let's Stop N Shop	CA	0.07
LONEP	Lonesome Pine Restaurant	OR	0.07
OLDWO	Old World Delicatessen	AK	0.07
RATTC	Rattlesnake Canyon Grocery	NM	0.07
SAVEA	Save-a-lot Markets	ID	0.07
SPLIR	Split Rail Beer & Ale	WY	0.07
THEBI	The Big Cheese	OR	0.07
THECR	The Cracker Box	MT	0.07
TRAIH	Trail's Head Gourmet Provisioners	WA	0.085
WHITC	White Clover Markets	WA	0.085

NewCustomers : Table — Record: 1 of 13

Creating an Append query

Append queries are a little more complex to create than the other Action queries. Append queries use both the table you append data to and the table you append from. I have faith that you can work with me on this.

Since Canada shares so much with the U.S.A., I am going to append the Canada data from the Customers table into the NewCustomers table.

To start, create a new Select query. In the Show Table dialog box, select the Customer table to <u>A</u>dd; then close the dialog box. Now pull down the Aster-isk (*) and the Country fields. In the Country field, uncheck the Show check box. We just want to use this field for criteria. In the first Criteria row of the Country field, type Canada.

You have now created the necessary Select query and are ready to change it into the Append query.

1 Choose Query, <u>A</u>ppend Query from the menu or click the Append Query button. When you pick this command, Access 97 asks you which table you want to append to. This is the NewCustomers table.

2 Type NewCustomers in the Table <u>N</u>ame field (see Figure 16.11).

Fig. 16.11
Supply the name of
the table to append
to in the Append
Query dialog box.

3 Click OK. Access 97 adds a new row called Append To. In this row, Access 97 filled in the fields it believes you want to append. This can be a very handy feature. However, in this case, Access 97 filled in the Country field twice—once with the * and once in the individual Country field. If you ran this query now, Access 97 would give you the "Duplicate output destination" error.

Q&A *What do I do if the field names don't match up?*

All you have to do is select the fields from the list in the Append To row.

Q&A *Can I use calculated fields?*

You bet! Simply create the calculated field in the Field row, and pick the field to append to from the list in the Append To row.

4 Select Country in the Append To row and delete it. Now the query should look like Figure 16.12. Access 97 uses this QBE grid column for criteria only.

Fig. 16.12
The Append query ready for business.

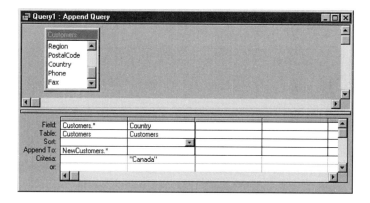

5 Click the Run command. Once again, you get a message letting you know the query is going to append records—three in this case.

6 Click Yes to complete the query. Then close and save the query as qryAddCanada.

The Append query has now added the Canadians to the NewCustomers table.

Creating a Delete query

The Delete query is actually one of the easiest to create. In this example, all the customers from California (CA) decide to call it quits. You need to remove them from the NewCustomers table.

To start, create a new Select query, choosing NewCustomers from the Show Table dialog box. Now pull down the Region field and type CA in the first Criteria row.

 Choose Query, Delete Query from the menu or click the Delete Query button. You see a new row called Delete. If you have two or more tables in the query, this row will contain two choices: Delete (From) this field's table or use it as Criteria (Where). When you have only one table, Access 97 deletes both rows.

The query is now ready to delete the customers from CA (see Figure 16.13).

Fig. 16.13
This Delete query is ready to do its damage.

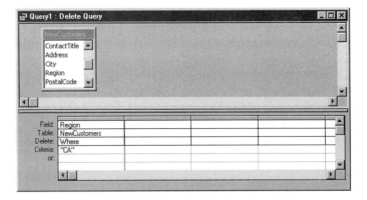

 CAUTION **Delete queries make me very nervous. Be very sure you have** everything correct before clicking the Run buttons when dealing with them.

Oh, what the heck. Go ahead and click the Run button. Access 97 gives you the standard dialog box telling you that it will delete your record(s). Click Yes. They're gone!

Now close and save the query as qryDeleteCA. When you open the NewCustomers table, you won't see any California customers listed.

Part V: Working with Forms

17

Creating Forms the Quick Way

● **In this chapter:**

- **What is a form and why do I need it?**

- **Creating a form with a click (or two) of a button**

- **Walking through the Form Wizard**

- **Picking and choosing styles for forms**

Creating forms is so easy with the Forms Wizard, you don't even have to know what makes a form work. . . . . ➤

nputting information directly into a table is okay, **when you are the only one who has to use it. However, that approach is very** limited when you're combining tables and trying to maintain accurate data.

When you first start using Access 97, you can get by without forms, but eventually you will want to use them. Fortunately, Access 97 makes creating them pretty painless.

To start, let's open up the VideoLib database.

Creating a form with one or two clicks

In the Tables tab of the Database window, select the tblTapes table (if it isn't already selected). That's one click.

Next, click the New Object: AutoForm button. Shazzam, you created a new form (see Figure 17.1).

Fig. 17.1
This form was created using the AutoForm feature.

Record Selector

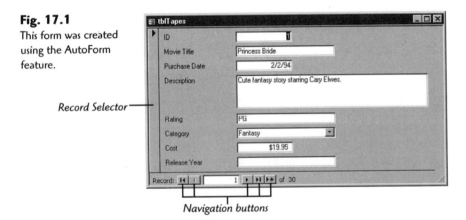

Navigation buttons

Figure 17.1 is a good example of what appears on most forms. Forms share some of the same controls you see when working with datasheets, such as navigation buttons and record selectors. They also use the same commands for editing fields. For information on these controls and commands, reread Chapter 6, "Maintaining Your Information with Datasheets."

Moving around a record in a form

One of the differences between forms and datasheets is the way you move around the record. Before, when you used datasheets, you saw records, one on top of the other. Now, in forms, you work with one record at a time.

In Table 17.1, you can see the navigation keys you use to move around in the form.

Table 17.1   Keys that move you around a record

To move to	Press
Next field	Tab, right arrow, or down arrow
Previous field	Shift+Tab, left arrow, or up arrow
First field	Home
Last field	End

Adding a new record in a form

Adding a new record in a form is similar to using the datasheet method. Click the New Record navigation button. A new blank record appears (see Figure 17.2).

Fig. 17.2
Click the New Record button to go to a blank record.

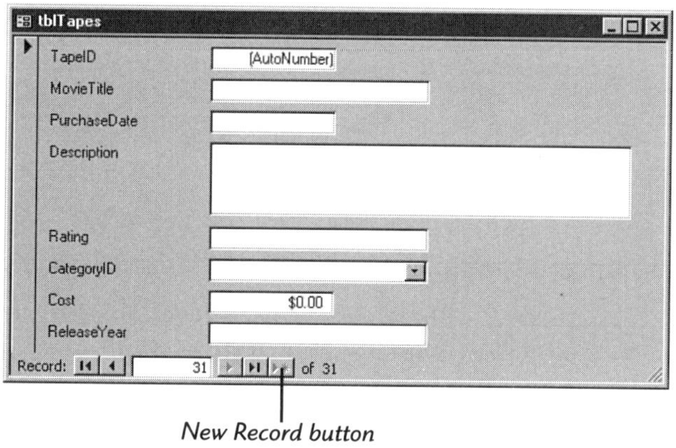

New Record button

Other ways to create quick forms

While the AutoForm button is great when you are in a hurry, there are better ways to create forms. Although the process may take a bit longer, you have more control over the look of the form. Close the form you have just created; don't bother saving it.

Click the Forms tab in the Database window; then click <u>N</u>ew. The New Form dialog box appears. Toward the bottom portion of the dialog box, there is a combo box that tells you to pick a query or table to base the form on. Pick the tblTapes table (see Figure 17.3).

Fig. 17.3
With the New Form dialog box, you have many ways to create forms.

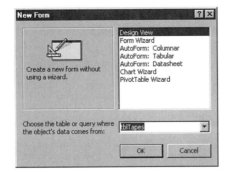

 TIP   **Whenever possible, base your forms on queries. That way, you** can include only the fields used on the form. You will have better performance and you can also use criteria.

Let's take a look at the items listed in the New Forms dialog box.

- **Form Wizard**—A quick way to create forms. By walking you through a set of questions, Access 97 creates an attractive form that is a great starting point. In the next section, you will walk through the Form Wizard step by step.

- **AutoForm: Columnar**—The AutoForm method you used at the beginning of the chapter, with one change: This version has a background rather than just appearing gray. It's a very quick way to create a form. The fields appear down the form. This is the Single Form view where a single record appears at a time. If you want to see what it looks like, select this choice and click OK.

- **AutoForm: Tabular**—Not to be confused with "Tubular Dude." This is another quick way to create a form. The fields appear across the form. The form style, called Continuous Form view, is where multiple records appear one at a time, but not like in the Datasheet view.

- **AutoForm: Datasheet**—The name says it all. This creates a quick Datasheet view form. Access 97 even calls the form Datasheet Form view.

Go ahead and play with the three AutoForm Wizards using different record sources (tables and queries). When you finish, we will go on to the Forms Wizard.

Using the Form Wizard for a more complete form

The Form Wizard gives you more options so that you can customize the form to your own preferences. This wizard, like the other wizards, takes you through step-by-step questions asking how you want to create the various pieces that make up a form. Highlight the Form Wizard and click OK. The first screen of the Form Wizard appears.

Choosing fields with the Form Wizard

With the same buttons used for moving fields, select all the fields in the tblTapes table except TapeID (see Figure 17.4).

 TIP An efficient way to pick all but one or two fields is to use the >> button (All Fields Right) to move all fields. Then select the field to back out, in this case TapeID, and click the Move Left button (<). This way, you only click two buttons instead of a dozen.

Fig. 17.4
Choosing fields to use
on your form with the
Form Wizard.

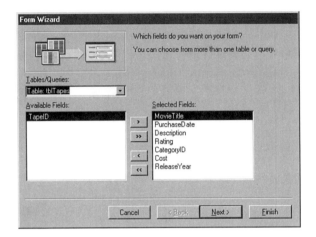

Q&A ***The dialog box says that I can create forms from more than one table or query. What does this mean?***

This lets you create a mainform/subform type form in which the main form contains information from one source, such as orders, and the subform contains information from another source, such as order details. The way to create this form is too advanced for right now, but you will learn more about it in Chapter 20, "Controls that Especially Enhance Forms."

For now, click <u>N</u>ext to go to the next screen.

Choosing a Layout

This screen gives you four choices for field layout on the form. The first three choices match the choices you have in the AutoForm Wizards. But the fourth is a new one called <u>J</u>ustified (see Figure 17.5).

The Justified type screen lines the fields from left to right, top to bottom, with the label over the field.

Choose <u>J</u>ustified and click <u>N</u>ext.

Fig. 17.5
Select the field layout on your new form.

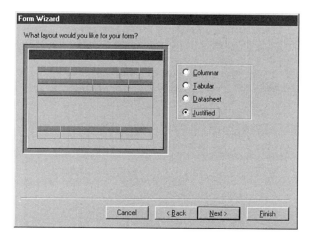

Adding style to the form

This is the screen where you can select the styles for your form. By clicking the different styles (see Figure 17.6), the picture will reflect the selected style. You can now select a style that you want to use.

Fig. 17.6
My favorite style is Dusk, which shows the Seattle skyline.

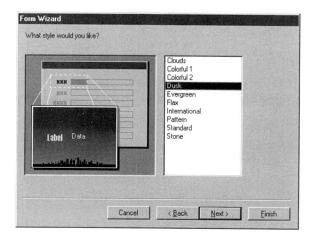

TIP **I recommend sticking with one or two styles for any given** application. Too many different styles ruin an attractive interface.

After choosing the style you want, click <u>N</u>ext.

Choosing a title for the form

This screen lets you create the title you want for the form. After you change the title, click <u>F</u>inish, and Access 97 generates the form (see Figure 17.7).

Fig. 17.7
Here is the final form generated by the Form Wizard.

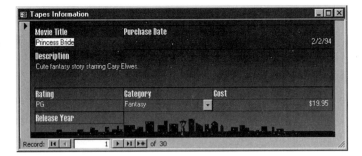

After you finish admiring your form, choose <u>C</u>lose from the <u>F</u>ile menu. You will now see your new form in the list of forms.

 Q&A *I notice that it made the name of the form the same as the title on the form. Is this a good idea?*

No. Go ahead and rename the form by right-clicking it and choosing Rena<u>m</u>e from the shortcut menu. Then type in the name frmTapesInformation and press Enter.

 TIP **When renaming the various objects in the Database window, you** can use the standard Windows 95 way to rename the object by clicking the object once to select it; then click once more to put you in the rename mode. Don't double-click the object or it will open.

18

Introducing Forms Design and Properties

● In this chapter:

- ● **Overview of Form Design view**

- ● **What are properties in Access 97?**

- ● **How do properties affect my forms?**

- ● **A look at important form properties**

- ● **Modifying form properties**

Creating forms is a little more complex than creating other objects you have seen so far in Access 97. The good news is that forms add a great deal of control when entering data and are just darn fun to work with . . . . ▶

Access 97 forms are some of the most fun and powerful features you can use. Unfortunately, these forms are some of the tougher features to work with. The good news is that once you understand them and get comfortable with them, you can take what you learn and apply it to reports, which use a similar design tool.

We will use the VideoLib database and revisit the frmTapeInformation form you created in the previous chapter.

Getting an overview of the Form Design view

You can see an example of each of the windows that might appear on your screen when you work in the Design view (refer to Figure 18.1).

Fig. 18.1
Here are the various tools that make up the Form Design view.

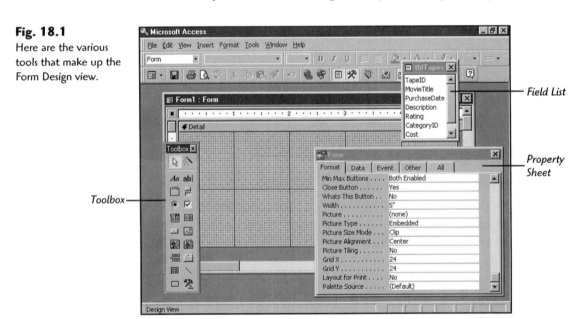

Here is a list of the different tools used with a form, and what they do for the form:

- **Toolbox**—Contains all the controls that you use on your forms. You use controls to input and display information based on the type of information. For more information on controls and using the Toolbox, check out Chapter 19, "Working with Controls on Forms."

- **Field List**—Similar to the field list used in the Query Design view. The fields that appear in the Field List depend on the record source (table or query) you base the form on. Using the mouse, you can pull fields from the Field List onto the form, similar to a query.

- **Property Sheet**—Property sheets are where you find the properties for an object. Properties describe the object they belong to (in this case a form). Examples of properties are: Caption, Record Source, and so on. You can find more discussion on properties in the "Understanding and using properties" section.

You will work with each of these items when you create forms. Getting back to the frmTapeInformation—open the form in Form Design view by selecting the form and clicking the <u>D</u>esign button in the Database window.

Once in the form, locate the buttons for each of the items just discussed and see if you can toggle them on and off.

Understanding and using properties

As I mentioned, properties are your way to describe how you want an aspect of an Access 97 object to appear. Most of the objects in Access 97 have properties, although they may differ depending on the object.

Properties can be as simple as a Caption (title) on the form, or the Picture that you use as the background for a form. You can see these two properties for frmTapesInformation in Form view.

Categories of properties

In a moment, you will change the two properties just mentioned. Before changing these properties, let's look at the category tabs in the Property Sheet.

If you have the Field List open, close it by either toggling the Field List button or clicking the Close button on the window.

Double-click in the Form Selector. The Property Sheet for the form appears (see Figure 18.2).

Fig. 18.2
Use the Form Selector when you want to make sure you are pointing to the form itself.

Form Selector ─

Property Sheet

Notice that the Property Sheet has tabs. Use these tabs to categorize the properties that you use in Access 97. These categories will be the same on the various objects you use in Access 97, although the number of properties in each category will vary. The categories are:

- **Format**—Specifies how various aspects of the object look. Examples are Width, Min Max buttons, Close button, and Picture properties. You can see some of these Format properties for frmTapesInformation in Figure 18.2.

- **Data**—Specifies how Access 97 uses data with the object. The RecordSource form tells which table or query you want to use for the form, as well as the Filter, Order By, and so on (see Figure 18.3).

Fig. 18.3
The Data properties for the form frmTapesInformation, with the RecordSource set to the tblTapes table.

- **Event**—Allows you to assign commands to different events that occur to an object. An example of an event is the OnClick event for a command button. This means that when you click the command button, Access 97 performs the task you tell it to do. You can see some of the Event properties for the form in Figure 18.4.

- **Other**—Any other property that doesn't fit into the other categories (see Figure 18.5).

Fig. 18.4
The Event properties for the form frmTapesInformation.

Fig. 18.5
These properties don't fit into the other categories.

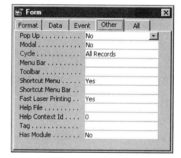

Q&A ***Do I have to set all these properties?***

No. Don't panic. Access 97 does a great job of setting the values of the properties. The defaults usually cover most of the bases.

You will probably need to use the majority of these properties at one time or another. The cool part about them is that they can be changed when necessary but they default to smart values for your convenience.

Changing properties in forms

I mentioned in the last section that we were going to change a couple of properties on the frmTapesInformation form. The first one is simple.

Changing the Caption property of a form

To change the Caption property, click the Format tab of the Property Sheet. You see the Caption property listed at the top of the Property Sheet (see Figure 18.6).

Fig. 18.6
The Caption property changes the title of the form.

Q&A ***When I click the Format tab in the Property Sheet, I don't see the Caption property. Why?***

One of two things occurs, or both. First, make sure that the top of the Property Sheet displays: Form. If it says something else, you have accidentally clicked elsewhere on the form. Click the Form Selector (refer to Figure 18.2 again) to make sure the form is the object of focus.

If you still don't see the Caption property, click the top of the scroll bar located along the right edge of the property sheet.

Change the Caption property from Tapes Information, as it currently reads, to Testing the Caption Property (see Figure 18.7).

Fig. 18.7
Changing the Caption property to display a new title.

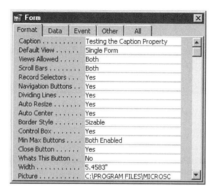

After typing in the new Caption property, click the View button to open the form in Form view. You see the new Caption property displayed in the title of the form (see Figure 18.8).

Switch back to Design view. Change the Caption property back to Tapes Information.

Fig. 18.8
Here is the finished product. Congratulations on changing a caption.

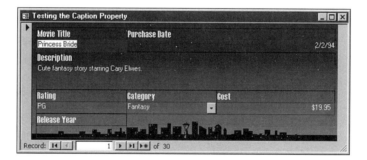

Changing the Picture property of a form

The next property takes a little more work because you use another dialog box. Let's start:

1 If the Property Sheet is not opened, double-click the Form Selector. Then click the Format tab in the Property Sheet.

2 Scroll down the properties until you get to the Picture property; then place the cursor in it. A builder button appears beside the property (see Figure 18.9).

You see the beginning of a path for the current picture that is in the Picture property.

Fig. 18.9
Click the Builder button to change the Picture property.

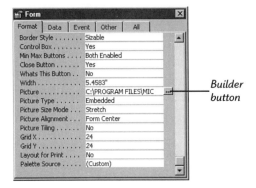

Builder button

 Q&A ***Why can't I read the full path in the Zoom dialog box?***

I will have to answer this one with the answer I give my kids: "Because you can't." There are some properties such as Picture that aren't actually text and therefore you can't edit or view them using the Zoom dialog box. Read on to see how to find out the full path.

3 Click the builder button. Access 97 opens the Insert Picture dialog box. This dialog box lets you point to various types of graphic files you can include as the background of your form. By default, the Insert Picture dialog box points to the My Documents folder. Follow the path down to the style graphic files for Access 97. That path is \Program Files\Microsoft Office\Office\Bitmaps\Styles and the result appears in Figure 18.10.

Fig. 18.10
Follow this path down to the graphic files.

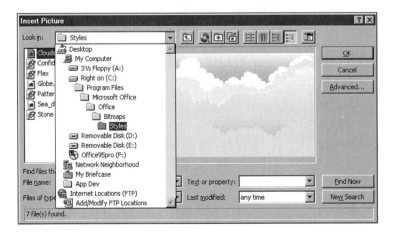

Q&A ***Why can't I find this folder when I look down the path
you display?***

The path displayed is the one that Office and Access 97 install into by
default. If you change the default path on installation, then you need to
find out where you put it.

Q&A ***I found the correct folders and see the file names. But
how do I see the graphic like you do?***

Notice the Preview button in Figure 18.11. Click this button and Access 97
displays the graphic, called a thumbnail, beside the files.

4 Select the graphic you like and click <u>O</u>K. You return to your form; you
see the background change. I decided to change the Picture property to
Flax.bmp (see Figure 18.11).

Preview button

Fig. 18.11
Picking a new graphic
for the form.

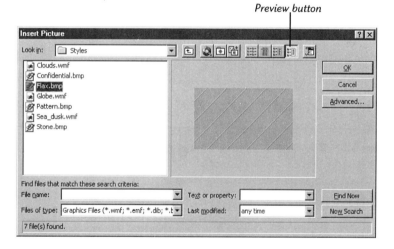

5 Switch to Form View to see the new form background as shown in
Figure 18.12.

Fig. 18.12
The final form with the new background.

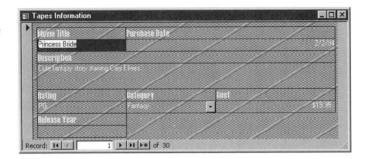

Notice that the graphic in Figure 18.12 appears stretched. There are other properties that affect how a graphic looks. Along with the Picture property, they are: Picture Type, Picture Size Mode, Picture Alignment, and Picture Tiling.

Looking at important form properties

We have looked at some of the easier properties to understand. There are a few more to discuss before jumping into controls in the next chapters.

The properties and a brief description of each follow. Whether you use them or not depends upon your situation. At this time, don't mess with the ones not listed, if the default is okay.

Form Data properties

Some of the following Data properties in Table 18.1 can help when you work with forms.

Table 18.1   Form Data properties

Property	Description
Record Source	The property that determines what you use as a base for your form.
Allow Edits	Choose Yes or No to determine if people can edit information on the form.
Allow Deletions	Choose Yes or No to determine if people can delete records.
Allow Additions	Choose Yes or No to determine if people can add new records.

Form Format properties

There are many useful properties in the Format category. Table 18.2 gives you a brief description of each. You have already seen the Caption and Picture properties, so they are not in this table.

Table 18.2   Form Format properties

Property	Description
Default view	Whether you want the form to open in Single Form (one record on the screen), Continuous (multiple records), or Datasheet.
Form view	You can look only at Form view or Datasheet, or both. Great way to limit people in what they can use.
Scroll bars	Display scroll bars vertically, horizontally, or both.
Record selectors	Display them (Yes or No).
Navigation buttons	Display them (Yes or No).
Auto Resize	If you set this to Yes, Access 97 automatically makes the border size of the form window match the size of the form. Access 97 recommends that you leave this Yes.
Auto Center	Automatically centers your form, no matter what size the monitor is. Very nice.

Q&A   *Why didn't you mention the Width property?*

Some properties such as the Width property can take care of themselves. You can affect the Width property just by sizing the form, discussed in the next chapter.

Form Other properties

There are two very important, and potentially dangerous, properties on the Other tab: Pop Up and Modal.

- **Pop Up**—Makes the form stay on top whether or not it has the focus. A form has the focus when the cursor is flashing in it and the title bar is lit up. Pop Up forms allow you to go to other forms but still stay on top.

- **Modal**—This forces a form to keep the focus until you close it. About boxes (forms that show credits) are usually a Modal form, as well as message boxes, meaning that you have to press OK to get out of them.

CAUTION **If you make a form both Modal and Pop Up, you have to make** sure you have a command button that lets you close the form; otherwise, you have to press Ctrl+F4 to exit. You will see how to make a command button to close a form in the next chapter, so for now don't mess with these properties.

Checking out other properties

There are other useful properties that help you control your forms. To get a good feeling of what properties are available, go through each of the tabs in the Property Sheet and play with some of the properties.

If you try a couple settings and switch to the Form view, and still don't know what they do, go back to Design view. Place the cursor in the property that interests you and press F1.

Don't get too bogged down in the Help text; otherwise, you may become confused. To learn more about the Access 97 Help features, see Chapter 3.

19

Working with Controls on Forms

● **In this chapter:**

- **What are controls?**

- **Placing controls on forms**

- **Moving and resizing controls**

- **Aligning controls**

- **Setting properties of controls**

Once you understand how to use controls on forms, you can make your forms more intuitive and user-friendly when looking for information or entering data . . . . ●>

Access 97 forms don't do you much good by themselves, since they are blank and very boring. Controls allow you to display data on both forms and reports, and input data on forms. Working with controls are a lot of fun when you understand them. By the end of this chapter, you will understand controls and how to work with them to enhance your forms.

What are Access 97 controls?

You use controls to make forms more user-friendly when finding information, and they make data-entry more efficient. Some examples of controls include command buttons, radio buttons, check boxes, combo boxes, and text boxes, as shown in Figure 19.1. You can find each control in the Toolbox, also displayed.

Fig. 19.1
In Design view, the frmControlsExample form shows many controls available to forms.

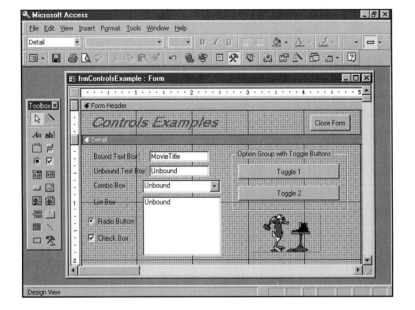

 TIP **You should be very familiar with these types of controls as they** appear in all of the Windows 95 and Office 97 applications, including Access 97.

This example has more types of controls than you would probably use on an average form. Rather than work through each of the types of controls, I am going to show you how to place controls on a form and then work with them. You will learn more about the different types of controls in Chapter 20.

Creating a form with controls

To create a form from scratch, rather than with a wizard:

1 Open the VideoLib database, and click the Forms tab.

2 Click the <u>N</u>ew button and the New Form dialog box appears.

3 Choose tblTapes for the record source, at the bottom of the dialog box (see Figure 19.2).

Fig. 19.2
Creating a form.

4 Choose Design View, and click OK. Access 97 creates a blank form and opens it in Design view (see Figure 19.3).

Q&A *Why isn't the Property Sheet showing?*

The settings for the various tools are the same settings you had when you last worked in Form Design. If you didn't have the property sheet open when you left Access 97, it isn't open now.

Fig. 19.3
A fresh, new form to
work with.

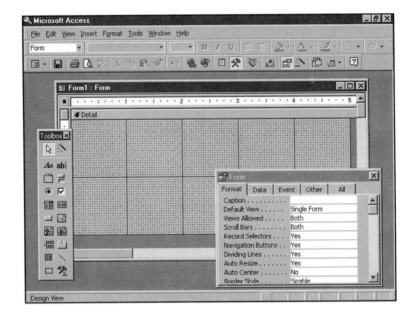

First, you need to add a field from the Field List.

TIP   **When you have a control based on a field in a record source or a**
calculation (as in our example), it is a bound control. The record source is a
query or table. To add a bound text box control, follow these steps:

5   Click the Field List button on the toolbar. The Field List appears.

6   Drag the MovieTitle field down to the form (see Figure 19.4) to the
position where you want it; release the mouse. The MovieTitle field
appears on the form, as shown in Figure 19.5.

TIP   **Sometimes, you have a control that requires something**
other than a text box. For instance, Yes/No fields are great as check
boxes. To use a check box, click the Check Box control type in the Toolbox;
then select and drag the intended field down to the form. You will then
have a check box control bound to the field you want to use.

Fig. 19.4
Drag and drop a field
on a form.

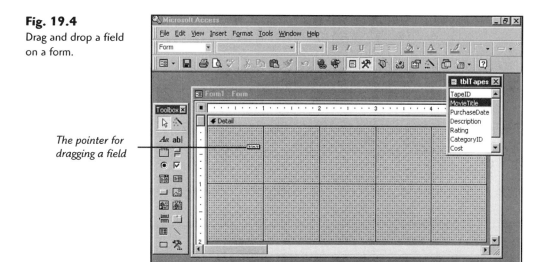

*The pointer for
dragging a field*

Fig. 19.5
A newly created
compound control: a
text box and its label.

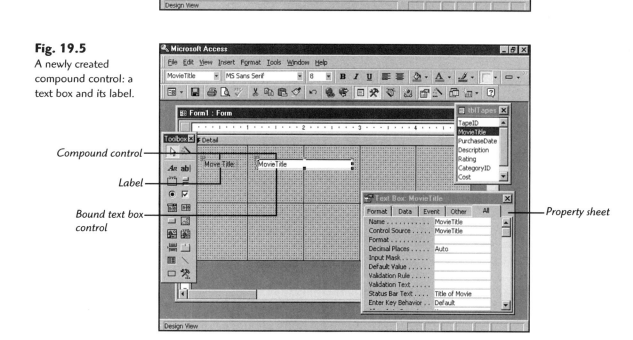

Compound control

Label

*Bound text box
control*

Property sheet

Plain English, please!

A **compound control** is a main control such as a text box, and a corresponding label used to describe the main control. If this is a bound control, then the control's name (or Caption property if filled in) will appear in the label.

Notice in the property sheet that the Control Source is MovieTitle. This is what the control is bound to. So when you change the form to Form view, the information in the MovieTitle field appears here. If the Control Source was blank, it was an *unbound* control.

You have created your first control. Notice that even though the control looks like it is two separate controls, they are one: a text box control with its label. The majority of the input controls have labels attached.

 TIP   **Notice that the label says Movie Title, yet the field itself is** MovieTitle (no space). This property was set at the table level in the MovieTitle field in tblTapes. By setting the Caption property of the field to Movie Title, Access 97 used that property for the label. This is *propagation*. Access 97 propagates quite a few fields to the properties of bound controls.

Because of propagating properties, it is a good idea to fill out the information for a field when you create your table, *before* you create a form or report. Once you create a control on a form or report, Access 97 will not necessarily propagate changes in the table field.

Moving and sizing controls

Controls are not much good if you can't move them and size them the way you want to. Access 97 has a method for moving and sizing that involves the handles on a highlighted control. You can see the handles in Figure 19.6.

Fig. 19.6
You can move and
resize this text box
control bound to
MovieTitle using its
handles.

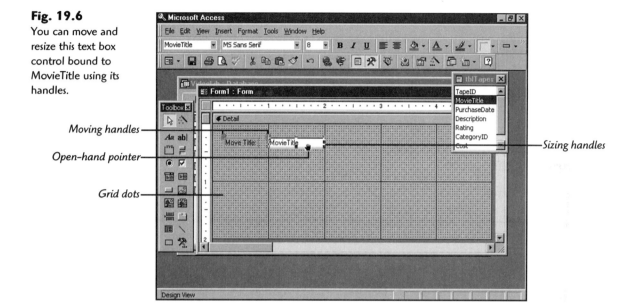

Moving handles

Open-hand pointer

Grid dots

Sizing handles

Moving compound controls

To move a control, there are a couple of techniques. For the first method, which moves the compound control, follow these steps:

1 Position the cursor over the control, either the label or text box. The cursor changes into an open hand (see Figure 19.6).

2 When you see the open-handed cursor, click and hold the left mouse button.

3 Drag the control to the new position on the form.

4 Release the mouse button when you have moved the control to the position you want.

Q&A   ***Why does the control seem to jump as I move it?***

If you look at Figure 19.6, there are Grid Dots on the form. The control jumps the space between these dots. This makes it nice when trying to line up multiple controls. Use the Snap to Grid to jump; you can toggle it on and off by choosing S̲nap to Grid from the F̲ormat menu.

TIP   **There may be times when you want to move a control a pixel** (the smallest measurement on the screen) at a time, rather than where the grid dots are set, but you don't want to change the method of movement permanently. To do this, highlight the control, hold the Ctrl key down, and use the arrows keys to move the control. Try it now!

If you hold the Shift key down and use the arrow keys, you can resize the control. This gives you even more control.

Moving controls independently

To move a control independent of its label, and vice versa, follow these steps:

1 Position the cursor on the move handle for whichever part of the compound control you want to move, either the label or text box. The cursor will change into a pointing finger.

2 When you see the pointing finger cursor, shown in Figure 19.7, click and hold the left mouse button.

3 Drag the control to a new position on the form.

4 Release the mouse button when you have moved the control to the position you want.

Fig. 19.7
Moving a control
without the label.

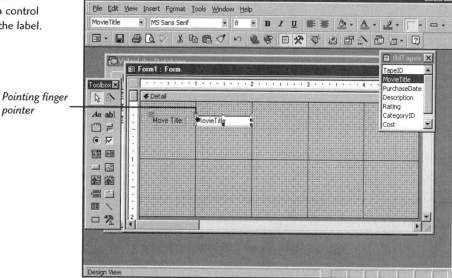

Pointing finger
pointer

Moving multiple controls

To show how to move multiple controls, you need to bring down a couple more fields. Bring down the Description and Rating fields.

To grab more than one field at a time, click the first field you want in the Field List (Description). Then, while holding down the Ctrl key, click the next field (Rating). Drag both fields down under the MovieTitle field on the form, and release the mouse. The fields then appear on the form.

To move multiple fields, follow these steps:

1 On the form, position the cursor down to the bottom right corner of the last control you want to move.

2 Click and hold the left mouse button.

3 Drag the mouse up and to the left, over all the controls you want to highlight; you see a frame stretching over the controls (see Figure 19.8).

Q&A *Why didn't you include all of every control when selecting the controls?*

You don't have to include all of a control in order for it to appear highlighted, if you set the Selection Behavior to <u>P</u>artially Enclosed. On the Forms/Reports tab of the <u>O</u>ptions dialog box in the <u>T</u>ools menu, you can change the selection behavior to F<u>u</u>lly Enclosed if you want to.

Fig. 19.8
Use the mouse to
highlight multiple
fields.

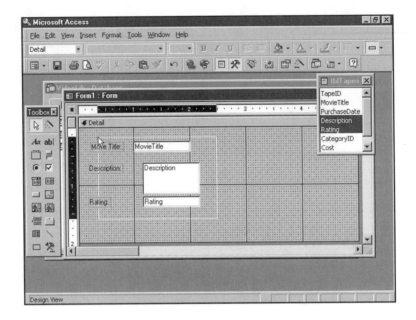

4 When you encompass all of the controls you want to move, release the
mouse.

5 Position the mouse over any of the controls you want to move. When
the cursor turns into the open hand, press the left mouse button and
drag the controls to where you want them.

Q&A **What if I don't want to include all the fields?**

You can toggle a control that you want included (highlighted) or excluded
(not highlighted) by holding down the Shift key and clicking the control
with the left mouse button.

You can also use this method for selecting multiple controls when sizing and
aligning multiple controls, as discussed next.

Aligning controls

In most cases, when you display controls on a form, you want to make sure
they line up evenly. Access 97 gives you an easy way to do this.

1 Highlight the controls you want to align using the selection method
explained in the previous section.

When you select the multiple controls for alignment or sizing, select only the part of the compound controls you want to align (or size). For example, Figure 19.9 shows that you want only the text boxes high-lighted. This way, you won't change the alignment of the labels and you can align (or size) them separately.

Fig. 19.9

When aligning or sizing controls, you can choose to change only one part of the compound controls at a time.

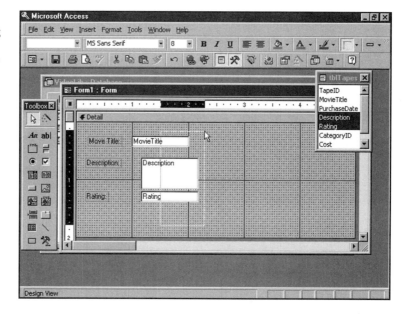

2 Choose Format, Align from the Form Design menu. You see the follow-ing choices for aligning the controls: Left, Right, Top, Bottom, or To Grid.

3 Pick Right from the Align menu. You then see the text boxes line up to the rightmost control (see Figure 19.10).

4 Following steps 1 through 3, align the labels for the controls by high-lighting them and aligning them to the left.

Fig. 19.10
These text box controls are right-aligned, but the label remains the same.

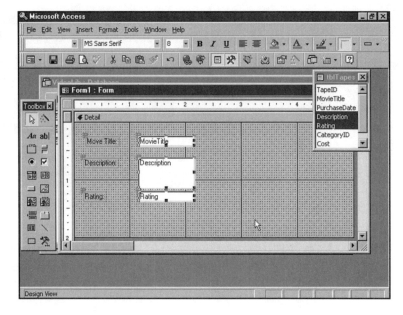

Sizing controls

When sizing controls, there are a couple of ways you can do it, depending upon the number of controls you want to size.

To size an individual control:

1 Click the control to highlight it.

2 Move the cursor over a Sizing handle. When you have it over a Sizing handle, the cursor changes into a set of arrows that point in different directions, depending upon which way you size the control (see Figure 19.11).

3 Holding down the left mouse button, drag the control handle; you see it stretch or shrink, depending on which direction you move it.

Fig. 19.11
You're ready to size
this control.

Sizing pointer —

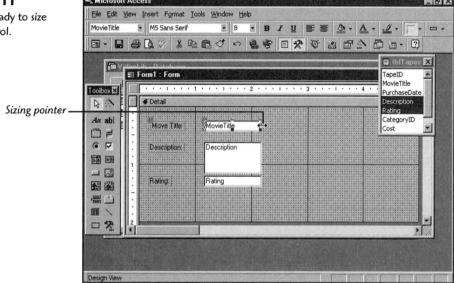

When sizing multiple controls, you can highlight the controls you are interested in, then:

- Use the method just described in the last section.

  Or

- Choose Size from the Format menu. Then choose from: To Fit, To Grid, To Tallest, To Shortest, To Widest, and To Narrowest.

Working with control properties

Just as you can work with a form's properties, you can also change a control's properties. In Figure 19.12, you can see the property sheet for the MovieTitles text box.

Fig. 19.12
The Property sheet and
Formatting toolbar for
Form Design.

Formatting toolbar —

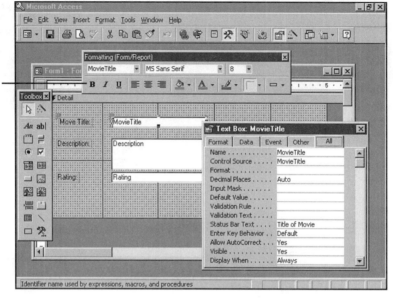

To see how to change one of a control's properties, let's change the Status
Bar Text property to display something new. To do this:

1 Place the cursor into the Status Bar Text property in the property sheet.

2 Replace the current text in the property by typing: This is the Movie
Title.

3 Switch to Design view.

Now, when you enter the MovieTitle field, the text you typed in will be
displayed in the Status Bar at the bottom of the Access window.

The formatting toolbar allows you to change the way your controls look. Play
with the buttons on the Formatting toolbar and change your controls to meet
your needs.

20

Controls that Especially Enhance Forms

● **In this chapter:**

● Using control wizards

● Using combo boxes to limit choices

● Command buttons allow you to have Access 97 perform tasks for you

● Tab Control for displaying multiple pages

● Subforms for displaying information from other sources

There is a control for just about every type of data entry that you need to do. . . . . ●>

Y ou have learned how to create forms and learned about form properties. You have also seen how to add controls to forms and to manipulate them by moving and sizing the controls. Now it's time to put them to work. Let's create a form that uses quite a few controls and is very productive as well. Once you create this form, you'll have a good idea of the flexibility and usefulness of controls and a better understanding of which control types are best for certain kinds of information. "Whoa, what a concept!" you say.

Table 20.1 shows some control types I recommend using for various types of data entry.

Table 20.1 Control Types for Data Entry

Control type(s)	Type of data entry
Text Box	Freeform text entry. This is the most common type of data entry, including everything from names and addresses to longer entries such as comments and notes.
Option Group	A small set of options, probably six or less, that you can choose among, for example, if you had three set mail carriers to choose from, you could have option buttons before each company's name, and then choose one or another.
Combo Box, List Box	Data that has a specific list to choose from, and you want to limit the choice to that list. One example would be assigning a customer to an order.
Check Box	Great for Yes and No type data entry; for example, Member or Non-Member.
Tab Control	Displaying multiple pages of information on one form.
Command Button	To have Access 97 perform tasks such as opening another form or report.
Subform Control	Relating information from one record source to another. The example shown in this chapter displays all the people who have borrowed a specific tape in the Tape Information form.

You can see some of these types of controls, along with the form you will create in this chapter. This form consists of two pages of information, displayed using the Tab control. As mentioned earlier, the Tab control allows you to display and edit multiple pages of information on one form rather than opening separate forms.

The first page of the tab, shown in Figure 20.1, displays some of the main information about the individual tape, such as title, purchase date, and so on.

Fig. 20.1
Believe it or not, this form took about 15 minutes to create.

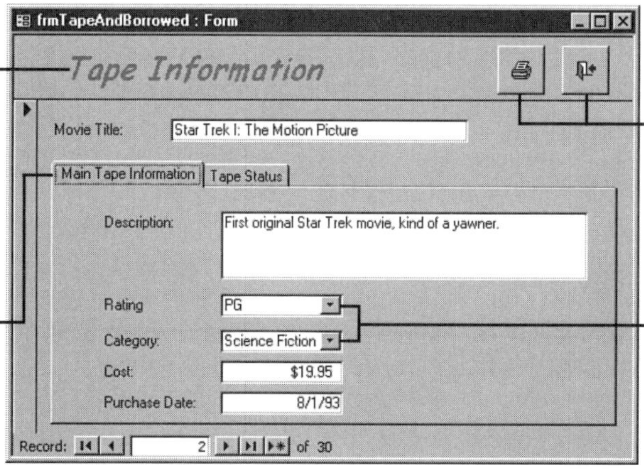

Form header

Tab control (Page 1)

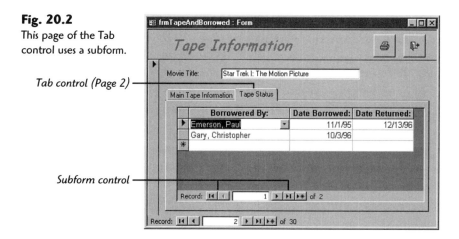

Command buttons

Combo boxes

The second page of the Tab control, shown here in Figure 20.2, uses a subform control to display a history of who has borrowed the tape. It also lets you add a new borrower.

Fig. 20.2
This page of the Tab control uses a subform.

Tab control (Page 2)

Subform control

You can see from the controls pointed out in both figures that you have your work cut out for you. So, to start with, let's create a new form.

Creating the base form

When you create any form, set its properties up from the start, specifying how you want it to behave. For instance, in Figures 20.1 and 20.2, properties were set so there is a Form header and no scroll bars. Once you've added a number of controls on the form, it may be more trouble to set some form properties.

Another good rule of thumb is to start from the top down when creating forms. Again, this helps you to remember everything that you want to include on the form, and logically see the flow of the form as you lay it out.

When creating forms, don't use too much color. You don't want people to have to wear sunglasses to look at screens. With colors, less is more.

Align your controls rather than have the controls uneven. Also be careful adding a control in the middle of existing controls, since this will throw off the order in which the tab flows through the controls on the form. How to align your controls and reset the tab order once a new control has been added was discussed in Chapter 19.

Setting the initial form properties

You can break up forms into various sections:

- **Form Header**—Use the form header section to display a title for the form, such as information and controls that are relevant to all records. This would include a label describing the form's purpose and command buttons to perform tasks.

- **Detail**—Here, place the information to be edited for each record, such as last name, first name, and so on. Place the controls to be used in a logical order on your form. For instance, place the last and first name text box controls side by side. Then, group address text boxes below (address on one line, city, state, ZIP Code on the line below). These can look just like they would on a piece of paper. In fact, it is a good idea to take a paper form you have now and emulate it with the Access form.

- **Form Footer**—You can use the Form Footer to display summary information for all the records. Some people also place their command buttons here instead of the Form Header.

TIP **As you create your forms, be consistent about where you place** controls such as command buttons. This will help everyone become efficient in using your forms.

To create the new form:

1 Click the Forms tab in the Database window. Click the New button, and then choose tblTapes once again as its record source in the New Form dialog box. Click OK. You will see the Form Design view.

2 Now choose View, Form Header/Footer from the Form Design menu. Access 97 then places a new section on the form called Form Header (see Figure 20.3).

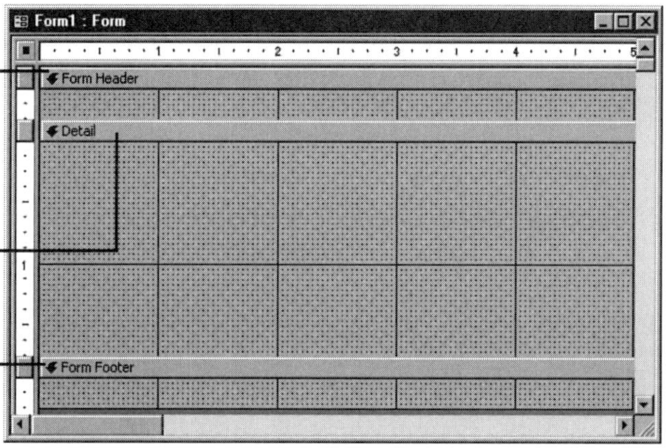

Fig. 20.3
Form Header sections are good places for titles and command buttons.

Form Header section ─

Form Detail section ─

Form Footer section ─

3 Place the cursor at the bottom of the Form Footer section. You will see the cursor change into a bar with two arrows coming out of it (see Figure 20.4). Holding down the left mouse button, slide the Form Footer up so that it disappears. You aren't going to be using that section of the form.

4 Take the mouse and grab the bottom of the Form Header section (at the top of the Detail section) in the same manner as you did the Form Footer section. Hold down the left mouse button and pull down on the mouse, making the Form Header section a bit taller.

Fig. 20.4
Sizing sections is very convenient.

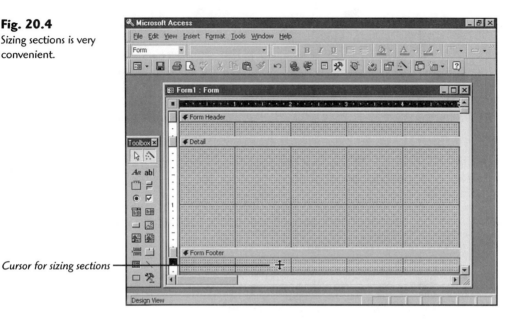

Cursor for sizing sections ———

5 Click the Properties button on the toolbar, and locate the Scroll Bars property in the Format tab. Since we don't need any scroll bars to appear on the form, set the `Scroll Bars` property to Neither. The reason we don't need any scroll bars is that all the data is going to fit on the form, so we don't need to worry about scrolling.

Q&A *I clicked the Properties button, but couldn't locate the Scroll Bars property. Why not?*

Chances are that Access 97 is no longer looking at the forms properties but at the Form Header or Detail section properties. To select the form again, click the Form Selector displayed in Figure 20.4, and then try step 5 again. No matter what object is currently selected, the Form Selector will point back to the form itself.

Adding a Text Label for a title

Go ahead and close the property sheet for now. The next task is adding a title to the top of the form. You will want to add a Label from the toolbox. To do this:

1 Click the Label control in the toolbox. The cursor will then turn into a plus sign and a big A.

2 Place the cursor in the Form Header section, at the top-left corner where you want the label to appear. Holding the left mouse button down, drag the cursor over and down (see Figure 20.5). When you have the cursor where you want it, let go.

Fig. 20.5
Adding a Label control.

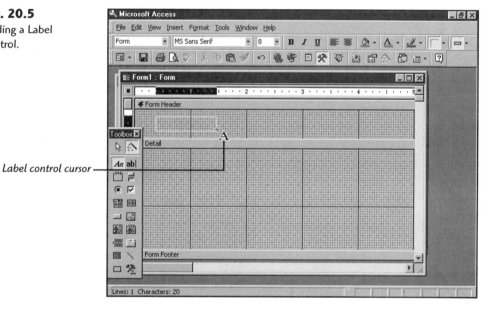

Label control cursor —

Q&A ***Why is it that I created the label and saw it appear, but when I clicked somewhere else on the form, it disappeared?***

After creating the Label control, you have to type the text into it right away; otherwise, Access 97 assumes that you don't want it and deletes it.

3 In the Label control, type in the text "Tape Information" and press Enter. You have a Label now, but it's pretty small and boring, isn't it?

4 Highlight the control once again if it isn't already. Then, using the Format toolbar, change the label to look like you want it. You can change the Font and Font Size to start with, then play with the colors.

Q&A   ***What do I do now that I've made the Font Size bigger and can't see the text?***

Place the cursor on the lower-right corner of the control, then double-click. Access 97 will perform Size To Fit on the control. This will set the size of the label to fit the length of the text.

Now it's time to add Command Buttons to the form.

Using the Control Wizard to create Command Buttons

Command buttons are different from other controls that you will use. Their sole purpose is to perform commands when you click them, such as closing or printing a form. Other controls are used for displaying information, entering or changing information, or both.

We'll use the Control Wizard to create a Command button for printing:

1 Click the Control Wizard button in your toolbox. When the Control Wizard is "on," the button appears depressed.

2 Click the Command Button tool in the toolbox. The cursor will then appear as a plus symbol along with a small command button.

3 Click the cursor to the right side of the Form Header section in the Grid Dots. You don't need to drag the shape, since Access 97 will shape it anyway. When you release the button, Access 97 will start the Command Button wizard, and you will see the first screen (see Figure 20.6).

4 In the Categories list, click the Record Operations, then Print Record in the Actions list (see Figure 20.6). Look at the sample on the left side of the dialog box to see what the control will look like on your form.

5 Click <u>N</u>ext to move to the next screen, which will ask if you want to display picture(s) or text (see Figure 20.7). You can use the Browse button to choose your own graphic. We'll use the selected printer for our example.

Fig. 20.6
Choose various
operations that you
want assigned to
command buttons.

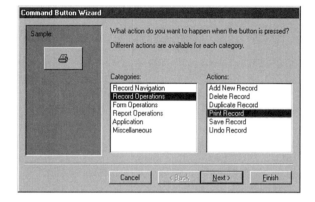

Fig. 20.7
You can display either
text or a picture on a
command button.

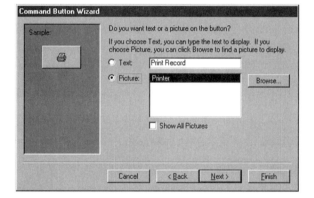

TIP **Windows recommends not using bitmaps on command buttons.**
If you want to make your database application look more like other
applications, don't use graphics on the command buttons; use text.

6 Click Next to go to the next screen. Access 97 asks you to name the
button. Type in the name for the command button control: "cmdPrint"
(see Figure 20.8).

7 Click Finish. Access 97 creates the control and places it on the form.

You have now created your first command button. If you switch to Form
view and click the command button, you get a blank page printed out at this
point.

Fig. 20.8
Prefacing command button names with cmd helps you locate them later.

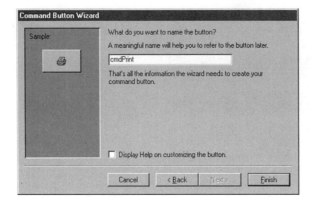

Go ahead and create a button for closing the form. Run the Command Button Wizard again and choose Form Operations from Categories and Close Form from Actions on the first screen. Then name the command button cmdClose. Place the button to the right of the Print button on the form.

You can see the finished command buttons in Figure 20.9.

Fig. 20.9
Here are the completed command buttons.

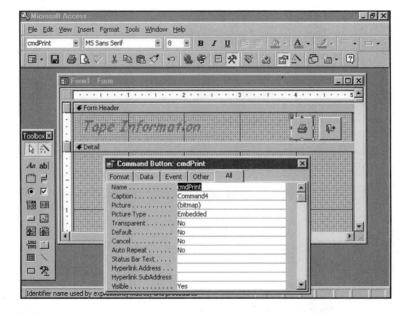

Adding a text box control (Revisited)

You learned how to add a text box using the Field List button in the last chapter. Our example includes a text box for Movie Title in the Detail area of the form.

 Click the Field List button. Then pull the MovieTitle field down onto the form from the Field List. Place the control in the Detail section, under the Title. Resize it so that it's wide enough to display the titles. You're all done; isn't that getting easy?

Now comes the fun part—inserting a Tab control onto the form.

Working with the Tab control

 The Tab control lets you work with multiple pages of information on one form, showing one page at a time. This is much more convenient than opening up a separate form for each page, or paging through multiple pages on a form using another control called the Page Break control and code. Using the Page Break control, located in the Toolbox, can be quite cumbersome.

Various dialog boxes in Access 97, such as the Options dialog box and the database window, use their own Tab controls to present their information in an organized way so you can find what you're looking for quickly and easily.

Using the Tab control is still a little tricky but not nearly as complicated as it used to be. It is also what I consider to be essential to a good-looking multipage form.

Inserting a Tab control

To insert a Tab control onto the form:

 1 Click the Tab control button in the toolbox. The cursor changes to a Tab control with the plus symbol.

2 Click the form on the place where you want the Tab control to appear. In our example, the Tab control is just below the Movie title text box.

3 Holding the left mouse button down, stretch the cursor down and to the right. This allows you to size the control when you are creating it.

4 When the control is the size you want, release the mouse button. You have now added a Tab control to the form with two tabbed pages (see Figure 20.10).

Fig. 20.10
A newly added Tab control.

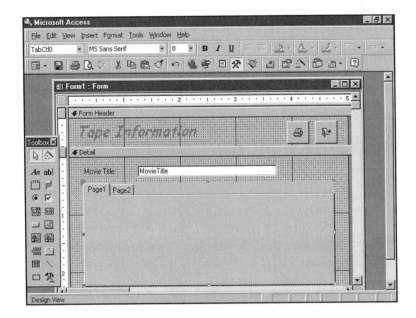

Working with the Tab control is different than working with other controls. There are property sheets, not only for the Tab control but for each of the tab pages as well. You will also click the individual tabs in Design view to add controls to the individual pages.

Take a look at Figure 20.11 (Page 1). Notice that the tab caption appears highlighted when it is in front or when it is the *active* tab.

Q&A ***When I added pages into my Tab control, why did they come up with different numbers other than 1 and 2?***

It depends on how many Tab controls you have created on the form. If you have placed two Tab controls on the same form, the first will have pages 1 and 2, the next 3 and 4—even if you delete the first to start over. They still work correctly, however.

Fig. 20.11
Page 1 of the Tab control is the active page.

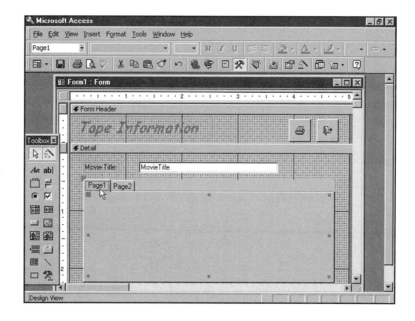

Regarding the multiple property sheets, except for changing the captions for each of the tab pages, you don't have to worry about dealing with the property sheets. In order to change the Caption property, you have to go into the property sheet.

Changing properties on the Tab control

To change the Caption properties on the individual pages of the Tab control:

1 Open the property sheet by clicking the Property Sheet button on the toolbar. Click the Format tab.

2 Click the Page1 tab. You can see the Caption property appear in the property sheet.

3 Type in: "Main Tape Information."

4 Click the Page2 tab. Notice that the first tab now has the new caption displayed.

5 In the Caption property for Page2, type: "Tape Status" (see Figure 20.12).

Now you are ready to add controls onto the Tab control pages. Close the property sheet for now to get it out of the way.

Fig. 20.12
Updating the Caption
properties for the
individual tab pages.

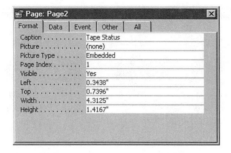

Adding controls on Tab control pages

Adding controls (bound text boxes, combo boxes, and so on) to the pages of
the Tab control is not much tougher than adding them to the form, as long as
you keep track of which page you are on.

1 Click the Page1 tab (Main Tape Information).

2 Click the Field List button to open it.

3 Drag the Description field onto the Tab control. When you do this, you
will see the inside of the Tab control darken, confirming you are placing
a control in the Tab control (see Figure 20.13).

4 Repeat step 3 for all of the other fields. Then rearrange them so they
look as they did in Figure 20.1.

Q&A   ***How do I get the vertical spacing even between fields,***
without driving myself crazy?

Highlight the nonlabel part of the group of controls you want to arrange.
Choose Vertical Spacing from the Format menu. Then choose Make Equal
from the Vertical Spacing submenu. Make sure that you don't include the
Tab control or it will get ugly.

After you create the controls as specified, if you click the Tape Status tab,
you may notice that the fields seem to disappear. They haven't. Remember
that the Tab control is broken up into pages; you are just looking at the
second page. Click the Main Tape Information tab to see the fields again.

Fig. 20.13
Adding a control to
the Tab control.

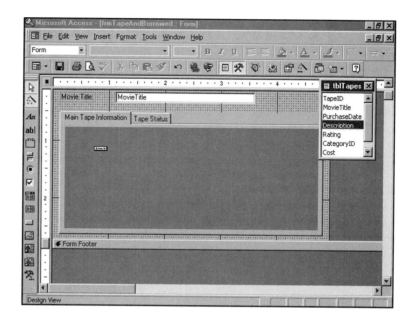

Q&A *In Figure 20.1, both fields look like combo boxes. When I am creating the form, why is the CategoryID field a combo box, but the Rating field is a Text Box control?*

Figure 20.1 was the completed form, shown ahead of time. If you remember way back in Chapter 9, we made the CategoryID field a Lookup field and specified the combo box at the table level. Access 97 then propagated the field to the form. We haven't done anything with the Rating field yet. In the next section, we create a combo box. Note that in real life you would probably treat the Rating field the same way as the CategoryID field, making it a Lookup field.

Let's make the Rating text box a combo box.

Creating a combo box using the Combo Box Wizard

Combo boxes are one of the handiest of the controls available. Although somewhat more complicated than some of the other controls, the Combo Box Wizard makes it painless to create them. To create a combo box:

1 Delete the current Rating Text Box on the form by highlighting the control and pressing the Delete key.

2 Choose the Combo Box control from the toolbox.

3 Now, with the cursor looking like a plus sign and combo box, drag the Rating field down from the Field List to the same location of the previous Rating control. Provided you had the control wizards still on, Access 97 will fire up the Combo Box Wizard (see Figure 20.14). This is the same wizard (Lookup Wizard) you saw in Chapter 9.

Fig. 20.14
The first screen of the Combo Box Wizard.

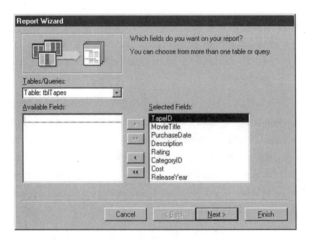

The first screen is where you want the combo box to get its values. Leave the default, which is to have the combo box look up the values in a table or query.

4 Click Next to go to the next screen. This screen asks you which table or query you want to use for the row source of the combo box.

5 Select the tblRatings table and click Next. The next screen asks you which fields you want to include.

6 Select All Fields (>>); Access 97 will move both the Rating and Description field over.

7 Click Next to go to the next screen. On this screen, you will be doing something a little different than before.

Normally, Access 97 hides the Primary Key field in a combo box (see Figure 20.15).

Fig. 20.15

Access 97 automatically hides the key column in a combo box.

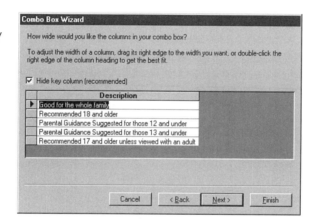

This is usually great, but in this case, you want to see the key column, which is the Rating field, so remove the check in the Hide key column (recommended) check box. Access 97 then displays the Rating field.

8 After this screen, you will use the default values of the wizard, so simply click Finish. Access 97 then displays the combo box on the form.

Q&A *Why is it that when I switch to Form view and tab through the fields, Rating is out of tab order?*

By adding the Rating combo box after the other controls on the form, Access 97 automatically puts it at the end of the tab order. (The tab order is where you move from control to control when you press Tab or Enter. It has nothing to do with the Tab control itself.)

To change the tab order of the controls, in Design view choose Tab Order from the View menu. You will then see the Tab Order dialog box. Click the Auto Order button and Access 97 reorders the controls top-down and left-right.

9 Save the form as frmTapeAndBorrowed, and then close it.

The second page of the Tab control consists of a Subform control.

Creating subform controls

Subform controls allow a form to display another form within itself, and link the two forms on a common field. Taking another look at the second page of the Tab form (see Figure 20.16), you will see that the subform is actually the tblBorrowTapes table with a combo box for the Borrower's information.

Fig. 20.16
Page 2 of the Tab control contains a subform.

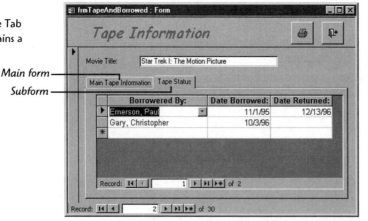

Here is a summary list of tasks you need to do to add a subform control to a form. We will then go into detail, showing each step.

- Create a form that will be used as a subform. This form will be created just as any other form. This will include creating the record source (possibly a query) that the form will be based on.

- Create the main form to be used.

- Use the Subform Control Wizard to create the subform control on the main form.

We have already performed the second bullet by starting the main form. In order to create a subform control, you first have to create the form that will be used as the subform.

How difficult it is to create subforms depends on how difficult the form used in the subform is to create. Often, you can create a subform in the main form. This time, however, you are going to prepare the form used in the subform ahead of time.

Preparing the form used for the subform

The form used in the subform was displayed in Datasheet view in Figure 20.16.

Q&A *Why don't I see the TapeID on the form?*

When you create a subform control, you have to link the forms based on a field, in this case, TapeID. Remember that the main form is based off the Tape Information, so you don't need to repeat the TapeID in the subform.

The only thing special about the form is that there is a combo box based off a query called qryBorrowersFullName, which we create in the following steps. This will be used in the tblBorrowersID field. To create the subform shown in Figure 20.17:

1 Create a Query for the combo box, as shown in Figure 20.18. If you need more help with creating queries, refer to Chapters 12 and 13.

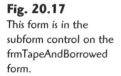

Fig. 20.17
This form is in the subform control on the frmTapeAndBorrowed form.

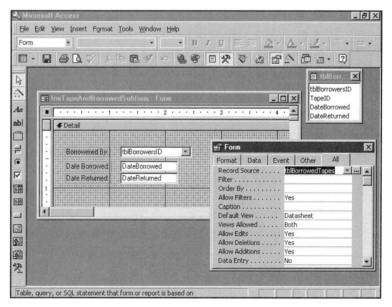

Fig. 20.18
This query, called
qryBorrowersFullName,
uses a calculated field
as described in
Chapter 13.

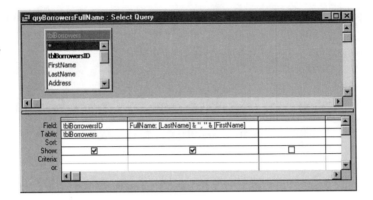

2 To create the frmTapeAndBorrowedSubform form, choose the tblBorrowedTapes as the Record Source property. The first control you want to place on the form is the combo box control for the tblBorrowersID.

3 With the Controls Wizards button toggled on, select the combo box control from the toolbox. Then pull the tblBorrowersID field down from the Field List onto the form. The Combo Box Wizard begins.

4 Accept the default settings and click Next on the first screen of the Combo Box Wizard. On the next screen, pick the source for the combo box.

5 Click the Queries option button, and highlight the qryBorrowersFullName (see Figure 20.19). Click Next to go to the next screen. This screen lets you pick which fields you want to include in the combo box.

Fig. 20.19
The Combo Box
Wizard uses either
tables or queries.

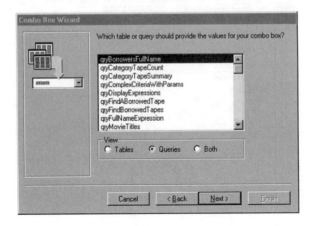

6 Select all fields by clicking the double arrows button (>>). Click Next to go to the next screen.

7 You will be asked how wide you want each of the fields displayed in the combo box. Since it's not important to show the tblBorrowersID field, you can hide it from view. Place the cursor on the right edge of the first field. When the cursor changes to a vertical line crossed with a double-headed arrow, drag the column edge to the left until the tblBorrowersID column is hidden (see Figure 20.20).

8 Click Next three times until you reach the dialog box that asks you to supply the name of the label for the combo box. Type in: "Borrowers" for the label; then click Finish. You have created the combo box for the subform.

Fig. 20.20
Adjust the width to hide the first field used in the query.

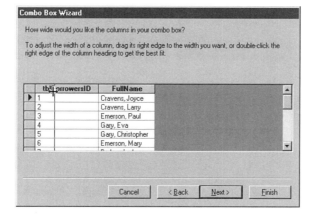

9 Drag the DateBorrowed and DateReturned fields onto the form. Close and save the form as frmTapeAndBorrowedSubform.

Creating the subform control

Subform controls are used for displaying and editing information from a different, yet related, record source. The example used here is to display the people who have borrowed a particular tape with the tape's information.

1 Open the frmTapeAndBorrowed form in Design view.

2 Click the Tape Status tab of the Tab control.

3 With the control wizards toggled on, select the Subform/Subreport control button from the toolbox.

4 Click the left mouse button in the Tab control and drag the mouse pointer down and to the right (see Figure 20.21) and then release the mouse. The Subform Control Wizard will begin. The first screen of the Subform Control Wizard gives you a choice of using a table/query or a form for the object source.

Fig. 20.21
You can drag and drop the Subform as you can other controls.

Creating the subform control

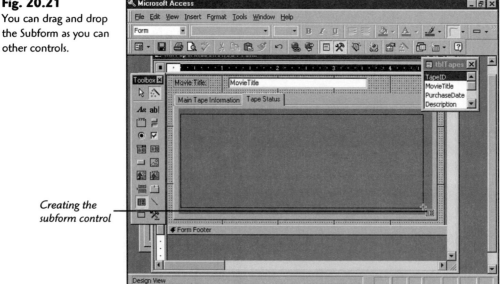

5 Click the Forms radio button, and pick frmTapeAndBorrowedSubform for the form (see Figure 20.22). This is all the information you need to create the subform. Click <u>F</u>inish.

Fig. 20.22
The Subform Control Wizard lets you select what to use for the control.

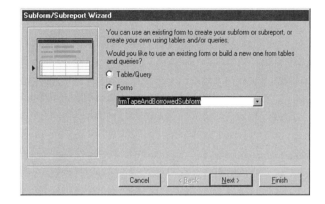

When you go back to the main form, all that is left to do is delete the Label the control wizard includes. Simply click the frmTapeAndBorrowedSubform label and then press Delete.

If you look at the form with the Property Sheet displaying the Subform controls properties, you see that the Object Source is set to frmTapeAndBorrowedSubform, with the Link Master Field (from the main form) set to the ID field and Link Child Fields (from the subform) set to TapeID (see Figure 20.23).

Fig. 20.23
Here is the final Subform control.

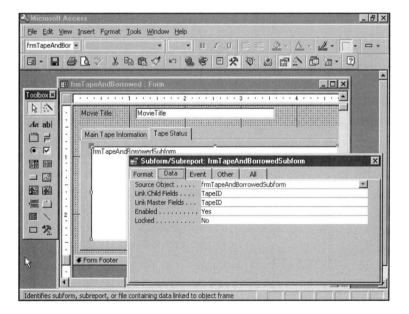

Part VI: Reporting Information

21

Reporting Made Easy with Wizards

● **In this chapter:**

- ● **Creating reports the fast way**

- ● **Discovering the type of reports**

- ● **Using Print Preview to get a better picture**

- ● **Printing your reports**

- ● **Specifying a printer to use**

Access 97 gives you the ability to create attractive reports with just two clicks of the mouse. . . . . ⮞

R eports are a big part of Access 97. Just as forms help you input and maintain your data, reports help you present your data in a meaningful way. Access 97 gives you a hand in creating reports very quickly. In this chapter, there are two methods for creating quick reports: AutoReport and the Report Wizards. To learn how to modify reports you create, see Chapter 22. When creating even highly customized reports, you will generally start with one of the methods described in this chapter and build on that report.

Creating reports using the two-click method

It takes two clicks to get a quick report in Access 97. With the table high-lighted, in this case tblTapes, click the New Object drop-down selection on the toolbar. Then select AutoReport. Access 97 then generates a quick Columnar report and opens it in Print Preview mode (see Figure 21.1).

Fig. 21.1
This report was quick to create but is kind of plain.

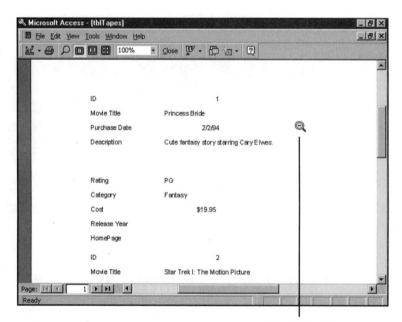

Magnifying Glass cursor

If you look at the New Object button, it now defaults to AutoReport. This will default to the last New Object used.

There you have your first report. You'll learn more about using the Print Preview feature and how to print your reports later in the chapter. You may notice that this report, while displaying the necessary information, is pretty boring. The AutoReport feature is great for creating quick reports, but as mentioned in the beginning of the chapter, you will want to modify and enhance the report. This is discussed in the next chapter.

You can quickly create more attractive reports by using the Report Wizards.

Taking a look at the Report Wizards

Access 97 has some wizards that will help you create reports. To take a look at them, in the Database window, click the Reports tab. Then click the New button. Access 97 opens the New Report dialog box.

The New Report dialog box is similar to the New Form dialog box because it lets you specify the record source (table or query) for the report you want to create. Choose tblTapes for the record source (see Figure 21.2).

Fig. 21.2
Take advantage of Access 97's Report Wizards.

The AutoReport reports listed (see Figure 21.2), Columnar and Tabular, are nice, quick ways to create reports. These reports are easier to read and look more professional than the one we created at the beginning of the chapter (see Figure 21.1). Figure 21.3 shows the same report we created in the beginning of the chapter, but created using the AutoReport:Columnar option in the New Report dialog box.

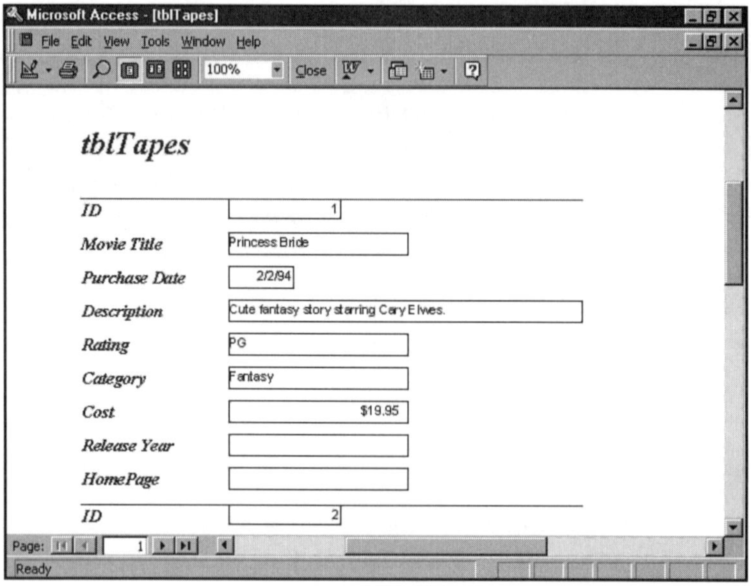

Fig. 21.3
This report is much nicer than the report generated at the Database window AutoReport.

Here is the same report, this time using the AutoReport: Tabular option in the New Report dialog box (see Figure 21.4).

Fig. 21.4
The AutoReport: Tabular option creates great list-style reports.

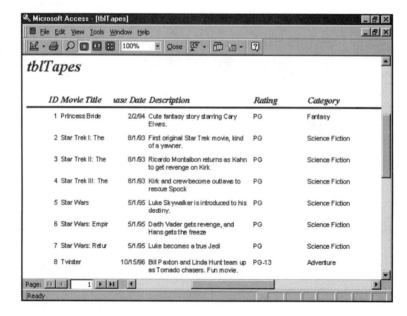

TIP **After you have created the report and are through viewing it,** click the Design button. You will now see the report in Design view, and you can modify and customize it further. I will be discussing Report Design view in the next chapter.

Refining your report using the Report Wizard

Previously, you learned to create a report using all the information in the tblTapes table with the "canned" format that you couldn't change. Now you'll learn to select and format the report for presentation.

In the Reports tab of the database window, choose <u>N</u>ew. In the New Report dialog box, choose tblTapes for the record source, select the Report Wizard, and click OK. Access 97 starts the Report Wizard.

Selecting fields to include in the report

On the first screen, pick all the fields you want to include on your report. Select all the fields (>>), and then click <u>N</u>ext (see Figure 21.5).

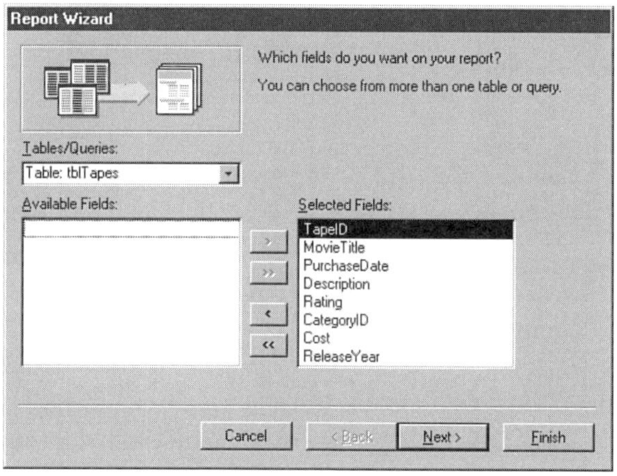

Fig. 21.5
Select the fields to include in your report.

Report Wizard

Which fields do you want on your report?
You can choose from more than one table or query.

<u>T</u>ables/Queries:
Table: tblTapes

<u>A</u>vailable Fields:

<u>S</u>elected Fields:
TapeID
MovieTitle
PurchaseDate
Description
Rating
CategoryID
Cost
ReleaseYear

Cancel   < <u>B</u>ack   <u>N</u>ext >   <u>F</u>inish

Once you choose the information you want in your report, you may decide that it would be easier to understand if it were organized differently. You can do this in the next wizard screen.

Grouping and sorting information

The next screen lets you choose how you want to group the data. This gives you an opportunity to display the fields in different orders. By grouping the data, you tell Access 97 which fields you want displayed "as a group," as well as how to summarize the data. Sorting it places the data in a specific order in the report. You can see in Figure 21.6 that the data displays by Rating.

Fig. 21.6
Grouping data by rating using the Report Wizard.

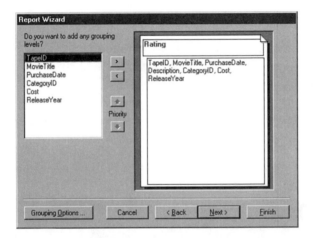

TIP **You can also use CategoryID as another logical choice for group-** ing for this report. Also, which field is chosen by default depends on the order they were picked in the previous screen. For example, if CategoryID were chosen before Rating, then CategoryID would be used as the default grouping.

To change the grouping, use the select buttons displayed on the screen. Click Next to accept the choice Access 97 made. You will then see a screen that asks how you want to sort the detail records. Select MovieTitle and click Next.

TIP **If you decide you want to change the grouping and sorting order** of your information, you can click the Back button at any time and change your options.

Selecting layouts for the report

This screen lets you decide what kind of layout you want to use in your report; make a slick from the various Layouts. Access 97 displays a sample of the layout you have chosen in the graphic on the left. You can also pick whether you want to use Landscape or Portrait on this screen (see Figure 21.7).

Fig. 21.7
Use the various layouts to make your report interesting.

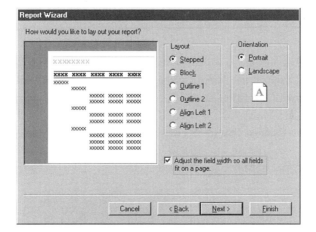

On this screen, you can choose if you want all your fields squeezed onto one page. If you don't want to fit all the fields on one page, Access 97 will print them on two pages. Once you choose your layout, click Next.

Adding style to the report

In this screen, you can choose various styles from a list. A report style adds a consistent look and presentation to your information appropriate for the audience of the report. For example, you may choose the Corporate style if you plan to distribute the report to colleagues at work; however, if this report is for personal use, perhaps the Casual style is the better choice.

Fig. 21.8
Choosing a nice style
makes your report
much more attractive.

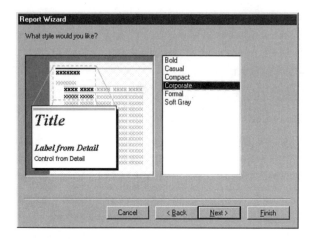

Click <u>N</u>ext to go to the last screen. Type Tape Listings by Ratings for the
title of the report. Access 97 uses the title you choose on this page in Print
Preview in the title bar and for the name of the report itself.

TIP **Before you click <u>F</u>inish, make sure you double check your choices**
by clicking the Previous button. Once you click <u>F</u>inish, you can only modify
the report manually.

Click <u>F</u>inish. Access 97 creates the report and opens it in Print Preview.
Close the report. You learn more about the Print Preview options later in this
chapter.

Just as with forms, you will want to rename the report to be something that is
more like the Access 97 object standard. Since the report is currently named
Tape Listing by Ratings, rename it to rptTapeListingByRatings. The reason
for calling it the original name was because that is also what is displayed on
the report itself, and it's easier to rename the report, rather than changing the
label and caption in the report.

There's one other wizard in the New Report dialog box worth mentioning
here. It's the Mailing Label Wizard, and I think you'll find it useful.

Creating mailing labels with the Mailing Label Wizard

The Mailing Label Wizard has long been one of my favorite wizards to use
since it is so easy, yet powerful. The Mailing Label Wizard supports the Avery

Label standard, although you can create your own customized label as well. If you go to your office supply store and pick the look and number across of the labels that you want, you can then find the Avery number in the list mentioned in the next section.

Using the Mailing Label Wizard, you can create labels for people who have borrowed your movies. To do this, while in the Reports tab in the database window:

1 Click the New button.

2 Pick the tblBorrowers for the record source; then highlight Label Wizard (see Figure 21.9). Click OK.

Fig. 21.9
Getting ready to create mailing labels.

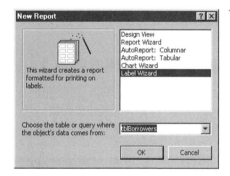

TIP Instead of always highlighting a command and clicking OK, simply double-click the command.

After you click OK, Access 97 starts the Label Wizard.

Selecting an Avery number to use

The first screen asks you the Avery number that you want to use for your mailing labels. Avery is the standard when it comes to creating mailing labels with printers.

Choose Avery number 5096 from the list, which prints three labels across the sheet (see Figure 21.10).

Make sure to select the correct Avery number to begin with. Once you click Finish in the wizard, you will have to start over again to change the label size. (This is true with all the wizards; you can't go back once you have finished.)

Click <u>N</u>ext to go to the next screen.

Fig. 21.10
You have a lot of
choices when creating
mailing labels.

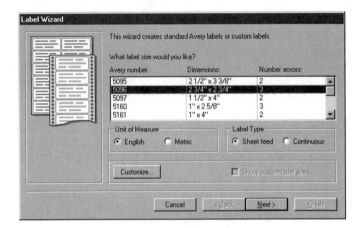

Picking fonts and sizes for your labels

The next screen lets you pick what kind of fonts and sizes you want for the
text in the label (see Figure 21.11). Click the down arrows next to all the font
options and view the results in the sample window.

Fig. 21.11
You can pick and
choose the look of the
text on your labels.

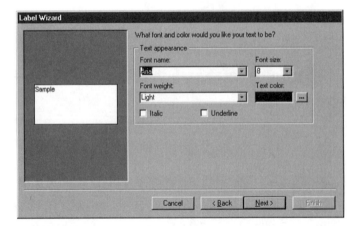

After picking the font options you want to use, click <u>N</u>ext to go to the next
page. This is the page that requires the most work.

Filling in the label information

Here, you can set up your label exactly the way you want it, by choosing
fields and typing in the necessary text.

Fill in the prototype label as shown in Figure 21.12. Either double-click the desired fields, or highlight them and click the select button (>).

Fig. 21.12

Set up your label here.

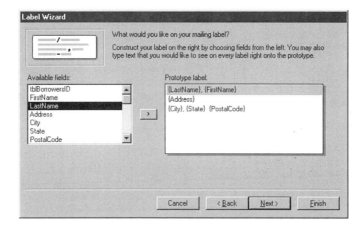

Here are the steps to create the label in Figure 21.12:

1 Double-click the LastName field. The text {LastName} appears in the prototype label.

2 Type a comma and then a space in the label after the {LastName}.

3 Double-click the FirstName field.

4 Press Enter. The highlighted line in the label will move to the line below the text you just entered.

5 Repeat the steps just given for the rest of the text and fields in the label.

Q&A *I made a mistake; how do I correct it?*

If you make a mistake, highlight the problem text, and then press the Delete key. To add text, position the cursor where you want the text added; then either move the field over or type in the text.

When you have filled out the label to match Figure 21.12, click Next to go to the next screen.

Deciding which fields you want to sort

This screen allows you to pick and choose which fields to use in sorting the mailing labels. Choose the LastName and FirstName fields. Highlight them and click the move right (>) button (see Figure 21.13). Click <u>F</u>inish to complete the labels.

Fig. 21.13
Selecting the fields to sort.

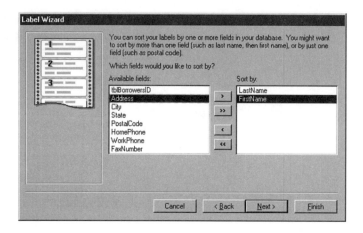

Access 97 then generates the labels shown in Figure 21.14.

Fig. 21.14
Here is the final product.

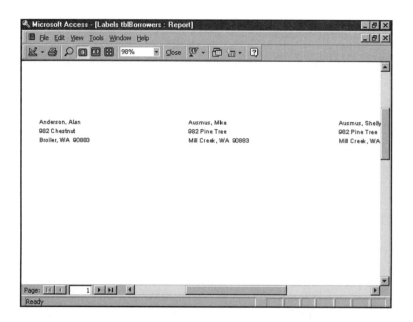

There you have it. It is extremely easy to create labels for different arrangements within the same table.

Printing reports

Access 97 follows Windows' standard in giving you the option of either previewing reports on the screen using the Print Preview feature, or directly printing to the printer. It also gives you a dialog box for printing the report to different printers. Before discussing the Page Setup and Print dialog boxes, let's look at previewing reports.

Using Print Preview

Previewing reports before you print them is always a good idea, because you waste a lot less paper and save a lot of time checking out the report on the screen first. This is especially true when you are making a lot of format changes. I recommend you preview all reports on the screen first, since you can then print them from the Print Preview screen.

Once in Print Preview, you can use several commands in the toolbar. Refer to Table 21.1.

Table 21.1 The Print Preview toolbar commands

Toolbar button	Command	Description
	Print	Lets you "quick print" your report from Print Preview.
	Zoom	Lets you toggle between Fit, which sizes the report to the window, or the size percentage as shown in Figure 21.15.
	One-Page Zoom	Toggles the zoom back to one page of the report.
	Two-Page Zoom	Toggles the zoom to view two pages. This is nice when you want to see how a report will look from the front and back. It is mainly good for formatting purposes, although you can also use the cursor and click into a specific area of the report.
	Multiple Pages Zoom	This button lets you choose to view one to six pages of a report on the screen at once, as well as how you want the pages laid out. Figure 21.16 displays six pages on the screen at a time along with a display option menu.

continues

Table 21.1 Continued

Toolbar button	Command	Description
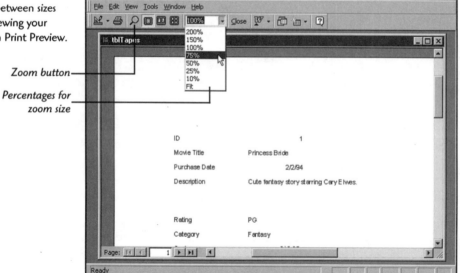	Office Links	Lets you link your report to the Word and Excel Office products. This feature will be discussed, along with other ways of using Office products with Access 97, in Chapter 25, "Using Access 97 with Other Office Products."
	Database Window	Takes you to the Database dialog box, from which you can select other objects in your databases. Once in the Database window, click the Preview button to return to Print Preview.
	New Object	If you decide to create a new object for your database, click the down arrow on this button and select the object from the drop-down list. If you change your mind, click Cancel in the New Object dialog box to return to the Print Preview screen.
	Office Assistant	If you've turned off the Office Assistant, click here to bring it back to the screen, ready to help you with a problem. Click the Close button on the Office Assistant to remove it.

Fig. 21.15
Toggle between sizes
when viewing your
report in Print Preview.

Zoom button

*Percentages for
zoom size*

> **TIP** **The Zoom button performs the same task that the Magnifying**
> Glass cursor performs (back in Figure 21.1), when you click with the left
> mouse button. It is more convenient to use the cursor since it will also focus
> on the specific area you point to.

Fig. 21.16
Access 97 can show up to six pages on the screen at a time.

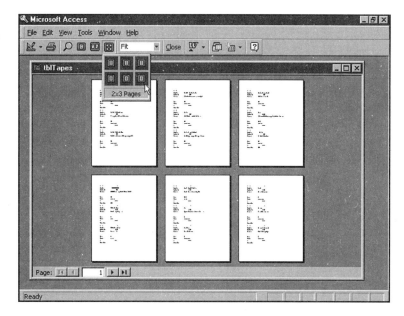

Understanding the options in the Print dialog box

While in Print Preview or Report Design view, if you click the Print toolbar button, the report prints directly to the printer. This is very convenient. However, if you have any questions about which printer the report will go to, or how it is set up, you need to choose File, Print. This opens the Print dialog box, as shown in Figure 21.17.

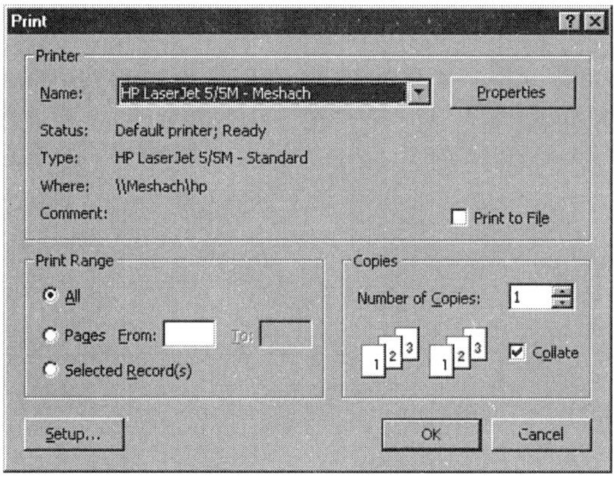

Fig. 21.17
The Print dialog box lets you specify which printer to use, as well as the pages of the report you want to print.

Here are the main options in this dialog box:

- **Printer**   Using the drop-down list of available printers installed for your computer, you can choose which printer you want to use. The default printer for your computer is initially displayed. You can modify specific options on your printer by clicking the Properties button. Since this will be different for each type of printer, we will not go into that in this book.

 TIP   **Unless a specific printer is necessary for a unique task, leave the** printer choice to the default printer. That way, whichever computer the database application runs on will use the default printer of that computer. Otherwise, the computer that the database application runs on will attempt to use the specific printer you designated, and will end up with an error if it is not available.

- **Print Range**   Allows you to specify the number of pages you want to print. This is specified by choosing either All or indicating the From and To pages. The last choice, Selected Record(s), allows you to print specific records you have highlighted in a Datasheet.

- **Copies**   Lets you choose how many copies of the report you want to print. You can also choose to Collate the copies, which either prints the copies in sets or prints them with all the same page number together.

One other useful button on this screen is the Setup button. When you press this button, Access 97 opens the Page Setup dialog box (see Figure 21.18), allowing you to change the page margins for the report.

To change the page margins, type the new value for the specific margin you want to change. The page margins are in one-inch increments, but you can also use decimals.

Fig. 21.18
Adjust the settings
and prepare your
page for printing.

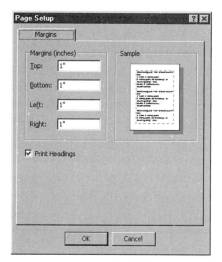

22

Enhancing Reports with Report Design Tools

● **In this chapter:**

- **Creating reports the smart way!**

- **Introducing the Report Design tools**

- **Changing controls and format in your reports**

- **Adding calculated fields and other enhancements**

As with Access 97 forms, you can create your own attractive reports and change their properties and controls . . . . ❯

n the last chapter, you learned how to create reports using AutoReport and Report Wizards. That is a good place to start when creating custom reports.

In this chapter, you will create an AutoReport and customize it. In doing so, you will see how to work with controls on reports. As I mentioned earlier, once you understand how to create forms, reports are a piece of cake. They both use controls to display information. The difference is that reports don't allow you to input information; they just display it.

Using AutoReport or Report Wizards

There may be times when you create a particular report that won't benefit from an AutoReport or Report Wizard. However, I am hard pressed to think of them, and for most reports you may as well take advantage of the tools available and save time and energy.

It is usually a good idea to create reports initially using the wizards. Then you have a standard style already in place.

An overview of Report Design tools

Access 97 gives us a number of tools for working with reports that look very much like the Forms Design tools. Before jumping into those tools, let's create a report using the AutoReport feature learned in the last chapter:

1 Click the Reports tab in the Database window.

2 Click New. Access 97 opens the New Report dialog box.

3 Pick tblTapes as the record source and AutoReport: Tabular (see Figure 22.1).

Fig. 22.1
Starting a new report
with help from
AutoReport.

4 Click OK. Access 97 runs the report in Print Preview.

5 Click the View button to change to the Design View window.

Before continuing with this report, let's look at some of the tools used in the
Report Design screen, shown in Figure 22.2. These are very similar to the
ones used in Form Design (see Chapter 18).

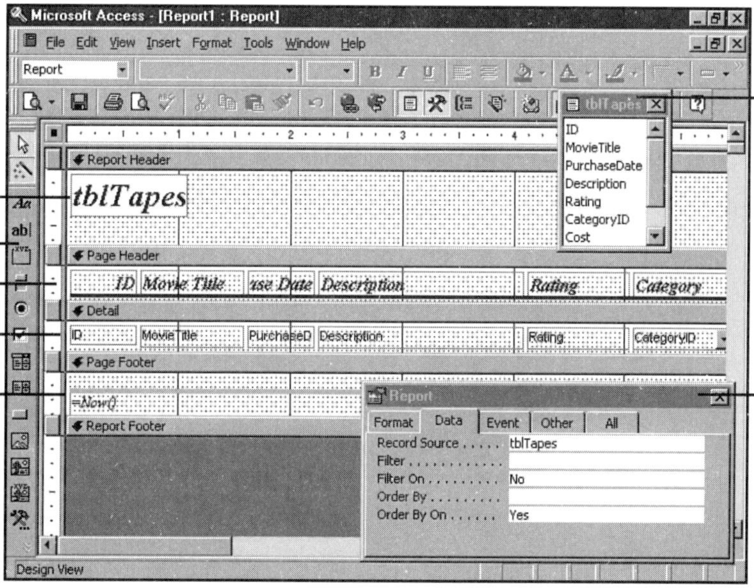

Fig. 22.2
Some of the same
tools are the same for
creating reports and
forms.

Field List

Report Header section
Toolbox
Page Header section
Detail section
Page Footer section

Property
Sheet

Here is a list of the various tools and sections that you see in Figure 22.2. I have noted any differences or similarities between Report Design and Form Design.

- **Toolbox**   Where you will find all the controls that you will use in the report. This is exactly the same Toolbox that you use when you design forms, although some of the controls don't make as much sense on a report as they do on a form. For instance, it doesn't do much good to put a Tab control on a report since you can't tab to another page.

- **Field List**   Contains all the fields in the underlying recordset for the report. This is also the same in Form Design, including the way you pull fields down to the sections.

- **Property Sheet**   Displays all the properties for the various objects used in the report, such as controls, sections, and the report itself. Again, the same tool as in forms. The properties, however, will be different, since they reflect those that are more useful on reports.

- **Report Header section**   Similar to forms, this is mainly useful on reports when you want to create a cover page for the report.

- **Page Header section**   The same as in forms but more useful in a report, since you will place column headings in it. You will also place the report title here if you want it repeated on each page of the report.

- **Page Footer section**   Useful for page numbers; some people like to put page summary numbers at the bottom of each page.

- **Detail Section**   The same as in forms; use for displaying the individual records of the recordset used for the report.

Enhancing the report

This section will show you how to change and improve your reports.

Here are the items I want to clean up; we will be walking through them step by step in the next sections.

- Move the label in the Report Header to the Page Header section, and create a better title.

- Change the Caption property of the report. Remember that the Caption property appears in Print Preview, so you don't want it to say tblTapes.

- Delete any fields you don't want to include in the report.

- Resize any fields that need it.

- Add a graphic to spruce up the report.

Let's get busy.

Resizing sections and moving controls

Sometimes, you have a report that doesn't include a title page, but you want the title of the report included on each page. To do this, you need to move the title from the Report Header section to the Page Header section. In order to move the title label down to the Page Header section, you first need to increase the height of the Page Header section. Next, you have to move the fields that are in the Page Header section out of the way.

Sizing the Page Header section

1 Place the cursor at the bottom of the Page Header section until you see the bar with the up and down arrows.

2 Press the left mouse button, and holding it, slide it down until the section is about two and a half times its original size (see Figure 22.3).

Fig. 22.3
Sizing the Page Header section.

Page Header section

Section Sizing cursor

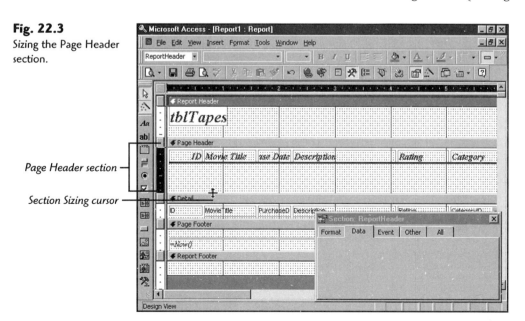

Now you need to move the controls in the Page Header section down to make room for the title label.

Highlighting and moving multiple controls

Here is a new method for highlighting controls that works on forms as well as reports.

1 Click the left ruler, to the left of the controls in the Page Header section.

2 Holding the left mouse button down, slide the cursor down until the ruler highlights all the controls (see Figure 22.4).

Fig. 22.4
Highlighting controls using the ruler.

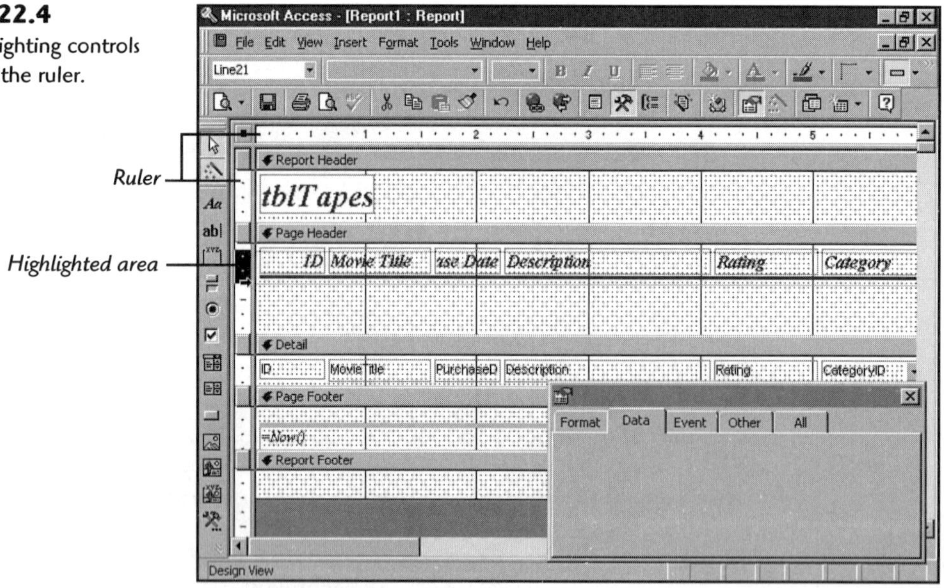

Ruler

Highlighted area

3 Release the mouse. You should see all the controls highlighted in the section. If not, try again.

4 Position the cursor over any of the controls until you see the Open Hand cursor, then drag the controls down to the bottom of the section (see Figure 22.5). You will also see that the highlight along the ruler follows the controls.

Fig. 22.5
Move the controls to make room for the Title.

Highlighted area

Open Hand cursor

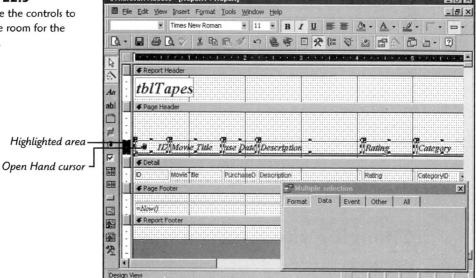

Moving the Title Label and removing the Report Header section

The next task is to move the Title Label from the Report Header down to the Page Header. Click the Label control; then drag and drop it into the Page Header section. Click the Label again, and change the text to read: **Tapes Listing**.

Now choose View, Report Header/Footer from the menu. The Report Header and Footer disappear, and the report looks like Figure 22.6.

Fig. 22.6
No more Report
Header and Footer.

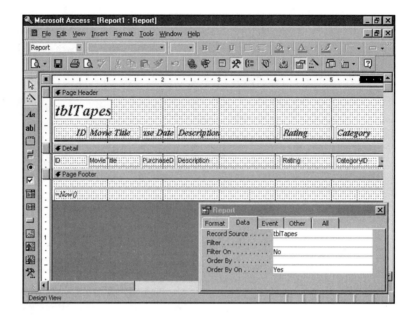

Changing the Caption property of the report

Since you don't want the caption of the report to say tblTapes, open the Property Sheet. Click the Format tab and change the Caption property so that it says the same thing as the title label: **Tapes Listing** (see Figure 22.7).

Fig. 22.7
Changing the report's
caption.

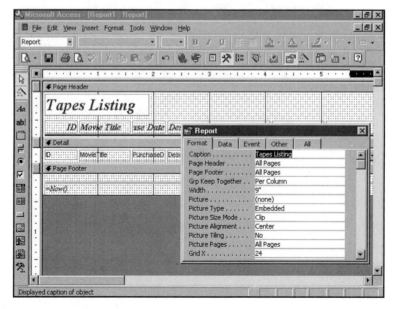

The title changes in the Page Header of the report. The next time you open the report in Print Preview, the title will reflect the new caption.

Removing a column from the report

Notice that Access 97 includes the ID field on the report. This is kind of useless since it doesn't mean anything to you when you look at it. Having a couple of unnecessary fields is common when you use the AutoReport method to start your report.

 TIP You can take care of the problem of unwanted fields by using the Report Wizard instead of the AutoReport method. That way, you can just tell Access 97 not to include any fields that you don't want.

When you delete a column from a report, you are actually going to be deleting two separate controls: the text box and its label. Click the ID Text Box. While holding the Shift key down, click the Label above that says ID.With both controls highlighted, press Delete. Both controls disappear.

 Q&A *Oops, what if I deleted the wrong control?*

Just as with most other editing commands, you can choose Undo Delete from the Edit menu to bring the control back.

Aligning controls on a report

You can use the Align feature on a report just as you can on a form. In fact, aligning columns on reports is one thing you will spend a lot of time doing.

For an example of this, move the label that says Movie Title all the way to the left of the report, where the ID label was. Then holding the Shift key down, click the Movie Title text box. Now choose Align from the Format menu, and pick Left from the Align submenu (see Figure 22.8). Access 97 then aligns the Movie Title column.

Fig. 22.8
You can Align controls on the report as easy as on a form.

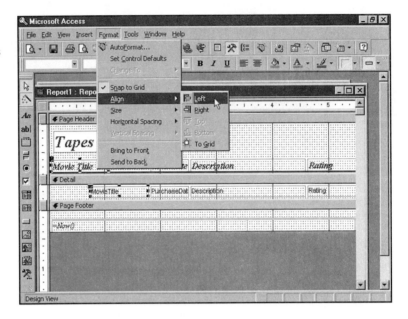

Sizing a control on a report

Now go ahead and size the Movie Title text box a little wider by highlighting it, grabbing the right sizing handle, and pulling to the right. Don't go all the way to the PurchaseDate, however, since you will want to increase that label as well.

Play with the rest of the columns to get them lined up and sized the way you want them. When you finish tweaking the report, click the Print Preview button, and view the report (see Figure 22.9).

Q&A ***When I clicked the Print Preview button, the drop-down list showed another button called Layout Preview. What is that?***

Layout Preview is useful for situations where you have a really large report that takes a while to run, but you want to see what it will look like. With Layout Preview, you will get the first couple of pages for the report, although none of the data is necessarily going to be accurate.

Close and save the report as rptMyFirstReport.

Fig. 22.9

Here is the cleaned up report, which is easier to read than the original.

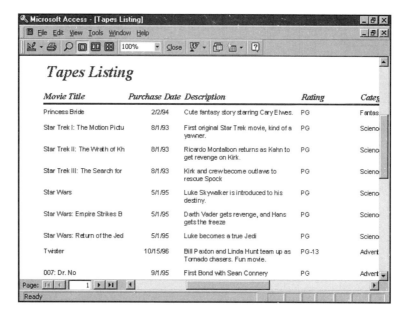

I now want you to make a copy of the report you just created. In the Database window:

1 Highlight the report.

2 Choose Edit, Copy from the menu. This copies the report to the Clipboard.

3 Choose Edit, Paste from the menu. This opens a dialog box asking you to name the new report.

4 Type "rptTapeListingByCategories" for the new report and click OK. You now have a new report to use in the next section.

Additional report features that add class

There are some other features in reports that can add a lot of class to your reports.

Adding groups and sorting

Access 97 gives you the ability to group information on your reports. In doing so, you can create Headers and Footers for each group to display summary information. We're going to create a group for Categories in the copy of the report you just made.

1 Open the rptTapeListingByCategories report in Design view.

2 Click the Sorting and Grouping button. Access 97 opens the Sorting and Grouping dialog box.

3 In the first column of the dialog box, type "CategoryID." (Because of the Autofill feature, Access 97 actually fills in the field when you type C.) Then press Enter. You will notice immediately that the Group Properties appears in the lower pane, and Ascending appears in the Sort Order.

4 Set the Group Header property to Yes (see Figure 22.10). A new Group Header section (called CategoryID Header) appears on the report.

Fig. 22.10
Here is how you can specify groupings and sort orders.

TIP **When you have multiple lines in your header or footer and want** to make sure that they don't get cut off or split at the bottom of a page, set the grouping property, Keep Together, to Yes.

5 Click the Group Footer section and choose Yes. Close the dialog box.

You now have a blank section above (CategoryID Header) and below (Page Footer) the Detail section. Move the Category label and text box into the CategoryID Group Header. Go ahead and set the font size of the CategoryID text box to 12 point (see Figure 22.11).

Fig. 22.11
The Group Header for
CategoryID is now
complete.

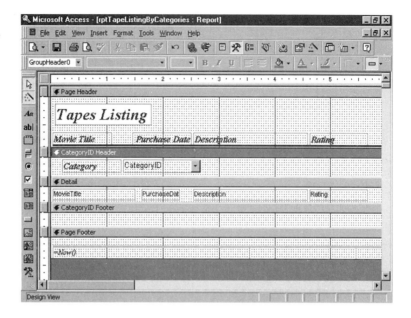

When you switch to Print Preview, you will notice a gap between the groups. This is the Group Footer section for CategoryID. This is a good place for creating calculated fields on reports using some useful function that Access 97 provides.

Creating calculated fields on reports

You have seen how to create calculated fields in queries and forms. Now it's time to learn how to use them in reports. Remember that a calculated field is a field that is made up of Access 97 functions as well as fields, and not just bound to one field. To add a calculated field, perform the following steps:

1 Place a Text Box control in the CategoryID Footer section.

2 Double-click the label and set the Label caption to say: **Number of Tapes**.

3 For the Control Source property of the Text Box, double-click the text box and type in: **=Count(*)** for the control source.

Now your report looks like Figure 22.12 in Design view and Figure 22.13 in Print Preview.

Fig. 22.12
Notice how the
Control Source
property is in this
Text Box.

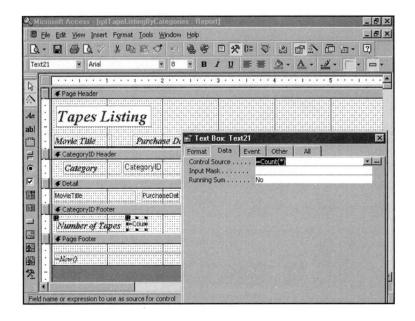

Fig. 22.13
Groups can tell you a
lot if you include the
right information.

There are other functions you can use besides Count ( ). You can use Sum(fieldname), (Sum the values), and Avg(fieldname) that gives the average. For more discussion on calculated fields, review Chapter 13, "Using Calculated Fields in Your Query."

 TIP **You may have noticed in Figure 22.13 that some of the movie** titles were chopped off. You can change this so the entire title appears without taking up a lot of space. There is a property on Text Box Property sheet controls called Can Grow. If you set this to True, the Text Box will "grow" another line if it has to.

Adding a page number or Date/Time to the report

To add a page number to the report:

1 In Design view, choose Insert, Page Numbers from the menu.

2 Access 97 displays the Page Numbers dialog box (see Figure 22.14) from which you can choose the type and location of the page number. Set the following:

- Format   Page N of M

- Position   Bottom of Page (Footer)

- Alignment   Right

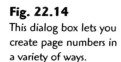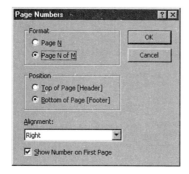

Fig. 22.14
This dialog box lets you create page numbers in a variety of ways.

3 Then click OK. Access 97 places a text box in the bottom right corner of the report in the Report Footer.

TIP **To delete the page number added by AutoReport (bottom-right corner),** select it and press the Delete key.

You can do the same thing with date and time by choosing Date and Time from the Insert menu.

Changing your style

Say your boss comes along and doesn't like the style of your report. Don't fear. By choosing Format, AutoFormat from the menu, Access 97 lets you change the style of your current report and will continue to use the new style (see Figure 22.15).

Fig. 22.15
Wouldn't it be nice if we could change our style this easily?

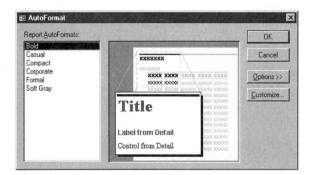

Part VII: Rounding Out Your Database

23

Fine-Tuning Your Database Application

● **In this chapter:**

- Suggestions for creating a good database application

- Performance tips

- Creating a switchboard to tie your objects together

- Having Access 97 use your switchboard when opening the database

You have had glimpses of how to use all the major objects in Access 97. Now we will tie them all together . . . .

R ight now, you know enough about Access 97 to get it to perform quite a few tasks for you. You can use Tables, Queries,
Forms, and Reports. At this point, you still have to go through the Database
window to perform all these tasks.

In this chapter, I discuss items that span quite a few areas of Access 97. What
all of them have in common is the fact that they will help you to fine-tune
your database.

What makes a good database?

Right now, you're thinking, "Why didn't Scott tell me this in the beginning of
the book?" Frankly speaking, you weren't ready for it.

I am going to give you a list of ideas, "watch outs," and "gotchas" filled with
terminology from throughout the book. If I'd thrown this at you in the
beginning, you would have been overwhelmed and probably stressed out.
I'm sure I would have been.

Check your relationships

Remember in Chapter 7 when I discussed using One-to-Many relationships?
Use them. Try to make your data conform correctly so you can use them;
they will make your life easier in the long run.

There is a tool called the Table Analyzer Wizard that is an advanced tool,
located on the Tools, Analyze submenu. From this submenu, choose Table.
The Table Analyzer Wizard (see Figure 23.1) takes your tables and checks to
see if they are Normalized, or, set up correctly for Relations. Use the Table
Analyzer Wizard...

Use the Table Analyzer Wizard whenever you create a new table to make
sure you are not creating a table structure that will cause you problems.

Fig. 23.1
Use the Table Analyzer
Wizard to look at the
tables you create to
make sure you have set
them correctly.

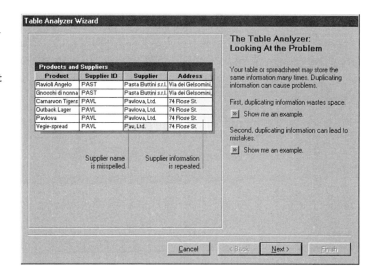

<h2>Plain English, please!</h2>

A database is **Normalized** when it follows a set of established rules used for relational databases. When databases are not normalized, you can have tables that include redundant (repeated) information (shown in Figure 23.1) and information that just comes out to be garbage. Refer to the misspelled names in Figure 23.1.

Referential Integrity helps to normalize a database by not accepting data when a related record does not exist.

The nice thing about this wizard is that it has examples every step of the way.

Use indexes to test performance

You can use indexes to make your queries perform faster. Use them generously. By making the queries faster, the forms and reports perform better. To read more on indexes, see Chapter 9, "A Closer Look at Field Properties."

You may think you have fine performance when you first begin; but remember, you will add data, and the tables will get larger. Choose either Cancel or Finish to close the Table Analyzer Wizard.

There is another wizard you use to see how your database is set up for performance. It is aptly called the Performance Analyzer Wizard (the command is <u>P</u>erformance), from the command <u>T</u>ools, Analy<u>z</u>e.

This wizard gives you suggestions for most of the different objects in Access 97 including Tables, Queries, Forms, and Reports. Figure 23.2 shows you the opening screen that allows you to choose what you want to analyze, with the All (objects) tab selected.

Fig. 23.2
The Performance Analyzer Wizard lets you choose which objects to analyze.

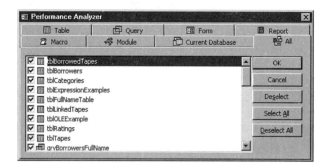

After choosing the objects you want to analyze, click OK. Access 97 analyzes all the objects you have chosen and displays a screen with Recommendations, Suggestions, and Ideas (see Figure 23.3).

Fig. 23.3
Using the Performance Analyzer can save a lot of time when trying to optimize your database.

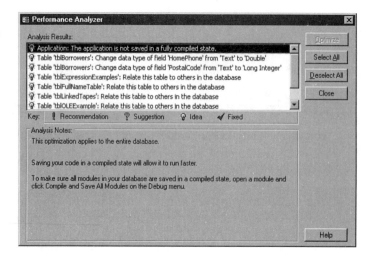

If you see that Access 97 can automatically optimize an object, highlight the line and click Optimize. Access 97 makes the change if possible.

Fields propagation

Don't forget to fill in all the field properties that you want propagated to forms and reports. Field propagation means that some of the properties you set on the fields, at the table level, will establish the initial properties of controls that are bound to those fields, when used on forms and reports. Once you create the form or report, you have to change the property setting manually in each form and report.

Consistency in your forms and reports

If you create an application that others will use, make sure you use the same style for the various forms and reports. There is nothing more frustrating for a user than having to figure out how to move around the different forms when they are all set up differently.

Another good thing to include in your database application, for both consistency and ease of use, is the use of switchboards.

Tying your application together with switchboards

Wouldn't it be nice to group and open the various objects in a nice logical manner, instead of having to jump around in the Database window? There is a way to do it easily and make it very manageable.

Switchboards are as important to Access 97 as the main menu used to be to DOS programs. You can see an example of the main switchboard in Northwind in Figure 23.4.

You may be thinking that you don't know how to program something like that. The nice thing is you don't have to. Access 97 has a wizard called the Switchboard Manager to help you.

Fig. 23.4
This switchboard, used
in Northwind, is
attractive.

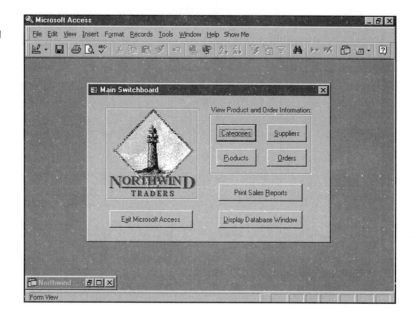

Starting the Switchboard Manager

To call up the Switchboard Manager:

1 In the main database window, choose the Tools, Add-Ins, Switchboard Manager.

2 If this is the first time you have run the Switchboard Manager in the database, Access 97 displays a message telling you it can't find a switchboard and will ask you if you want to create one (see Figure 23.5).

Fig. 23.5
The first time you
create a switchboard in
the current database,
you see this message.

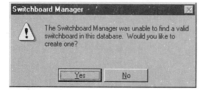

3 Click Yes. The Switchboard Manager screen appears, which displays a switchboard called Main Switchboard (the default) as shown in Figure 23.6.

Fig. 23.6
Here is the Switch-
board Manager main
screen.

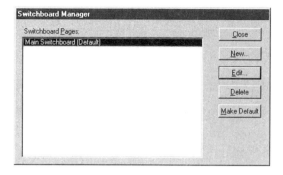

4 Click Edit to edit the Main Switchboard.

Adding commands to the Main Switchboard

Once you are in the Edit Switchboard Page, you are ready to add commands
to the switchboard. To do this, click New. You now see the Edit Switchboard
Item dialog box, as in Figure 23.7.

Fig. 23.7
Here is the Edit
Switchboard Item
dialog box.

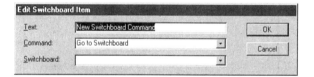

This dialog box has two, possibly three fields displayed. The first field is
Text, where you will type in the description of the switchboard command.

The next field, Command, has eight possible settings:

- **Go to Switchboard**   Opens another switchboard, the one specified in
  Switchboard text box in the Edit Switchboard Item dialog box.

- **Open Form in Add Mode**   Opens a form in Data Entry mode, specified in Form.

- **Open Form in Edit Mode**   Opens a form in add, edit, and delete
  mode that is specified in Form.

- **Open Report**   Opens a report specified in Report.

- **Design Application** Opens the switchboard manager to edit the switchboards. This command should be used only on an administrative switchboard.

- **Exit Application** Leaves the application.

- **Run Macro** Runs a macro specified in Macro.

- **Run Code** Runs a Visual Basic for Applications routine specified in Function Name.

 Q&A ***How come I don't see the fields such as Report and Form you mention?***

These fields will all appear in the third field. The third field changes based on the setting of Command.

For now:

1 Type Tapes Information Form in the Text field.

2 Set the Command field to Open Form in Edit Mode. The Form field appears below the Command field.

3 Set the Form field to frmTapesInformation (see Figure 23.8).

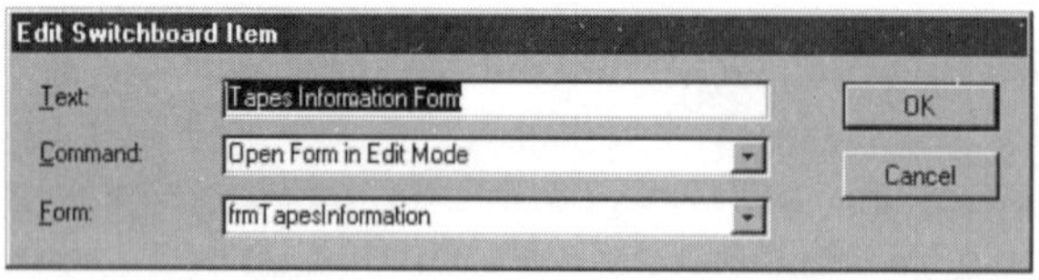

Fig. 23.8
Adding a switchboard command to open the frmTapesInformation form.

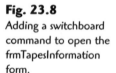

4 Click OK.

Access 97 brings you back to the Edit Switchboard Page screen, and you see Tapes Information as the only entry in the Item on the Switchboard list. Let's add the second command that will open the report we created in Chapter 22:

1 Click New.

2 Type "Print Tape Listing by Categories Report" in the Text field.

3 Set the Command field to Open Report. The Report field appears below the Command field.

4 Set the Report field to rptTapeListingsByCategories. Your settings will now look like Figure 23.9.

Fig. 23.9
Adding the command to open the frmBorrowers form.

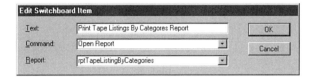

5 Click OK to accept the settings.

Lastly, we need to add a command that lets you exit the application:

1 Click New again.

2 Type Exit Application in the Text field.

3 Set the Command field to Exit Application.

4 Click OK. Click Close twice to close the Switchboard Manager.

Checking the results

From the database window in the Forms tab, double-click the Switchboard form. You see the beginning of a main switchboard (see Figure 23.10).

Fig. 23.10
The main switchboard you just created.

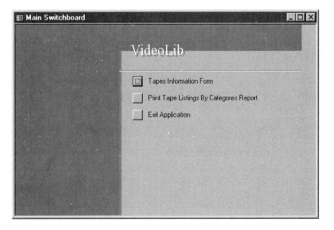

Go ahead and test each button to make sure it brings up the information you expect.

Setting Startup properties to run your switchboard

Now that you have created a nice switchboard to open the various objects in your database, it would be nice to have the switchboard start up when you open the database.

To do this, in the database window choose <u>T</u>ools, Start<u>u</u>p. You see the Startup dialog box, which lets you set some properties for starting your database (see Figure 23.11).

Fig. 23.11
These properties let you customize how your application will start.

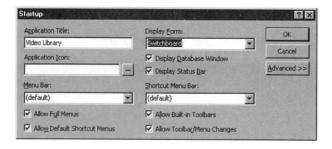

The properties of interest are:

- **Application Title**   Places the name of your application on the title bar. Type: **Video Library**.

- **Display Form**   Open immediately when the database opens. Set this to Switchboard.

You can set the other properties as you want.

 TIP **If you don't want the Database window to open when you start** the database, remove the check for the Display <u>D</u>atabase Window property. You can always use F11 to display the Database window later.

24

Importing, Exporting, and Linking Information

● In this chapter:

● Working with other file types

● The difference between linking and importing data

● What is exporting?

● Creating reports

When you have non-Access 97 applications out there working away, Access 97 can read the data right where it sits . . . . . ➤

A s powerful as Access 97 is, it's still a fairly new product in the world of databases. That means that there is a good chance some of the information you need is already stored in another file format.

Access 97 gives you several ways to read the information from other file formats and to write information to those formats.

How to find out the file formats that Access 97 installed

Just as Access 97 stores its information into an *.mdb file format, other database products store their information into their own formats. Access 97 can read some of these formats. Which file formats you can use depends on which drivers you included when you ran the Office setup.

To see Access 97's drivers:

1 Go to the Windows Control Panel and choose Add/Remove Programs. The Add/Remove Programs Properties dialog box appears.

2 Highlight Microsoft Office 97, Professional Edition (see Figure 24.1).

Fig. 24.1
This dialog box allows you to add or remove options to your applications after the initial setup.

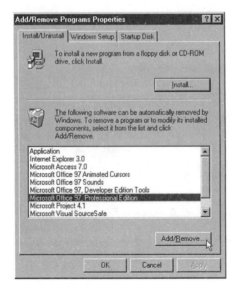

3 Click the Add/Remove button. At this point, you need to insert your Microsoft Office CD, unless you installed off the network.

4 At the main Setup dialog box, choose Add/Remove. You now see the Maintenance screen that has all the Office products displayed in an Options list (see Figure 24.2).

Fig. 24.2
Add or Remove Office options.

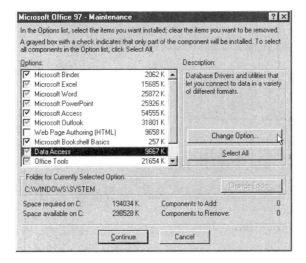

5 Highlight Data Access; then click the Change Option button. You are then taken to the Data Access screen.

6 Highlight Database Drivers, and then click the Change Option button. The Database Drivers screen appears. This is where you can see the available database drivers (see Figure 24.3).

TIP **You can add or remove database drivers simply by clicking in the** check box beside each driver's descriptions. I recommend clicking Select All if all the drivers aren't already chosen. That way, you're ready for all the file formats supported by Access 97.

Fig. 24.3
Determine which types of files Access 97 can use.

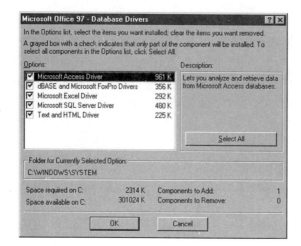

Working with other file formats

Access 97 has three ways to deal with data from other file formats:

- **Exporting**—When you export data, you take the data in the Access 97 database and make a copy of that data into another file. Access 97 can export table and query data from Access 97 to other file formats and other objects such as forms, reports, macros, and modules to other Access 97 databases. Remember, when you export your data, you make a copy of it. Access 97 will not see changes to that data. Once again, Access 97 will not export Access 97 objects other than tables to other file formats, including database formats.

- **Importing**—This allows you to make a copy of other data, either in Access 97 or the other file formats, and to bring that data into your Access 97 database. The table that Access 97 creates or adds to is a copy, separate from the original, just as an exported file is.

- **Linking**—You can create a link to the original data, in its original format. This means that when you add and change information in the linked table, the original application accesses those changes. The original indexes also update. You will see a name entered in your list of tables in the database window, but it will have an arrow pointing to a logo representing the type of file. For example, Excel spreadsheets have the arrow pointing to the Excel logo. Access 97 tables merely have an arrow pointing to the table symbol.

Q&A ***When do you use linking versus importing?***

When you need to change the information but you don't want to affect the original information, then import. When you have a system that has been out there for a while (called legacy systems), and you just want to plug into the information and update it, then link.

Exporting information

I am going to show you how to first export the tblTapes table to an Excel spreadsheet, and then how to export the same table to an Access 97 database.

Starting to export

Wherever you are exporting to, start the exporting by clicking the Tables tab in the Database window; then highlight the tblTapes table. Choose File, Save As/Export. Click OK in the Save As dialog box and accept the To An External File or Database default (exporting the file out of the database).

Choosing the name and type of file to export to

You should now be in the Save In dialog box, where the title is currently Save Table 'tblTapes' In.

For the Save as type property, choose Microsoft Excel 97. Access 97 automatically names the file tblTapes.xls (see Figure 24.4).

Click Export. Access 97 exports the data. To see the data, you have to start up the application that reads that type of data, in this case Microsoft Excel (see Figure 24.5).

TIP **If you are exporting data to Word or Excel, it is faster to use the** Office Links feature found in the Database window. This is covered in the next chapter.

Fig. 24.4
Exporting to an Excel
spreadsheet.

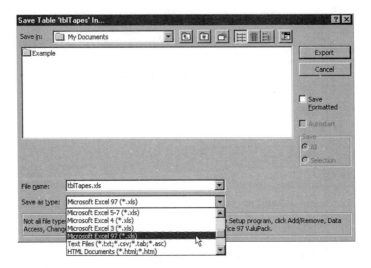

Fig. 24.5
Viewing the exported
data in Excel.

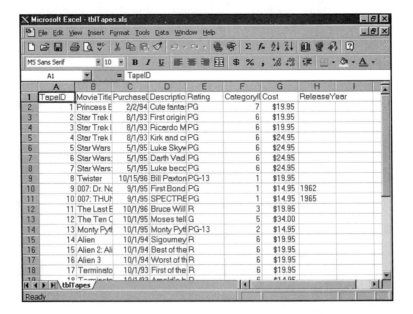

Exporting the table to another Access 97 database

Exporting an object into another Access 97 database isn't any tougher than
exporting into a different format. You begin the export the same way you did

in the section titled "Getting the exporting started." When you get to the Save In dialog box, the title is: Save Table 'tblTapes' In…

In this dialog box, leave the default for the Save as type property, which is Microsoft Access 97. Then locate the database you want to export the table to, in this example, Northwind.mdb (see Figure 24.6).

Fig. 24.6
Selecting
Northwind.mdb to
export the tblTapes
table into.

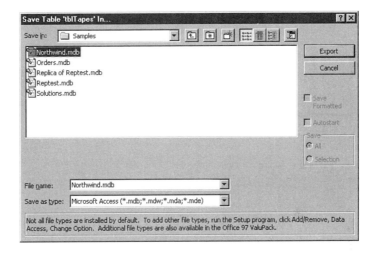

When you click Export, you go to the Export dialog box. This asks you what you want to name the table in the new database. With tables, you also get the choice of exporting both the structure of the table and the data, or just the structure.

Click OK. Access 97 exports the table to the new database.

Q&A ***What happens if the file/table already exists?***

If the object already exists in the database you are exporting to, Access 97 tells you and lets you decide to overwrite the table or cancel the export.

Importing information from other formats

As I said, importing information is much easier when you use the wizards that walk you through step-by-step. We're going to import the spreadsheet you exported earlier in the chapter.

1 In the main database window, choose File, Get External Data. Access 97 gives you the choice of Import or Link Tables.

2 Choose Import. Access 97 then presents the Import dialog box.

3 For the File of type property, choose Microsoft Excel(*.xls). Locate the tblTapes.xls file created earlier (see Figure 24.7).

4 Click Import. The first screen of the Import Spreadsheet Wizard appears (see Figure 24.8).

Fig. 24.7
Importing the tblTapes.xls file.

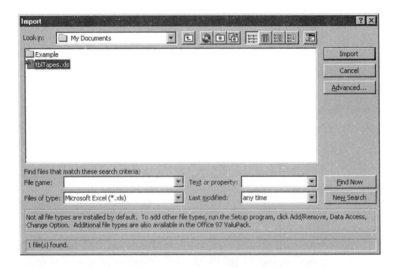

Fig. 24.8
Choose a worksheet from the list.

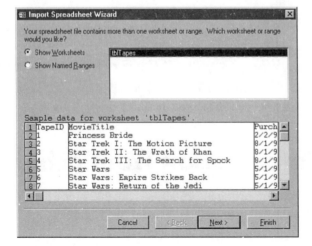

5 Since there is only one worksheet in tblTapes.xls, click Next.

6 There are times when the first row of the imported file contains the headings for the fields. If this is the case, you need to click in the check box on this screen. When you do, the first row changes to column headings (see Figure 24.9). Click Next to go to the next screen.

Fig. 24.9
Here, the first row
contains field headings.

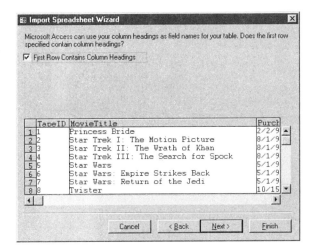

7 This next screen gives you the option to create a new table to put the data in, or adding it to existing data. If you specify a new table, Access 97 asks you to supply a table name at a later screen. For now, click Next.

8 The next screen allows you to specify information about each of the fields being imported into the database. This is useful if the first row doesn't contain field names, because you can specify them here (see Figure 24.10). You can also specifiy the omission of one or more fields, if you do not want to include them in the import. Click Next to go to the next screen.

TIP **In Figure 24.10, you may notice that the ID field has the Indexed** property set to Yes (Duplicates OK). Normally, this would raise a red flag, since this index should be unique (No Duplicates). We actually take care of this in the next section by using the wizard. To review indexes, see Chapter 9, "A Closer Look at Field Properties."

Fig. 24.10
Here you can work
with each field.

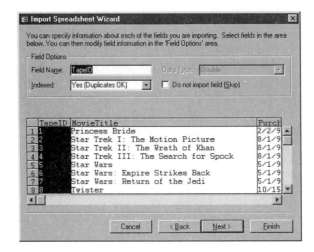

9 The next screen of the Import Spreadsheet Wizard lets you choose a
field for Access 97 to use as the Primary Key field. You can also let
Access 97 create one for you. Select the Choose my own Primary Key
option; Access 97 will then default to the ID field (see Figure 24.11),
which is what you want. Click Next.

Fig. 24.11
Pick a field for the
Primary Key.

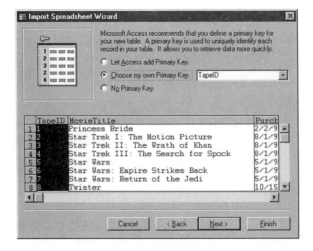

10 This is the screen that asks you to name the table. Type "tblNewTapes"
(see Figure 24.12), and then click Finish.

Fig. 24.12
Name your table on
this screen.

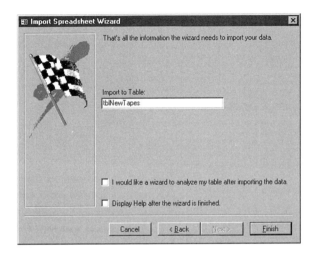

Be sure to name your table something unique; otherwise, Access 97 asks
if you want to overwrite the table that already exists under that title.

Importing an Access 97 object from one Access database to another

When it comes to importing objects between two Access 97 databases, the
process is very streamlined.

Choose File, Get External Data. From this submenu, choose Import. Access
97 then presents the Import dialog box. For the File of type property, leave
Access 97's default. Then locate the Northwind.mdb. Once you locate it,
choose Import.

Access 97 shows you the custom Import Objects dialog box used for Access
97 objects. From here, you can pick and choose objects by using a container
that is similar to the Database window you have been using. Click the
appropriate tab and choose your objects from the Northwind database (see
Figure 24.13).

When you finish choosing objects, click OK. Access 97 then pulls them into
your database.

Fig. 24.13
Pick any of the objects
from the Northwind
database.

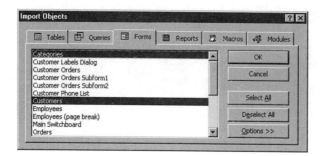

TIP   **This is a great way to "borrow" ideas from the sample database.**
Once you import them, you can modify them to suit your needs.

Linking tables

The steps for linking tables are not much different from importing. In Access
97, you can link tables to spreadsheets and text files, which is very handy.

To link to the tblTapes.xls spreadsheet:

1 Choose File, Get External Data. This time, pick Link Tables. The Link
dialog box appears, which is identical to the other Export and Import
dialog boxes. Locate the tblTapes.xls.

2 On the first screen of the wizard, click Next, since there is only one
worksheet.

3 Click the First Row Contains Field Names option, and then click Next.

4 The last screen is where you name this link tblLinkedTapes, so you
don't overwrite the original tblTapes table. Click Finish.

Now when you look at the Database window, you see a table with an arrow
pointing to the Excel logo (see Figure 24.14).

Fig. 24.14
You can use linked tables just like native Access 97 tables.

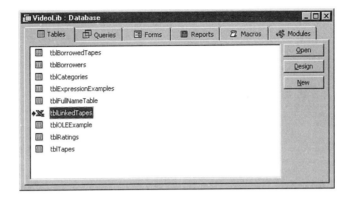

Issues with linking

There are some issues that you need to consider when you link tables:

- You can't modify the original table structure through the link. You can do so only by opening the table (or file) in the original application and modifying the structure there.

- You can use the linked table in queries, forms, and reports as if it were a table in the current database.

- When tables are linked to formats such as Fox Pro or dBASE, you need to specify the index files as well.

- Performance to a format such as dBASE is slower than an Access 97 table link.

25

Using Access 97 with Other Office Products

● **In this chapter:**

- **Sending reports and tables to Word and Excel**

- **Starting other Office applications from Access 97**

- **Attaching Access 97 objects to e-mail**

- **Storing Office documents in Access 97 tables**

- **Merging information with Word using Mail Merge**

You are not restricted to using only Access 97 when working with your data. You can also take advantage of the other Office applications! . . . . ➤

You have learned quite a bit about how to squeeze power out of Access 97, but there are some things that Access 97 can't do as well as other products. For example, you just can't beat Excel for number crunching or Exchange for mailing information. So why not use these other tools with Access 97 to enhance your application all that much more?

You can use other Office applications throughout Access 97's forms, reports, and even the Database window. Take a look at a couple of ways to use other Office applications from within the main Window database.

Looking at the Office Links feature

Besides exporting and importing various file formats, Access 97 allows you to use Access 97 data with features from other Office products.

 When you have a table or query highlighted, one of the features on the toolbar is the Office Links drop-down list. When you click this drop-down list, you have the following choices:

- **Merge It with MS Word**   This command takes the record source you highlight and merges it with a Mail Merge document in Word. The next section walks you through this feature.

- **Publish It with MS Word**   Creates a Rich Text Format file (a file standard that keeps all the fonts and settings used by word processing applications) for Word; then opens it. To see an example of this, highlight the tblTapes table, and choose Publish It with MS Word. Access 97 creates the file and opens Word (see Figure 25.1).

- **Analyze It with MS Excel**   Creates a spreadsheet that opens in Microsoft Excel. To see an example of this, switch back to Access 97 and, leaving tblTapes highlighted, choose Analyze It with MS Excel. Access 97 creates a spreadsheet file and opens Excel with the file displayed.

Fig. 25.1
Using Word with
Access 97 is as simple
as clicking a button.

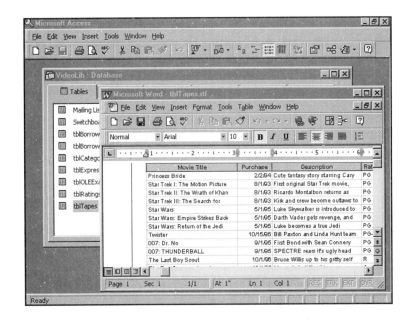

Q&A ***The Office Link to Word seems to work fine, but Excel gives me an error. What do I do?***

When working in other applications with Access 97, you have to deal with their problems as well as Access 97's problems. The best solution, when you have a problem between two applications talking to each other, is to reinstall Office.

You can also use the Office Links feature in Print Preview.

Using Mail Merge between Access 97 and Word

When you learn to use the Office Link feature of <u>M</u>erge It with MS Word, you actually learn to use the Mail Merge feature of Word. There is very little Access 97 involved.

Word uses two documents in Mail Merge. The first is your data document, which Access 97 creates for you. The second is a Mail Merge document that you create.

To start, highlight the tblBorrowers table, click the Office Links button, and then choose the <u>M</u>erge It with MS Word command. Access 97 starts the Microsoft Word Mail Merge Wizard.

On the first screen, you have two choices:

- <u>L</u>ink your data to an existing Microsoft Word document, which basically means you have already created a Mail Merge document before and just need to link to it. (If this is the case, why are you reading this?)

- <u>C</u>reate a new document and then link to it. You need to create a new Word document in which you will merge the Access 97 data.

Click the last option and click OK.

Word opens and creates a blank document in Word's Mail Merge mode. You will be left with the blank screen; it's up to you to create the Mail Merge document.

 TIP For help on using Word 97, check out *Using Microsoft Word 97.*

Creating the Mail Merge document

Insert Merge Field ▾ In the toolbar just above the document, you can see a drop-down list that says <u>I</u>nsert Merge Field. If you click this drop-down list, Word lists the fields from the table or query you told it to use (see Figure 25.2).

You can then click the fields you want to include, and Word inserts them into the document surrounded by double curly braces {{ }}.

When you want to add text, simply type it in. Try it, creating the document as seen in Figure 25.3, which combines fields and text.

Fig. 25.2
Use fields from the
Access 97 table or
query.

*Fields from
Access 97*

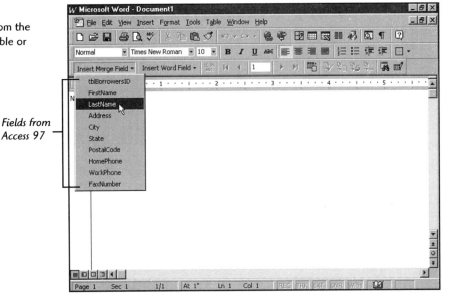

Fig. 25.3
It's up to you to create
the merge document.

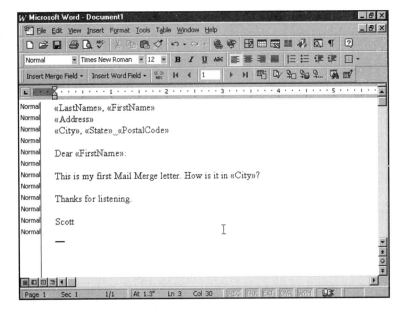

Creating a merged document

Once you enter the text and fields that you want, create the merged document. To perform this task, click the Merge to a New Document button on the Mail Merge toolbar. Without further ado, Word creates the merged document (see Figure 25.4).

Fig. 25.4
The finished document of the mail merge.

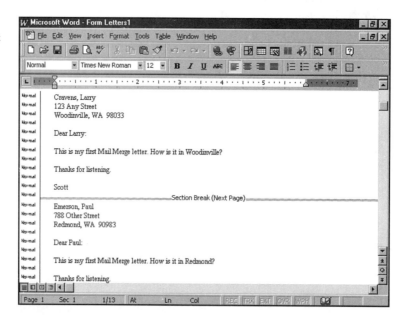

TIP Be sure to save the Merge Document containing the fields and text if you want to keep it for later use.

Sending Access 97 objects to Exchange

Another great feature is the ability to send objects from Access 97 through electronic mail to other users. To do this, highlight the object you want to send, in this example, tblTapes. Choose File, Send. Access 97 asks you what file format you want to send it as, listing the standard RTF, XLS, HTML, and so on. For now, choose RTF (Rich Text Format).

Your e-mail begins, whether it is Exchange, Outlook, or some other mail program, and creates an e-mail message with the object attached to it (see Figure 25.5). Your screen may vary depending on how you have your e-mail system set up.

Fig. 25.5
Sending a table
through the mail.

Copying and pasting from Access 97 to other Office applications

The various Office products are so integrated that copying data from one to another is as simple as copying it to itself.

Copying and pasting information into Word

Here are the steps for copying and pasting data into Word.

1 Open the tblBorrowers table in Datasheet view by double-clicking it.

2 Highlight some data by dragging over it (see Figure 25.6).

3 Choose Edit, Copy.

4 Start Microsoft Excel.

5 In a blank spreadsheet, place the cursor into one of the cells.

6 Choose Edit, Paste. The information from Access 97 is then pasted into Excel (see Figure 25.7).

Fig. 25.6
Highlighting data to
copy into Excel.

Highlighted fields —

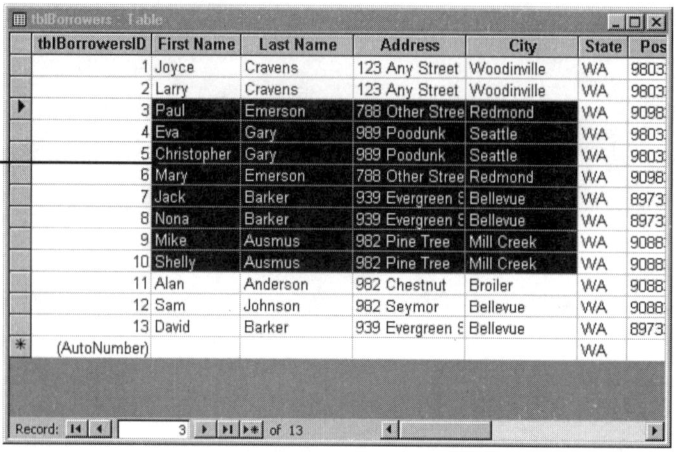

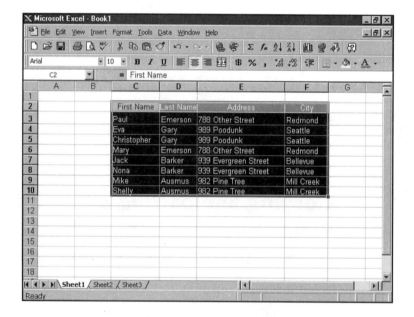

Fig. 25.7
This data came from
Access 97.

Copying information from Access 97 to Word

Copying data from Access 97 to Word isn't any more difficult. Since you still
have the data copied into the Clipboard, which holds data copied within
Windows, open Word; then choose Edit, Paste. The data is then placed into a
Word table (see Figure 25.8).

Fig. 25.8
This Word table is
courtesy of Access 97.

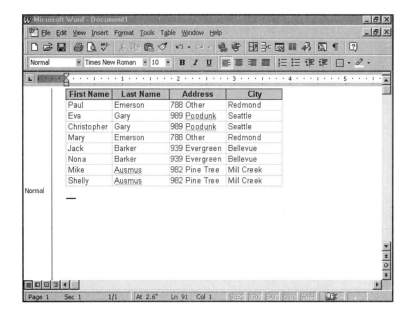

Storing Office documents in an Access 97 table

Office Documents can be many different types of files. Some examples of Office documents are spreadsheets (*.xls), Word Documents (*.doc), and so on.

Sometimes, it's more convenient to store various types of documents inside an Access 97 database. For instance, one application that I created keeps track of people who are being recruited for various jobs. Part of the application stores the résumés for the recruits in an Access 97 table.

Before adding a document to a table, the table needs to have an OLE Object-type field to accept. Create a new table by choosing the Tables tab and then clicking New. Add a field, called OfficeDocs, of OLE Object data type (see Figure 25.9).

Fig. 25.9
This field stores various
types of Office
documents.

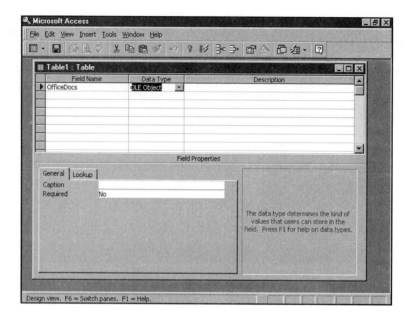

66 *Plain English, please!*

OLE (Object Linking and Embedding) is a standard used for physically
storing (embedding), or in some cases linking, various types of items
(objects) created in one application into another. An example of this is the
ability to store Excel spreadsheets or Word documents into an Access 97
table and then being able open them while in Access. 99

Now save your table and open it in Datasheet view. When asked about
creating a Primary Key, choose No.

In Datasheet view, the object looks boring. Place the cursor in the first
record. Now choose Insert, Object menu and Access 97 opens the Insert
Object dialog box.

Inside the Insert Object dialog box, click Create from File. You will see a field
where you can supply a path and file name to an Office document. You can
also click Browse to browse for the file (see Figure 25.10).

Fig. 25.10
With this dialog box, you can choose the Office Document you want.

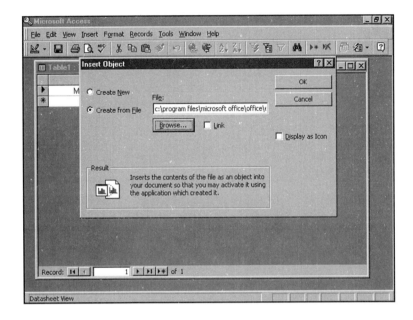

Q&A *What is the check box that says Link used for?*

That property is the Link in Object Linking and Embedding (OLE). If you click the Link property, a path is stored in the table out to the actual object. If not, the object is embedded in the table itself. There are pros and cons to each.

When you embed an object, your database will grow by the size of the object. If you link it and move the object, then you have to find it again. It depends on the situation whether you want to use Linking or Embedding.

There are other methods for accessing OLE objects through *Visual Basic for Applications*, but they are beyond the scope of this book. If you are interested, this is covered in my developers' book, *Access 97 Power Programming,* also published by Que. This book has an entire chapter on working with automation using Visual Basic for Applications (VBA).

When you locate the file you want, click OK. Access 97 places the file into the table. You can see it in an Excel spreadsheet in Figure 25.11. To view the document once it's stored in the database, double-click the field.

Fig. 25.11
This Excel spreadsheet is now stored in an Access 97 table.

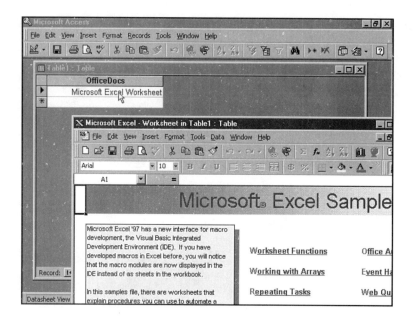

Starting Office Applications from Access 97 forms

Sometimes, you may need to start another application from within Access 97. You can create command buttons that open various applications and place them wherever you need them. This was covered in Chapter 20. Create a new form. Make sure that the Control Wizards are toggled on in the toolbox; then place a new Command button on the form. Access 97 starts the Command Button Wizard. If you choose Application from the Categories, you will see the applications you can run in Actions (see Figure 25.12). Choose an application, and click Finish. Access 97 creates the command button.

Fig. 25.12
Adding command buttons to call other applications is easy with the Command Button Wizard.

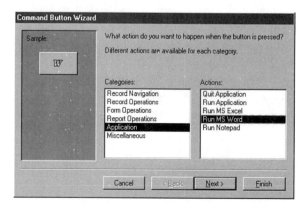

26

Access 97 and the Internet

● **In this chapter:**

- **What is the Internet?**

- **Using Access 97 with the Internet**

- **Access 97's Internet feature**

- **Working with hyperlinks**

With Access 97, you can take advantage of Internet features, like jumping to your favorite Web site and contributing or sending information to it, and receiving information from it. . . . . ▶

T he Internet is by far one of the hottest topics today. So it makes sense that Microsoft would incorporate Internet features into their Office products. Before going into the features Access 97 uses with the Internet, I want to give you a brief explanation of what the Internet is all about.

Because this book is about Access 97, we won't spend much time getting you up to speed on all the things to know about the Internet and the World Wide Web. We're assuming you already know something about setting up an Internet account and using a Web browser. If you need more information about the Internet and creating Web sites and pages, you should pick up a copy of *Using the Internet, Second Edition,* by Jerry Honeycutt or *Using FrontPage 97,* by Eric Maloney and Josh Nossiter.

Working with the Internet

The Internet is made up of a number of different carriers (service companies). They let you store information and let you create an interface so that people can see your information. This interface is a Web page. When you create a Web page that has your name or company name in it, you create a home page.

 Q&A **What is the difference between Internet and intranet?**

Just as the Internet runs over the World Wide Web, an intranet runs over your in-house network, or on a Wide Area Network.

Creating Web Pages

There are a number of tools available to help you create Web pages, as well as a huge amount of books to help you begin. You create Web pages by using a computer language called HTML, which stands for Hypertext Markup Language.

HTML is actually easy to understand as far as programming languages go. Access 97 also includes many ways to create Web pages from different Access 97 objects. We'll cover a couple of them later in the chapter.

Using a Web browser

In order to use the Internet, you need an account with an Internet service provider (ISP), or you need to belong to a service, such as The Microsoft Network. (That is the service I belong to. Convenient, isn't it?)

You will also need to use a Web browser such as Netscape or Internet Explorer (IE). You can get Web browsers for free from a number of places. I even know of some books that include them on their CDs. I use the Internet Explorer and will use it in my examples for this chapter.

Getting on the Web

To get onto the Web, you need to log on to your service (see Figure 26.1).

Fig. 26.1
Here is the Log On dialog box for The Microsoft Network.

Usually, your service will have its own service page, as well as a home page for you on the Web. Sometimes, when you log on, you initially see the home page of the browser (see Figure 26.2). You can set up your browser to the home page of your choice.

Fig. 26.2
Startup page for the
Internet Explorer.

Jumping to Web pages and applications with hyperlinks

Hyperlinks are one of the most well-known features used in browsers today. Hyperlinks have been used for years as HyperText in Help files. When you click a green underscored Help topic, the Hyperlink takes you to that definition. You can see this in Figure 26.3. Here, the user will click a word to jump to that help topic.

A hyperlink contains an address and a subaddress that the computer jumps to when you click it.

Creating the hyperlink data type in a field

You can create a field in your table to store hyperlink addresses so that you can click them later and go to an address. To try it out, create a field called HomePage in the tblTapes table (see Figure 26.4).

Now you can add a hyperlink address for the movie publishers' Web sites (home pages) to the information about the tape.

Fig. 26.3
Jump to the Help topic for hyperlink address.

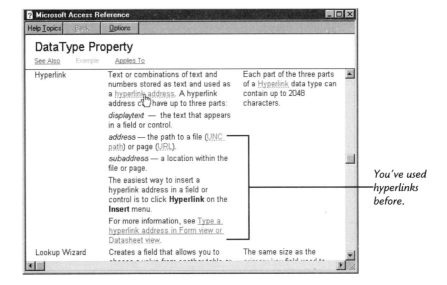

You've used hyperlinks before.

Fig. 26.4
Adding a hyperlink-type field to the table.

A hyperlink field

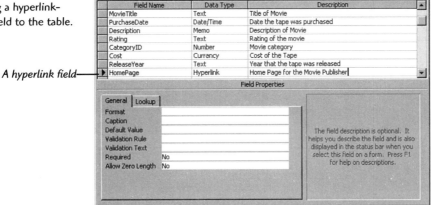

Before we create this address, you have to understand what makes up the hyperlink addresses.

What makes up a hyperlink address?

Hyperlink addresses can be either an Internet address or another application on your system. For instance, you can go to someone's home page on the Internet, open a form in another database, or even open one in the current database.

The hyperlink address is where you place the address of what you want linked. This address can be any of the following protocols:

\\ (UNC Path)	msn:
cid:	news:
file:	nntp:
ftp:	pnm:// (Real Audio Media)
gopher:	prospero:
http:	rlogin:
mailto:	telnet:
mid:	tn3270:
mms:// (Microsoft Media Server media)	wais:

The UNC (Universal Naming Convention) path is the absolute path used with network servers. Suppose that the VideoLib.mdb database is in the \Examples folder, assigned to the logical H: drive. The H: drive is assigned the share \\Abednego\Root. The UNC path would be:

\\Abednego\Root\Examples\VideoLib.mdb

Use the hyperlink subAddress to specify the object within the file you want to use. An example here may be a form within VideoLib.mdb—in this case, frmTapesInformation. For this example, the hyperlink subAddress would be:

Form frmTapesInformation

Another common protocol you will use is the http: protocol, which stands for Hyperlink Transfer Protocol. When using the http: protocol, you will see something like:

http: www.microsoft.com

where www stands for World Wide Web, and microsoft.com is the Web site. Another example of this is one of my companies; LBI has a Web site called LBIInfo.com for our conference information. The address for this is:

http: //www.LBIInfo.com.

Now, take a look at how to add an address to a hyperlink field.

Adding hyperlink address fields

To edit a hyperlink field that has an address out on the Web, follow these steps that show you how to get to Paramount's home page:

1 Open the tblTapes table in Datasheet view. Place the cursor in the HomePage field for one of the Star Trek movies.

2 Choose Insert, Hyperlink. Access 97 opens the Edit Hyperlink dialog box.

3 Type in the address: http://www.paramount.com/ (see Figure 26.5). Click OK.

You will see the address added in the field. You can then copy and paste this data to the other Star Trek movies just as you would any other data (see Figure 26.6).

Fig. 26.5
Adding a hyperlink address to the HomePage field.

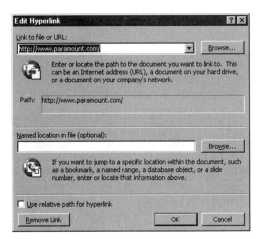

When you click the Hyperlink field, you will be taken to Paramount's home page (Figure 26.7). You can click one more time on the Motion Picture icon to get all the information you want about Star Trek (see Figure 26.8).

tblTapes : Table

TapeID	Movie Title	HomePage	Purc
1	Princess Bride		
2	Star Trek I: The Motion Picture	http://www.paramount.com/	
3	Star Trek II: The Wrath of Khan	http://www.paramount.com/	
4	Star Trek III: The Search for Spock	http://www.paramount.com/	
5	Star Wars		
6	Star Wars: Empire Strikes Back		
7	Star Wars: Return of the Jedi		
8	Twister		
9	007: Dr. No		
10	007: THUNDERBALL		
11	The Last Boy Scout		
12	The Ten Commandments		
13	Monty Python and the Holy Grail		
14	Alien		
15	Alien 2: Aliens		
16	Alien 3		
17	Terminator		

Record: 5 of 30

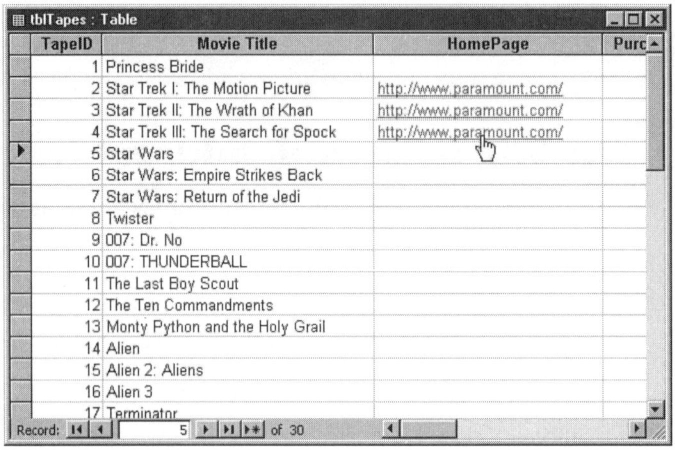

Fig. 26.6
The Hyperlink field, ready for business.

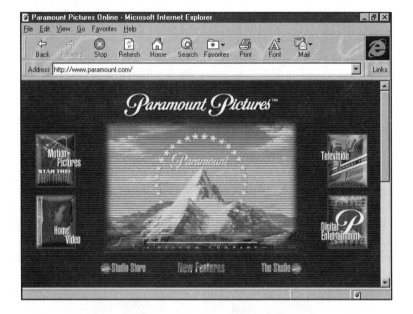

Fig. 26.7
Hyperlinking to Paramount's home page.

Creating hyperlink controls

Another way Access 97 utilizes hyperlinks is to let you turn other types of controls into hyperlink controls. The controls that you can change are Labels, Command Buttons, and Image Controls.

Fig. 26.8
Checking out Star Trek
from your database.

A common example for using a hyperlink for one of these controls is when
you want to have a button open another form, using no Visual Basic code or
macros. This is useful on switchboards, especially since hyperlinks turn color
when you use them once. This happens so that you will know whether or not
you have been to a form during a session. To see how this works:

1 Create a blank form. Make it unbound (no table or query) so you don't
   have to worry about a record source for it.

2 Turn off the Control Wizard by toggling it in the toolbox.

3 Place a new Command Button control on the form.

4 With the command button highlighted, open the Property Sheet to the
   Format tab. Here you see the HyperLink Address property.

5 Click the builder button beside the Hyperlink Address property. Access
   97 opens the Insert Hyperlink dialog box introduced in the last section.

6 Tab out of the Link to file or URL field into the Named location in the
   file field.

   By leaving the first field blank, you are telling Access 97 that you want
   to use the current database as the main address.

7 Click the Bro<u>w</u>se button. The Selection Location dialog box appears (see Figure 26.9).

Fig. 26.9
Locating a form to include as the subAddress.

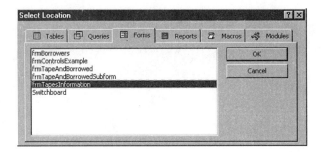

8 Highlight the frmTapesInformation form in the Forms tab, and then click OK. Access 97 inserts the name of the form into the second field on the Insert Hyperlink dialog box (see Figure 26.10). Click OK.

Fig. 26.10
The SubAddress is set.

Access 97 takes you back to the form, and the command button is bright blue and underlined like a hyperlink. If you look at the Hyperlink SubAddress property in the property sheet, you see Form frmTapesInformation.

You can change the caption of the command button to anything you want, simply by changing the Caption property. To check out the new Hyperlink command button, switch to Form view, and then click the command button.

Exporting to HTML the easy way

Access 97 allows you to take an object such as a table and export it to HTML so you can use it on a Web page. To export to an HTML file:

1 Highlight the tblTapes table in the Tables tab of the Database window; then choose <u>F</u>ile, Save <u>A</u>s/Export. This opens the Save As dialog box.

2 Click OK in the Save As dialog box to save the file to an external format. You will then see a dialog box where you can choose the File <u>n</u>ame and Save as type of the file to export to.

3 Choose HTML Documents for the Save as type field.

TIP In order to set the column headings in the HTML file, check Save Formatted, under the Cancel button. Then click Aut<u>o</u>start for IE to display the page right away if you want.

4 Click Export. If you click the Save Formatted option, Access 97 asks you for an HTML template. Click OK on this dialog box.

Access 97 then creates a file called tblTapes.html. If you click Autostart, it opens IE with the file (see Figure 26.11).

Fig. 26.11
The finished HTML product.

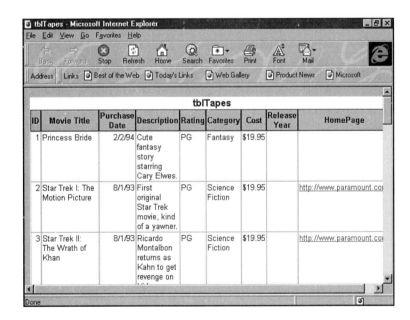

You can also Import and Link to HTML files, the same way you would to other type files.

Publishing to the Web

There is an alternative to simply exporting an object to the HTML file format. That is using the Publish to the Web Wizard (see Figure 26.12).

Fig. 26.12
Using the Publish to the Web Wizard.

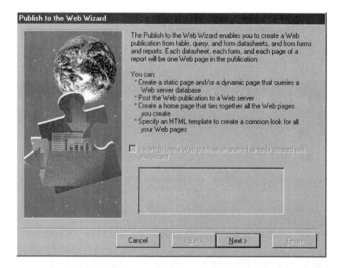

To start this wizard, choose File, Save as HTML. However, using this wizard, you need to know quite a bit more about setting up a database on the Web than I have described in this book—including knowing how to work with Web servers.

This is just a peek at what you can do using Access 97 with the Internet. It is also the end of this book. I hope you have learned a lot by reading this book. If you have, and you want to continue learning more about Access 97, look for my developers' book: *Access 97 Power Programming*, also published by Que.

Index

Symbols

& (ampersand) operator, 186
* (asterisk) wild card, 178, 207
<= operator, 133
<=Date() validation rule, 133
? (question mark) wild card, 207
[], field names, 185
... (ellipsis), 23

A

Access 97
  primary keys, 70
  programs
    information
      options, 40
    starting, 366
    starting Access, 14-19
Access window
  Office Assistant, 18
  status bar, 26
Action queries, 182, 222-224
Add/Remove button, installing drivers, 343
adding
  Access start button
    to Office shortcut
    bar, 15

columns in
  datasheets, 93
commands to
  switchboard, 337
controls to Tab
  control, 282
records
  to datasheets, 78
  to forms, 237
tables to Relationship
  window, 102
addition calculated field example, 188
Addition operator, calculated fields, 185
addresses on Web pages, hyperlinks, 371
aggregate functions, 216
aligning controls, 264-266, 321
ampersand (&) operator, 186
AND operator
  complex query
    criteria, 209
  filtering records,
    165-167
Append queries, 182, 223, 230-231
applications
  database, 5

Development Solu-
  tions demo data-
  base, 19
Northwind demo
  database, 19
Orders demo data-
  base, 19
**arguments in func-
tions, 191**
**ascending sort order,
146**
assistants, 31
**asterisk (*) wild
card, 178, 207**
**AutoForm feature,
236**
  Columnar option, 238
  Datasheet options,
    239
  Tabular option, 239
automating tasks, 11
**AutoNumber data
type, 70**
AutoReport feature
  Columnar option, 297
  Tabular option, 298,
    314
**Avery mailing label
options, 303**

B

**Back button, Data-
base Wizard, 50**
**background graphics
on forms, 250**

Complete and Return this Card
for a *FREE* Computer Book Catalog

Thank you for purchasing this book! You have purchased a superior computer book written expressly for your needs. To continue to provide the kind of up-to-date, pertinent coverage you've come to expect from us, we need to hear from you. Please take a minute to complete and return this self-addressed, postage-paid form. In return, we'll send you a free catalog of all our computer books on topics ranging from word processing to programming and the internet.

Mr. ☐   Mrs. ☐   Ms. ☐   Dr. ☐

Name (first) ☐☐☐☐☐☐☐☐☐☐ (M.I.) ☐ (last) ☐☐☐☐☐☐☐☐☐☐☐☐☐☐☐☐

Address ☐☐☐☐☐☐☐☐☐☐☐☐☐☐☐☐☐☐☐☐☐☐☐☐☐☐☐☐☐☐☐☐☐☐

☐☐☐☐☐☐☐☐☐☐☐☐☐☐☐☐☐☐☐☐☐☐☐☐☐☐☐☐☐☐☐☐☐☐

City ☐☐☐☐☐☐☐☐☐☐☐☐☐ State ☐☐ Zip ☐☐☐☐☐ ☐☐☐☐

Phone ☐☐☐ ☐☐☐ ☐☐☐☐ Fax ☐☐☐ ☐☐☐ ☐☐☐☐

Company Name ☐☐☐☐☐☐☐☐☐☐☐☐☐☐☐☐☐☐☐☐☐☐☐☐☐☐

E-mail address ☐☐☐☐☐☐☐☐☐☐☐☐☐☐☐☐☐☐☐☐☐☐☐☐☐☐☐☐

1. Please check at least (3) influencing factors for purchasing this book.

Front or back cover information on book .... ☐
Special approach to the content .... ☐
Completeness of content .... ☐
Author's reputation .... ☐
Publisher's reputation .... ☐
Book cover design or layout .... ☐
Index or table of contents of book .... ☐
Price of book .... ☐
Special effects, graphics, illustrations .... ☐
Other (Please specify): _____ ☐

2. How did you first learn about this book?

Saw in Macmillan Computer Publishing catalog .... ☐
Recommended by store personnel .... ☐
Saw the book on bookshelf at store .... ☐
Recommended by a friend .... ☐
Received advertisement in the mail .... ☐
Saw an advertisement in: _____ ☐
Read book review in: _____ ☐
Other (Please specify): _____ ☐

3. How many computer books have you purchased in the last six months?

This book only .... ☐   3 to 5 books .... ☐
2 books .... ☐   More than 5 .... ☐

4. Where did you purchase this book?

Bookstore .... ☐
Computer Store .... ☐
Consumer Electronics Store .... ☐
Department Store .... ☐
Office Club .... ☐
Warehouse Club .... ☐
Mail Order .... ☐
Direct from Publisher .... ☐
Internet site .... ☐
Other (Please specify): _____ ☐

5. How long have you been using a computer?

☐ Less than 6 months   ☐ 6 months to a year
☐ 1 to 3 years   ☐ More than 3 years

6. What is your level of experience with personal computers and with the subject of this book?

	With PCs	With subject of book
New	☐	☐
Casual	☐	☐
Accomplished	☐	☐
Expert	☐	☐

Source Code ISBN: 0-7897-1016-1

7. Which of the following best describes your job title?

Administrative Assistant .... ☐
Coordinator .... ☐
Manager/Supervisor .... ☐
Director .... ☐
Vice President .... ☐
President/CEO/COO .... ☐
Lawyer/Doctor/Medical Professional .... ☐
Teacher/Educator/Trainer .... ☐
Engineer/Technician .... ☐
Consultant .... ☐
Not employed/Student/Retired .... ☐
Other (Please specify): _____ ☐

8. Which of the following best describes the area of the company your job title falls under?

Accounting .... ☐
Engineering .... ☐
Manufacturing .... ☐
Operations .... ☐
Marketing .... ☐
Sales .... ☐
Other (Please specify): _____ ☐

9. What is your age?

Under 20 .... ☐
21-29 .... ☐
30-39 .... ☐
40-49 .... ☐
50-59 .... ☐
60-over .... ☐

10. Are you:

Male .... ☐
Female .... ☐

11. Which computer publications do you read regularly? (Please list)

_____
_____
_____
_____
_____
_____
_____
_____
_____

Comments: _____
_____
_____

Fold here and scotch-tape to mail.

MACMILLAN COMPUTER PUBLISHING USA

A VIACOM COMPANY

 **Technical** ---- **Support:**

If you need assistance with the information in this book or with a CD/Disk accompanying the book, please access the Knowledge Base on our Web site at **http://www.superlibrary.com/general/support**. Our most Frequently Asked Questions are answered there. If you do not find the answer to your questions on our Web site, you may contact Macmillan Technical Support **(317) 581-3833** or e-mail us at **support@mcp.com**.

Check out Que® Books on the World Wide Web
http://www.quecorp.com

As the biggest software release in computer history, Windows 95 continues to redefine the computer industry. Click here for the latest info on our Windows 95 books

Make computing quick and easy with these products designed exclusively for new and casual users

Examine the latest releases in word processing, spreadsheets, operating systems, and suites

The Internet, The World Wide Web, CompuServe®, America Online®, Prodigy® —it's a world of ever-changing information. Don't get left behind!

Find out about new additions to our site, new bestsellers and hot topics

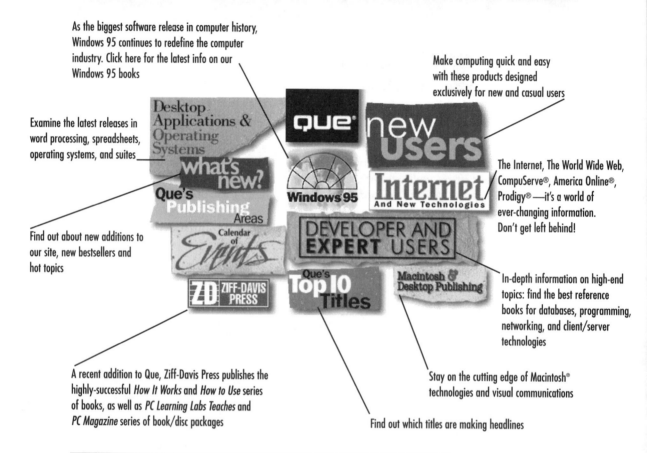

In-depth information on high-end topics: find the best reference books for databases, programming, networking, and client/server technologies

A recent addition to Que, Ziff-Davis Press publishes the highly-successful *How It Works* and *How to Use* series of books, as well as *PC Learning Labs Teaches* and *PC Magazine* series of book/disc packages

Stay on the cutting edge of Macintosh® technologies and visual communications

Find out which titles are making headlines

With 6 separate publishing groups, Que develops products for many specific market segments and areas of computer technology. Explore our Web Site and you'll find information on best-selling titles, newly published titles, upcoming products, authors, and much more.

- Stay informed on the latest industry trends and products available
- Visit our online bookstore for the latest information and editions
- Download software from Que's library of the best shareware and freeware